Minnesota's Lost Towns
SOUTHERN EDITION

Also by Rhonda Fochs:

Minnesota's Lost Towns: Northern Edition

Minnesota's Lost Towns: Northern Edition II

Minnesota's Lost Towns Central Edition

Wisconsin's Lost Towns

Minnesota's Lost Towns

SOUTHERN EDITION

Rhonda Fochs

NORTH STAR PRESS OF ST. CLOUD, IN.
St. Cloud, Minnesota

ISBN 978-1-68201-030-3

Printed in the United States of America.

Published by:
    North Star Press of St. Cloud, Inc.
    Saint Cloud, MN

    www.northstarpress.com

ACKNOWLEDGMENTS

Without the assistance, help and support of many, many people and organizations, this book would not have been possible. Early historians, known and unknown, wrote local and family histories, leaving them for later generations. They are an invaluable record of the times and people of the past. Their memories, letters, oral and written histories are a treasure-trove of memories, tales, anecdotes and facts that would be lost without their foresight and their efforts to record them. Without their contributions we would be severely limited in our knowledge and rich details of the past. It is a great debt, that I, that we, owe to those early historians.

I can't stress enough the importance of local historical societies and museums. These local repositories are true gems right in the midst of our local communities. With limited funds and resources, the staff and volunteers of these organizations preserve our past and ensure our future. I urge you to visit them, support them and perhaps even volunteer. Without them, and the people involved with them, we would be sorely lacking in our historical knowledge and legacy. Libraries are equally important. This book could not have been written without them.

To my family and friends, I thank you for your belief, support and your help in so many ways.

Ruth Klossner, thanks for all you do to preserve local history and for sharing that history.

Tom McLaughlin, your photos preserve the past for the future and they bring the long ago alive.

To Roger Langseth—your road trip journals show us how the bast lives on.

To those who contacted me and shared their places and their loved ones, thanks for sharing them with us.

To those who allowed me the use of their photos, thank you. Your credits are listed by your photos.

ORGANIZATIONS

Blue Earth County Historical Society
Brown County Historical Society
Cottonwood County Historical Society
Dodge County Historical Society
East St. Olaf Church
Goodhue County Historical Society
Houston County Historical Society
Immaculate Conception and Nativity
    Church
Lake Benton Area Chamber of Commerce
Le Sueur County Historical Society
Lyon County Historical Society
Manley Tire
Martin County Historical Society
Murray County Historical Society
Nicollet County Historical Society
Nobles County Historical Society
Okaman Elk Farm
Olmsted County Historical Society
Pilot Mound Design
Pipestone County Historical Society
Rice County Historical Society
Steele County Historical Society
Wabasha County Historical Society
Waseca County Historical Society
Watonwan County Historical Society
Winona County Historical Society
Winona County Soil and Water District

INDIVIDUALS

Jennifer Andries
Barba K. Best
Anthony Bianci
Andrew Bloedorn
J.C. Boice
Daryl Buck
Gaylene Chapman
Ruth Pettis Collins
Pat Demuth
Joshua Dixon
Linda Evenson
Connie Giles
Libby Glimsdal
David Goodell
Heather Harren
Audrey Helbling
Nicole Huss
Joyce Kaplan
Ruth Klossner
Fr. Paul Kubista
Roger Langseth
David Larson
James Marushin
Melissa McCarthy
Nancy McNab
Sandy and Dick Millerbernd
Daniel Moeckly

Kari Morford
Gina Moser
Andrew Pietenpol
Georgia Rosendahl
Joyce Resoft
Robert Sandeen
Barb Scottston
Jason Smith
Linda Taylor
Kathleen Keller Theisen
Karl Unnasch
Paul Vanderburg
Myrna Wesselman
Dan West
Errin Wilker

Table of Contents

MINNESOTA GHOST TOWNS

Minnesota ghost towns are different. They are not the stuff of Hollywood movie sets nor the iconic "Wild West" images branded into our minds. They don't have the dusty tumble-weed-strewn dirt streets lined with weather-beaten buildings. In the Midwest, our ghost towns are more of the vanished villages, lost locations, abandoned communities, and relocated town sites variety. I call them "places of the past."

In Minnesota, with our abundant natural resources, there are a multitude of these places of the past. Generally based on a one-industry, one-resource economy and the service-oriented support businesses, such as banks, retail establishments, saloons, and brothels, the communities thrived as long as the industry or resource did. Once depleted, the industry owners moved to the next location or people sought new resources. The supporting businesses then failed, the residents moved on, and the village faded, leaving few traces of its existence other than perhaps a wide spot along the highway, a clearing in the landscape, a crumbing foundation or two, decrepit weather-beaten buildings, and sometimes a cemetery. Disasters, wars, and changes in area economies also contributed to the loss of many towns and communities.

I've long had an interest and personal connection to the notion of ghost towns. My grandparents homesteaded in eastern Montana in a town that would fade into history in the 1920s. My aunt owned land upon which a booming early 1900s Wisconsin logging town was located. The town was abandoned after tornado and fire, leaving few remains.

In the 1970s my mother moved to Hackensack, Minnesota, and lived in a rustic basement cabin on Little Portage Lake. It was my first extended exposure to northern Minnesota, and it took root; I now live in Northern Minnesota full time and love it more each day.

To get to mom's place we needed to head north out of Hackensack, turn west at the intersection of Highway 371 and Cass County #50. Every time we turned at that juncture, Mom would talk of a long-ago town that once sat there. While I had a fleeting fascination, I was young then and hadn't fully developed my love of history. I guess I didn't have enough of my own history to appreciate the larger history of time and place as a whole. As years passed, I grew to treasure the past, eventually becoming a history teacher. But back then, I didn't listen as closely as I could have, should have. Not that Mom knew that much about the town. She just knew it used to be there and was intrigued by that fact.

Many years and lots of history have been added to my life since those days. In 2014, as I marked a mile-stone birthday, the big sixty, I decided to indulge my interest, pursue my passion and make it my mission to learn all I could, locate, document and visit Minnesota's places of the past, those places where lives were lived, children were raised, homes and businesses were created and for various reasons were packed up and moved elsewhere.

This is the story of many of those towns.

WHAT IS A GHOST TOWN?

With no clear-cut definition, determining what constitutes a ghost town is highly subjective, often a matter of degree and opinion.

Purists will define a ghost town—a true ghost town—as a town that has been completely abandoned. Others argue that a ghost town is any community that is a semblance, shadow—or "ghost"—of what it used to be.

At its core, on a basic level, the most agreed upon definition would be that of a human settlement that has been abandoned. With an arbitrary definition in place it is possible to further classify ghost towns into categories or classes based on definitive characteristics.

The most common breakdowns and classes with Minnesota examples are: **

CLASS A – Barren site, nature has reclaimed the land, no visible signs of former inhabitation (Lothrop)

CLASS B – Rubble, foundations, roofless buildings (Gravelville)

CLASS C – Standing abandoned buildings, no/rural population, hamlet, no viable organized community (Gull River)

CLASS D – Semi/Near Ghost town. Many abandoned buildings, small resident population (Lincoln)

CLASS E – Busy historic community—smaller than in boom days (Rose City)

CLASS F – Restored town, historically preserved status (Old Crow Wing – Buena Vista)

A seventh category could also be included:

CLASS G – town joined or was absorbed by neighboring/thriving city (Spina)

Many communities, whatever their class, did leave behind tangible remains in the form of cemeteries. The hallowed grounds are a visible record of the times and lives of the town's inhabitants. Many areas also carry the town's name.

** Modified from Gary Speck's *Classes of Ghost Towns*

Note: Classification is subjective into more than one class, or may not completely fit in any class.

LIFE-CYCLE OF A GHOST TOWN

Minnesota, with its abundance of natural resources, has a multitude of used-to-be-towns--ghost towns. Generally based on a one-resource, one-industry economy, the population and all town activity would be heavily dependent on that one factor. The town survived as long as the resource did. Once it was depleted, the industry/owners moved workers and equipment to new locations and new opportunities.

The Michigan Chronoscope E-press describes the process simply and effectively. After the owners/industry moved on, soon the supporting businesses (retail, banks, saloons, brothels, hotels) failed, and the owners closed shop. Residents moved on to new lives, new jobs, homes, and communities. Some towns were dismantled, packed up and shipped out, reassembled in new locations. Others were abandoned and reclaimed by nature. Most left no physical remains except a cemetery or place name.

The earliest settlements first appeared along major transportation routes, primarily rivers. As time would progress, other transportation routes provided prime locations for a town, along tote roads or railroad lines. Others grew in haphazard patterns, when and where there was an opportunity. Native American villages were among the first communities. Though many were seasonal, there were some permanent villages. As settlers moved in, the communities became more permanent.

While each town or community was unique and had its own personality, there was a definite pattern to their life-cycles. The only variable being the rate of progression or pace at which a town moves(ed) through the cycle. Depending on the commodity or resource, this time frame could vary greatly.

Economists, sociologists and historians have labeled this a "boom-and-bust" economy. Models have been created that include definitive characteristics and stages of such an economy. Mining towns, particularly Western mining towns, were the examples most often used in setting the model. In large part, mining towns moved through the progression as a rapid pace. Moving at such an accelerated pace, it was possible to make observations that fit most of the towns that were products of

a "boom and bust" economy. Michael Conlin, a business professor in Canada concisely lists the six stages of a "boom and bust" cycle in his book *Mining Heritage and Tourism*. The following are simplified modifications of his model as well as the process described by E-Press:

Stage One – Discovery and Growth
Resource is discovered and developed.
Size of the workforce is capped by workforce required to exploit the resource, often dictated by size and type of resource

Stage Two – Production
Highest level of activity

Stage Three – Decline
Production begins to decline--can be depletion of the resource or a decline in demand.
Can also be that costs have escalated making it unprofitable.
Decline may be rapid.

Stage Four – Abandonment
Owners move equipment and workers to new locations, closing down current production.
Supporting businesses fail/close shop.
Residents move on.

Stage Five – Decay
Town is either packed up or moved on, or buildings are left to decay.

Stage Six – Disappearance of Evidence of Occupation
Everything moved on or reclaimed by nature.

As the E-Press states, towns built on this model were doomed from the beginning to be ghost towns.

LIFE CYCLE BIBLIOGRAPHY

Conlin, Michael V., Lee Joliffe, ed. *Mining Heritage and Tourism: A Global Synthesis.*, UK, Routledge, 2010
"Ghost Towns of Newaygo." E-Press Chronograph Number II. Big Prairie Press. Winter 2007. Web. 16, Nov. 2012

GHOST TOWN CODE OF ETHICS

By their very nature, ghost towns are subject to the ravages of time and the elements. Harsh winter weather and humid summers in Minnesota all take their toll on the remnants of abandoned communities. Vandalism as well as accidental or unintentional damage adds to the deterioration of the sites. It is our duty and responsibility to treat these historic sites with respect and to do all we can to preserve the integrity of ghost towns. Use common sense and follow a code of ethics.

RESPECT PRIVATE PROPERTY.

Many former town sites are now located on private property. Please respect all private property.

Do not trespass—Do not enter private property without permission from the owner.

OBEY ALL POSTED SIGNS

Do not destroy, damage or deface any remains, buildings, or structures.

Do not remove anything from the sites.

Do not cause any disturbance to the foundations, vegetation, or land.

Do not litter. Remove and properly dispose of any trash you take into the area.

Always be courteous, respectful and SAFE.

TREAD LIGHTLY—TAKE ONLY PHOTOS—LEAVE ONLY FOOTPRINTS

Make as little impact on the environment as possible

Honor the past and preserve it for the future.

Blue Earth County

Beauford Creamery Today. (Courtesy of Tom McLaughlin)

Our Savior's Lutheran Church, Butternut. (Courtesy of Tom McLaughlin)

BEAUFORD (CORNERS)

1867 - 1980s

CLASS C

APPROXIMATE LOCATION:
12 Miles South of Mankato

Prior to their removal in 1863, the land on which Beauford was located had been part of the Winnebago Reservation. The first settler, a Scotsman, arrived in 1864 and within a few years the burgeoning community included a school, a sawmill, and a post office. The post office route was abandoned in 1875. After six years without a post office a new postmaster was appointed in 1882. Mail delivery in the earliest days was weekly. Daily mail service began in 1896 and lasted until the post office was permanently discontinued in 1904.

Though the post office was short-lived, Beauford as a community had a long life. The year 1884 saw the United Brethren Church established and served area residents until 1953 when a larger building was constructed and it became the United Methodist Church.

A creamery was established in 1895 and was successful from the very start. The original structure was replaced by a new building in 1935. The creamery closed in 1953, and the building remained vacant until 1961 when it was used as a mink farm's headquarters until the 1980s.

As with many lost towns, the lack of a railroad caused Beauford businesses to close and the town to decline. Better prices and more variety offered by nearby, larger towns accelerated the decline. As America transformed from a horse- to automobile-based economy, towns had little need for blacksmiths. Rural Free Delivery mail service eliminated the need for local post offices in every town. All combined to further hasten Beauford's demise.

In the 1950s the last general store closed its doors. Area students were bussed to Mapleton, and the Beauford school was closed in 1955. The mink farm closed in the 1980s. The majestic creamery building still stands. A small population and several buildings still call Beauford home, as do former resident's memories.

BUTTERNUT (VALLEY)

1894 - 1950s

CLASS C

APPROXIMATE LOCATION:
#22 West of Mankato

The year 1894 was a busy one in Butternut. That year the Lakeshore Creamery began operating. A post office, general store, and a blacksmith shop were also built. The settlement was established by Colonel Shaw of Butternuts, New York, and named in honor of his hometown. Warren Upham wrote that butternut trees were also common in Minnesota's southern river valleys.

Butternut commercial building. (Courtesy of Tom McLaughlin)

Long ago Butternut store. (Courtesy of Tom McLaughlin)

Beauford Postmark. (Author's Collection)

3

A busy 1895 saw the addition of a feed mill, harness shop, shoemaker, a meat market, livery, hotel and a town hall to the community.

While the post office lasted just six years and was discontinued in 1904, the creamery operated nearly sixty years, closing in 1953. In 1963, the population was twenty-six. Today the roadside hamlet still has several buildings standing that offer a glimpse into Butternut's history. The Our Savior's Lutheran Church is still active.

CAMBRIA

1881 - 1967

CLASS E

APPROXIMATE LOCATION:
South of Minnesota River and #6 and #68

Word has it that one can get a tasty burger and a cold drink at the Preri Bach Saloon in the busy historic town in Cambria. With a small population and several buildings Cambria still has a community feel.

Cambria's first settlers were from Cambria, Wisconsin. Thus the name. Cambria is also the ancient Latin name for Wales, and since many, if not all the early settlers were from Wales, the name was doubly fitting.

Those settlers came from a mining background and were ill-suited to building a farming community. They had few carpenters and even fewer tools. The harsh climate and swampy conditions added to the settlers' discomfort. The winter of 1853 was particularly harsh; some say it was the worst on record. Swampy conditions were ideal for producing a bumper crop of mosquitoes. One early settler's account tells that the mosquitoes were "as big as geese and were numbered in the millions per two cubic inches.) For four years a grasshopper infestation wreaked havoc and was the main reason the town declined.

Eventually Cambria's population and activity dwindled, yet the post office operated for nearly one hundred years from 1881 to 1967. The community still has an active Presbyterian Church, several residences, and a few standing buildings. A small population still calls it home. The Preri Bach Saloon displays vintage town photo, welcomes visitors and serves the best burgers around.

Vintage Cambria Building. (Courtesy of Tom McLaughlin)

Preri Bach Saloon. (Courtesy of Tom McLaughlin)

Early Cambria. (Courtesy of Dan West www.west2k.com)

4

Town View Early Cambria. (Courtesy of Dan West www.west2k.com)

Modern Woodsman Hall. (Courtesy of Tom McLaughlin)

FORT L'HUILLIER

1700 - 1702

CLASS A

APPROXIMATE LOCATION:
MN #66 just southeast of junction #66 and #90

Without any hard physical evidence, some say Fort L'Huillier is more of a fairy tale than a reality, more fiction that fact. Still, records, including early diaries, indicate the fort's actual existence and tell us the details of the fort.

The French fort was established by Charles Pierre Le Sueur in 1700 and was located on seventy-foot high natural mounds near the mouth of the Mankato River (now the Blue Earth River) and St. Peter's River (now the Minnesota River). Le Sueur sailed from Mississippi in a small sailing ship called a shallop and two canoes. He was accompanied by seventeen men. Arriving in September, winter provisions were the first priority. Four hundred buffalo were killed and stockpiled. Diaries note that the men suffered great indigestion from the new food source but after about six weeks their intestinal tracts equalized.

Possessing a ten-year mining and fur trading authorization from the king of France, Le Sueur and his men soon engaged in both activities. Mining 30,000 pounds of blue green dirt, which they were sure contained copper deposits, they sent 3,000 pounds of the soil back to France to be assayed. No copper deposits were detected. Some say the mining activity was merely a front to cover the real reason for Le Sueur's presence in the region, that of trading with the Dakota.

Departing to trade with the region's native tribes, Le Sueur left seven men behind to man the fort. In his absence, the fort was attacked by nearby natives. Three of the men were killed, the other four abandoned the fort, supposedly leaving behind a cache of goods, which, to this day, has never been found. Modern day treasure hunters dream of finding the stash.

In 1904, a local committee explored the site, finding no significant artifacts, thus the notion that the fort was merely fable. In 1926 a marker was placed at the site.

JUDSON

1890s - 1973

CLASS A/C

APPROXIMATE LOCATION:
MN #60 near NW end of Minneopa State Park

FORT JUDSON

In a land of few trees, alternatives to building materials had to be used. In building Fort Judson, the thick, dense grass sod of the region made do. The sod—cut into fourteen-inch-wide, eighteen-inch-long, four-inch-thick slabs—while far from perfect, worked well enough.

In 1863, during the height of both the Civil War and Minnesota's Dakota Conflict, settlers wanted added protection. The Ninth Minnesota Volunteers commenced building a fort on the western edge of the community of Judson. Using the sod, they began construction of the compound, layering the sod four feet thick at the base and tapering to eighteen inches at the top. The round structures were outfitted with port holes.

Over the ensuing years, wind, water and Minnesota's harsh elements eroded the sod walls. Those passing by in later years would be hard pressed to know that a fort had once stood at the site.

A bronze plate set in a concrete base marks the site.

JUDSON

GROWTH WAS RAPID, at least in the beginning for Judson, shortly after two brothers-in-law established the settlement on their 274-acre military bounty. The population swelled to fifty almost overnight. Buoyed by the boom, plans gave way to big dreams. The property was platted into ninety-seven lots of fifty by one hundred feet. Streets were to be seventy feet wide with twenty-foot alleys. Amenities were to include a public landing at the river and a centrally located park and town square. Lot sales were brisk in 1857, so much so that an additional forty-two acres were added to the town.

It is said that the people of Judson were noted for their religious zeal and pious nature. Judson itself was named after an early Baptist minister, Adoriram Judson. Judson was credited with translating the Bible into the Burmese language as well as with creating an English-Burmese dictionary.

Two views of the Judson Depot. (www.west2k.com)

Judson Bethany Lutheran Church Today. (Courtesy of Tom McLaughlin)

In 1857 Judson included a sawmill, two stores, and a small hotel. School was taught in a building next to one of the stores. Just two years later, in 1859, the town included thirty homes, a school, a sawmill, a blacksmith shop, a nursery store, and a ferry that operated between Judson and Eureka (a small settlement across the river in Le Sueur County).

During the summer of 1862, the Dakota Conflict was creating tensions throughout the region. A fort for added protection was built on the west end of town. The Civil War was also at its height. Thirty men from Judson enlisted. Financial difficulties in the late 1850s, the Civil War, and the Dakota Conflict took their toll on the small community.

The Chicago and Northwestern Railroad dealt Judson a fatal blow when it decided to build a short line rail line from Mankato to New Ulm, bypassing Judson. The new line ran just south of Judson and caused the settlement to be abandoned. A new community one-half mile south and west of "Old Judson" was laid out and was referred to as "New Judson." The new town surged in population with an all-time high of fifty-five. New businesses were established and included a cement factory, two creameries, a farm implement dealer, a school, and a restaurant among others.

Judson, in its new location, was booming. The 1910s and 1920s saw a spike in population with 125 residents in 1921 and 200 by 1930. A bank and rooming house joined the town.

Area historian Julie Schrader in her Blue Earth County Heritage book told the tale of President Coolidge visiting Judson. People flocked to the depot to see the president and his wife. As the train made its stop, the back door of the president's car opened. Out stepped Mrs. Coolidge and the couple's white collie. Silent Cal as the president was known, was extremely shy and didn't appear. The spectators didn't mind. "After all Mrs. Coolidge was nice and everyone can appreciate a good dog."

Judson's prosperity and growth, as well as that of the nation as a whole, would collapse with the 1929 Stock Market Crash. The railroad, in cost cutting efforts, changed its policy and no longer offered passenger service for towns as small as Judson, nor did it handle freight shipments of less than a carload. Those policies coupled with ever-increasing automobile traffic, dealt small towns, including Judson, a double blow. Nearby Mankato reaped the benefits and burgeoned as Judson gradually declined.

Throughout the 1940s, 1950s and 1960s businesses closed. The last creamery shut its doors in the 1940s. The school followed suit in the 1960s. The post office was discontinued in 1973. Traffic increased on the road to Mankato, and it eventually was paved and designated a state highway. Folks could easily travel to Mankato where lower prices and a wider variety of goods could be had.

Early Judson resident and former Mankato mayor, Vern Lundin, wrote his memories of growing up in Judson in a 1987 Blue Earth County Historical Society newsletter. He fondly recalled his boyhood days, the general store, the creamery and buttermilk, candy at the confectionary store and the sorghum mill. Summing it up, he wrote that in its early days "Judson had it all and was a full-service center." He concluded by stating "It was a great place to grow up."

MANKATO MINERAL SPRINGS

1864 - 1904

CLASS A

APPROXIMATE LOCATION:
Le Ray Township - 6 miles SE of Mankato

For years area Native Americans had visited the springs along the banks of Spring Creek, believing the waters had healing properties. Early settler Enoch Morse thought so too, and in 1864 he purchased the land on which the springs were located. After Enoch's death, his two sons inherited the property and laid plans to develop the property and the springs.

The first priority was to have the spring's waters tested. Learning that the water had a moderate concentration of acidity and that such minerals were said to treat liver, kidney, bladder and skin conditions, the brothers proceeded with their plans to develop a resort.

Area historian Steven Ulmen wrote in a Blue Earth County newsletter that the waters flowed at 40,000 gallons daily. The

Rural Judson Today. (Courtesy of Lee Koehler)

largest spring, by itself, flowed over 16,000 gallons daily. To control the waters, a six-inch cylinder with a gas dome was planted. The captured gas would be used to control water flow as needed.

A bottling house was constructed. The water was carbonated and bottled and sold for the first time in Mankato in 1890. A gazebo, with sitting benches was also constructed that summer. The gazebo was very popular as it allowed access to the springs without charge. The surrounding forty acres were platted with parks and lots. A large hotel with several cottages was also planned. Winter's cold didn't slow down the activities. Palmer writes that during the winter the water was frozen into molds and sold as frozen mineral water.

For reasons unknown, the hotel and cottages were never built. The land was sold to a partnership and later to a Dr. Macbeth who hoped to build a sanatorium. Again, the plans never materialized. All of the parties involved lost interest. In 1912 a cement tank was built over the springs. The gazebo was moved to a nearby knoll. Palmer concludes that, in 1886, when County Highway #28 was improved, the site was destroyed, the only remnant remaining the nearby gazebo.

MEDO (CREAM)

1866 - 1904

CLASS A

APPROXIMATE LOCATION:
Near Waseca County Line, South and East of Pemberton along #37

Carved out of the former Winnebago Reservation land, Medo, Winnebago for "small potatoes" was first established in Blue Earth County. With growth, the small community expanded into Waseca County and was also known as Cream. (*See* Cream under Waseca County.)

Settled shortly after the reservation lands were opened in 1863, Medo included a post office (1866 to 1904), a blacksmith shop, a general store, a feed store, and the Medo Lutheran Church and cemetery.

Mail was delivered by a stagecoach from Mountain Lake. The community was a busy trade center until the railroad chose nearby Pemberton for a station stop and depot. As Pemberton flourished, Medo declined.

MINNEOPA

1850s - 1900s

CLASS A/F

APPROXIMATE LOCATION:
Located within Minneopa State Park

Long before the Treaty of Traverse des Sioux opened the area for settlement, early Native American people had occupied the region. Known to them as "Makatosa," meaning "the goose," a native village sat at the mouth of the creek. It was also known as "Six" because of the six teepees grouped together.

Isaac Lyons, nicknamed "Buckskin" because of the clothes he wore built a cabin and sawmill on the creek in 1853, calling it Lyon's Creek. Next to the sawmill was a large artesian well. That same year covered wagons carrying eleven Welsh families from Watertown, Wisconsin, settled and built cabins along the creek.

Wildlife was abundant in the region, including buffalo. However, with settlement the number of buffalo rapidly declined with the last one being killed by a Civil War soldier in 1862. Bear were also known to habitat the surrounding area. According to an article in the Blue Earth County Historical Society's newsletter, one day a farmer heard his pig squeal. He saw a huge brown bear pick up a 350-pound pig, lift it over the fence and carry it away. Fifty to seventy-five armed men, with hunting dogs, tracked the bear. Two miles away the bear was shot and killed. The meat was divided up among area families. The bear was the largest grizzly ever shot in Blue Earth County. The claws are in the Blue Earth County's Historical Society's "Gallery."

Minneopa Depot. (Courtesy of www.west2k.com)

Seppman Mill. (Courtesy of Doug Wallick)

Minneopa Falls Postcards, (Author's collection)

Two views of Minneopa Park. (Courtesy of www.west2k.com)

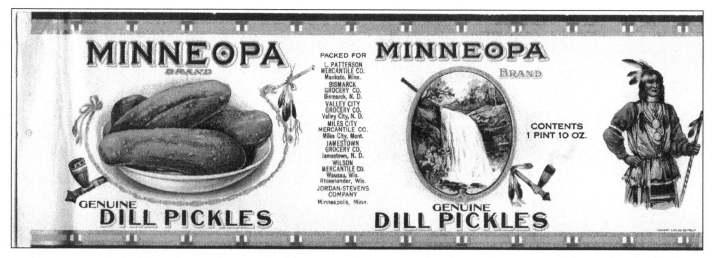

Minneopa Pickle Label. (Author's collection)

From the beginning, the area's scenic beauty and waterfalls attracted both settlers and tourists. The falls were a favorite subject for artists and later photographers and helped attract even more visitors. Minneopa, which the small settlement was known as, had the name shortened from Minneinneopa, which was a mouthful to say, let alone spell. The community was growing rapidly. The beautiful grounds surrounding the falls provided a perfect setting for the luxurious Minneinneopa Park Hotel, built in 1858 east of the waterfall.

Local landowner D.C. Evans, the first owner of the falls, built bridges and steps. Railroad tracks were laid along the creek by the St. Paul & Sioux City Railroad and a depot was built. The train agent convinced the railroad to advertise the falls, and soon four trains a day arrived from Mankato. The trains often carried 250 passengers each. Special group excursions were often planned with large groups participating, some with as many as 5,000 attendees.

Another early landowner, D.J. Alden, was quite famous. Dubbed "the shortest man on earth" Alden was said to be one-half inch shorter than Tom Thumb. At age twenty-two, Alden was thirty-five inches tall and weighed thirty-five pounds. Fittingly, he worked in the circus.

In 1862, local landowner Louis Seppmann built a stone windmill. At the base, the mill was thirty-three feet in diameter, twenty feet at the top. Four arms extended out thirty-five feet. Lightning hit the mill in 1873, damaging two of the arms. Using just two arms the mill operated until 1880.

The Civil War and the Dakota Conflict hampered travel during the 1860s. Still Minneopa prospered. In 1870, Evans platted Minneopa. The streets were named after the region's hills, summits, and native trees. Soon the village included the hotel, a store, a blacksmith shop, and a lumberyard. From 1873 for three years, nature and grasshoppers plagued the re-gion. Crops failed for several years. By the time the grasshoppers were gone, so was the town. Within a short time the town was abandoned.

Folklore provides an interesting anecdote. In September of 1876, after a botched robbery in Northfield, Minnesota, the James-Younger Gang was said to have taken refuge in the Minneopa area. The gang would have had to pass through the area as it was along the only road to Madelia and the only escape route. Supposedly they hid out under the bridge with blankets as camouflage. Approaching law enforcement men were so loud they alerted the gang allowing them to escape. The gang split up and moved out.

After the abandonement of Minneopa, Evans sold his land in 1885. A succession of owners followed. Even though the area was still a popular tourist destination, all efforts to develop failed. When the 1903 owners planned to clear cut the land, local citizens stepped in and organized efforts to have the land preserved. Hoping to secure status as a state park, a bill was introduced in 1905 to appropriate $5,000 to purchase the land. Originally twenty-five acres were purchased and in succeeding years more money was appropriated, and the park was able to expand its boundaries.

J.B. Hodges, the railroad agent who first touted Minneopa's beauty and tourism potential, became the park's first superintendent. Under his leadership and with state funding, the park was improved. Safety, accessibility, bridges, picnic shelters and stabilizing the falls were completed. The old train depot served as the ranger station for the park in its earliest days. Minneopa State Park was becoming a Minnesota treasure.

Improvements and expansion continued in the 1930s and 1940s. In 1931 the park acquired a non-contiguous parcel of land when the Seppmann Mill was donated to the park. The Works Progress Administration (WPA) further improved the park by building steps, shelters, restrooms and other structures between 1937 and 1940. Local sandstone was used in the construction of all of the structures. A fifty-eight-acre district, which includes all the WPA structures is on the National Register of Historic Places.

Local groups continued efforts to secure funding to expand the park. In 1967, three miles of river shoreline as well as land from the Seppmann heirs was acquired. The new land addition connected the Seppman Mill property to the rest of the park.

Today the scenic beauty still abounds. The park (and the falls) are still a tourist destination and now includes a campground, picnic area, a road to the mill, and a hiking and skiing trail system. A local group has undertaken the preservation and maintenance of the Minneopa Cemetery

PLEASANT MOUND (CERESCO)

1863 - 1902 1857/1900

CLASS A

APPROXIMATE LOCATION:
10 miles South and East of Madelia

Located on hill-shaped mounds that run north and south and stand forty-fifty feet above the surrounding prairie, the name Pleasant Mound came naturally. The first settlers, German Lutherans in the 1860s, lived a community-based existence. According to area historian, Steven Ulmen, the town sites of Pleasant Grove and Ceresco were closely intertwined and existed more as one community than separate and independent towns.

The close-knit communities of about one hundred families were led by Reverend Julius Miller. Religion and education were of great importance to the settlers and the community had its own church and school. Classes were conducted in both German and English languages and presided over by a professor hired from Wisconsin. School was held year-round with a two-week harvest time break.

Very unusual was the establishment of a community insurance company that insured for fire as well as livestock loss.

Both communities had post offices, and both were located in townships of the same names as the communities. The two town halls are still standing and in use.

RAPIDAN (MILLS)

1875 - 1960s

CLASS D

APPROXIMATE LOCATION:
Southwest of Mankato at intersection of #9 and #126

With a mission to preserve the history of Rapidan in artifacts, photos, and oral histories, the Rapidan Heritage Society has been working hard to do just that for almost fifteen years.

Early Rapidan was created in 1876 with the establishment of a general store. Growth was rapid after 1880 when the Chicago, Milwaukee, and St. Paul Railroad was granted a right of way to build a route through the area. The existing store

Two views of the Pleasant Mound (Ceresco) town hall, 2014. (Tom McLaughlin)

Rapidan Dam. (Author's Collection)

Rapidan Mill. (Author's Collection)

Bird's-eye view of Rapidan. (Author's Collection)

Rapidan Depot. (www.west2k.com)

and post office moved to be nearer the railroad. Over the following years, several businesses joined the settlement. The store and post office, which continued under a succession of owners and postmasters, was a community staple. In 1897 a grain elevator, a coop creamery, and St. John's Lutheran Church called Rapidan home. In the early 1900s a Woodmen's Hall was built. Three trains stopped daily in 1906. In 1912, the storekeeper installed a small telephone switchboard. Eggs were a big business in the early years. It is said that over thirty cases were shipped out each week. The Farmer's State Bank was established in 1913.

Harnessing the readily available water power supplied by the horse-shoe bend of the Blue Earth River, Northern States Power built Rapidan's first dam, providing the villagers with their first electricity. The dam has and remains to define the region, and it is a local landmark and recreational destination.

According to the Rapidan Heritage Society, the depot was moved to an area farm in 1958 where it was used as a storage building until 2002, when it was moved back to Rapidan and restored by the Heritage Society.

In 1922, four school districts consolidated, and a new school was built in Rapidan. In 1977, the post office was discontinued. Community spirit is thriving. The Heritage Society hosts several events throughout the year including a Memorial Day service, bake sales, Chautauqua Revivals, sleigh rides, and more. The nearby Rapidan Dam Store is in itself a destination, offering the best homemade pie for miles around.

SHELBYVILLE

1856 - 1881

CLASS A

APPROXIMATE LOCATION:
2 miles south of Amboy

It didn't take long for Shelbyville to prosper. Platted in 1856, by the early 1860s it was said to be the only town in Blue Earth County that could accommodate the county fair. By 1867, a hotel, a church, a school, a mill, two stores, a blacksmith shop, and a wagon shop were up and running. A post office operated from 1857 until 1881.

Social activities were important to area residents, and they had a wide variety to choose from, including lyceums, mock senates, church activities, and meetings.

In the late 1870s the railroad was making plans to lay rail lines through the region. Many communities vied for the route to come through their region. Some were even said to offer incentives to the railroad to enhance their location. Shelbyville was not one of the communities offering grants to the railroad. Records indicate that Shelbyville residents voted down one such enticement. Thus, in 1879, a nearby location was platted as Amboy. Amboy received the rail route, and Shelbyville began its descent. Today the former town site is a grain field.

SOUTH BEND

1856 - 1900

CLASS A

APPROXIMATE LOCATION:
Southwest of Mankato in South Bend Township

Aptly named because of the Minnesota River's "south bend," it didn't take long for South Bend to thrive. The first log cabin was built in 1853. The first school term was in 1855. A post office was established in 1856. By 1857 a number of stores were in operation and included a blacksmith shop, a plow works, a hardware store, a ready-made clothing shop, a shoemaker, a cooper shop, a doctor's office, a lawyer's office, a tailor, a harness shop, a cabinet shop, a real estate office, and at least four saloons. Within three years South Bend had over one hundred homes and a population of three hundred.

South Bend continued to thrive until the St. Paul and Sioux Railroad located depots at nearby Minneopa and Mankato, bypassing South Bend. At the time, area historians write, Mankato was not even on the map.

The loss of the railroad brought rapid decline to South Bend. Portions of the town were destroyed by a 1900 fire. The post office was discontinued in 1900. By 1909 one store, a school house, the Welch Congregational Church, and few dwellings were all that remained. The church was torn down in 1930 and was moved to Pemberton where it was reconstructed as an addition to a church there.

Today no buildings remain.

STERLING CENTER

1856 - 1904

CLASS A

APPROXIMATE LOCATION:
Near junction of 121st Street and 550th Avenue WSW of Mapleton

First spelled Sterling Centre from 1856 to 1893, the settlement boomed once rumors spread of a proposed rail line from Good Thunder to Winnebago City. The Sterling Center store opened in 1867 and was soon the area's gathering place. Folks would stop by to pick up their mail, which they could find in a bushel basket by the door. They would simply sort through the mail until they found their own.

A two-story building was constructed. The top floor had a community hall and a blacksmith shop, with a millinery and jewelry store on the first floor. As area historian Julie Schrader wrote, "It was an early mini-mall." Two grist mills were located at the confluence of Providence Creek and the Maple River. The post office operated under both spellings from 1856 to 1904. The store lasted much longer, closing in the mid-1960s.

VOLKSVILLE

1867 - 1902

CLASS A

APPROXIMATE LOCATION:
Section 20 Jamestown Township near the towns of Eagle
Lake and Madison Lake

Furniture wasn't the only thing the Volk brothers built. They also built a sawmill, a shingle and planning mill— all powered by water. The activity, in turn, created a small community surrounding a three-acre mill pond.

In 1867 a two-story building, known as Volk's Hall was constructed. Area historian Gail Palmer writes that the top story was a meeting hall and the first floor housed a cooper shop. On the south shore of the mill pond a furniture factory was added in 1869. The factory manufactured white-oak staves used in the cooper shop, wooden farm implements, and furniture.

In 1882, a devastating fire started in the furniture factory and destroyed the building. It was rebuilt. By 1902, the last of the factories was torn down.

WATONWAN CITY

1856 - 1908

CLASS A

APPROXIMATE LOCATION:
On Watonwan River

Considered a "paper town," Watonwan City was unusual in that it physically existed on land and not only on paper. With the construction of a sawmill on the Watonwan River, a small settlement grew. In addition to the sawmill, a school and post office began operating in 1858. Six years later, a store joined the community. In 1882, the post office name was changed to Blaine (1882 to 1889). The addition of a Presbyterian Church in 1894 was not enough to keep the community viable, and by 1908 the post office was discontinued, and Watonwan City, except for a few pilings in the river in 1986, existed only on paper and in history.

Brown County

Dotson Garage/Car Dealership. (Courtesy of the Brown County Historical Society)

Dotson bank vault and foundations. (Courtesy of the Brown County Historical Society)

DOTSON

1900 – 1940s

CLASS B

APPROXIMATE LOCATION:
5 Miles South of Springfield

From a distance, one might ask "What is it?" Even upon closer examination, the concrete structure isn't easily identifiable. Only when told that the massive cement block is the old bank vault does recognition come. The old concrete vault and foundation are all that remains of the Bank of Dotson, Minnesota. Shortly after the bank closed, people hauled away the façade and bricks, leaving the vault behind.

First named Bedford by the Western Iowa Lot Company survey crew, after one of the worker's Massachusetts home town, the name was changed to Dotson in 1901 after early settler Enoch Dotson.

The Iowa and Minnesota Railroad, which ran a line from Burr, Iowa, to Sanborn, brought early settlers to Brown County. Businesses were busy and plentiful and included, in addition to the depot, two elevators, a lumberyard, a blacksmith, a general store, a stockyard, a creamery, a bank, a garage and car dealership, a dance hall, a saloon, a school, and several homes.

The school was established in 1880. The first school building was constructed of wood and located near the intersection of Brown County #3 and a present township road. In 1921, the building was closed and moved. A new brick building was built and had a full basement, a fuel oil furnace, a cloakroom, a library, and one classroom. Enrollment reached a peak of thirty students. The school served the community until it closed in 1964, when students were sent to nearby Springfield. The school district was dissolved in 1965. One news account tells that the original school bell was sold at an auction and donated to the museum in Springfield. Nearly all school records have been lost.

Dotson was the social center for area residents. A town baseball team was popular in the 1920s and 1930s. Games were played nearly every Sunday afternoon during the summer. Many dances were hosted and were very popular, especially during the years of the Great Depression. It is said crowds were large and often rowdy. Dotson opened an open-air pavilion in 1918, and it quickly became a popular destination. Moonshine was readily available and often helped farmers supplement their incomes. In later years the facility was used as a roller rink. It was later torn down.

Increasing automobile use spurred the construction of a repair garage in 1922. A car dealership was operated in conjunction with the garage. Kessel Kars, made in Hartford, Wisconsin, and Minneapolis Moline tractors were sold as well.

At one time people thought a coal mine was in the region. A mining corporation was formed and equipment was brought in. The coal was most likely brought in and planted by someone playing a joke or by conmen.

Dotson was active until the 1940s. By 1963 the population was nine and consisted of one extended family. In later years a few remnants were left of the town, including the concrete vault, foundations, and rubble from the elevator, the garage/car dealership building, the creamery, the school, and one home.

GOLDEN GATE

1868 – 1900s

CLASS B

APPROXIMATE LOCATION:
6 Miles north of Sleepy Eye

Back in 1949 a young Brown County 4-H'er researched and wrote a report on the long-ago community of Golden Gate. According to her report, Golden Gate was said to be "rough and rowdy." Something was always happening on Saturday afternoons. Events ranged from horse races to ball games. If inclement weather put a damper on

Golden Gate mill. (Courtesy of the Brown County Historical Society)

Golden Gate site. (Courtesy of the Brown County Historical Society)

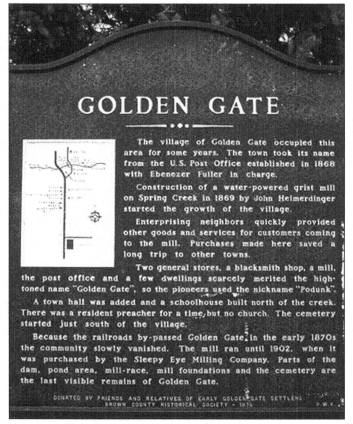

Golden Gate marker. (Courtesy of the Brown County Historical Society)

those activities, wrestling or boxing matches (without gloves) were held. Horseshoes were also a popular activity. The primarily Irish, English and Scottish settlers loved debate competitions and contests were held at area schools or at the social center of the community, the town hall.

Life in Golden Gate began with and centered on the mill. Built by John Heimerdinger in 1869, all construction for the mill, including the mill stones, were made, by hand, by Heimerdinger. In 1872 a second mill with a twenty-five-foot

water wells was constructed. When water in the small stream ran low, that water source was supplemented by several artesian wells. By 1882, Golden Gate was bustling and included two stores, a post office, a blacksmith, a dance hall, and a handful of homes. Dances were held every two weeks. Mail was delivered once a week, on Fridays.

Golden Gate's prosperity declined in 1902 with the Sleepy Eye Milling Company's purchase of the mill. The Golden Gate mill was dismantled. The former miller's house was renovated and became a company summer house. When the railroad chose to bypass Golden Gate, the community's fate was sealed.

By 1910, Golden Gate was no longer listed as a town in Minnesota directories. Most of the businesses were gone by the 1920s. Over the years, the historic Golden Gate Cemetery had become abandoned and was in dire need of maintenance. A historical group was formed in the 1980s. The dedicated preservation group worked to restore the cemetery as well as cleaning and repairing many of the stones. Efforts to place a historical marker were also begun. Golden Gate as a town may be long gone, but the community spirit and the preservation of history lives on.

IBERIA

1860s – 1900s

CLASS A/HISTORICAL MARKER

APPROXIMATE LOCATION:
5 Miles Southeast of Sleepy Eye near junction of County #24 and Stark Township Road

With a nickname like "Brimstone Corners" there has to be tales to tell, stories to hear. From all accounts, there are. Said to have all the characteristics of a Wild West frontier town there were fights, murders, elopements, robberies, political corruption, death (by Indians), grasshopper plagues, scandal, epidemics, and lives lived on the raucous side. Local folklore has it that Jesse James stole a horse in Iberia on his escape from the botched robbery in Northfield.

Prior to the community being established, tempers were high in the region due to the Dakota Conflict. The Shetak Trail went through the region, and settlers used the trail to get to New Ulm during the height of the tension. Wagon ruts could still be seen 130 years later. The cemetery shows evidence of several fatal attacks in the region. At least one tombstone tells that family members were "Killed by Indians." The

Blim (Bleum) Family Tombstone marker. All but one family member killed near Iberia 1862. (Courtesy of Curtis Dahlin)

Cottonwood River at Iberia Dam postcard. (Author's collection)

Blim (Bleum family), except for one lone survivor were casualties, and a marker in the cemetery tells the tale. His parents and siblings are killed.

Iberia began in 1862 and took the ancient name of the Spanish Peninsula. Iberia was also the name of a community

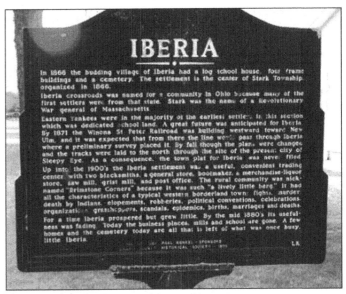

Iberia historical marker. (Author's Collection)

in Ohio that had been the first settler's home place. The first buildings went up in 1864. A log school was built in 1866. Expectations were high in 1871 with the rumor that the Winona and St. Peter Railroad planned a new rail line through the community. Preliminary surveys had the line going through the heart of the newly established community but for reasons unknown the plans changed, and the railroad line passed just north of Iberia. The change in route gave birth and growth to the community of Sleepy Eye.

Iberia continued on and even prospered as a busy trade center until the early 1900s. Businesses included two blacksmiths, a general store (with a short-lived post office) a bootmaker, saloon, liquor store, sawmill, grist mill, cabinet shops, and farm implement dealers. When the railroads plans changed and Sleepy Eye prospered, Iberia declined. A fatal blow was dealt to Iberia when a mill was built, in 1883, in Sleepy Eye. Iberia's mill declined rapidly and closed a few years later.

"Shooting the Anvil" appears to have been a common celebration in nineteenth-century communities, and Iberia partook of the festivities as well. An early settler wrote that a large acorn or burr was filled with gunpowder and placed on an anvil. Another anvil was placed on top of that. A line of gunpowder was poured from the burr between the two anvils to the ground. The trace line was lit and the gunpowder load exploded raising the top anvil as high as the load would carry it. Not only was the flying anvil dangerous, but when the acorn or burr would shoot out at dizzing speeds no one was safe. The result could be lethal. Fred Carpenter, early resident, recalled that one time, his infant brother, was asleep in the store across from the blacksmith shop. The burr, when lit, became a bullet.

Once it went through a window and over the sleeping baby's head.

Social activities were important to Iberia residents. One news report stated that the Iberia Annual Picnic was shortened due to caterpillars.

Iberia's cemetery was abandoned for years. In 1970 the Brown County Historical Society and a group of concerned citizens began restoring the cemetery. The grounds were cleaned up, and several tombstones were sent for repair and restoration. Public access to the cemetery was also addressed. The tombstones themselves told the history of Iberia. The earliest stones were dated 1859/1860.

The school closed in 1971. In tribute, the last class researched and wrote the town history. A historical marker is at the site.

LONETREE (LAKE)

1869 - 1904

CLASS A

APPROXIMATE LOCATION:
South of Upper Sioux Agency State Park

A lone cottonwood tree, with a diameter of at least five feet, marked the spot of the long-ago community and was a local landmark. It also was the source of the settlement's name.

Primarily a postal station with a succession of postmasters, Lone Tree was established in 1869 and discontinued in 1904. The post office operated under different spellings, Lonetree Lake from 1869 until 1894 and Lonetree from 1894 to 1905. A Presbyterian Church, with fourteen members, was organized in 1870. A church building was constructed at a cost of $1,500.00 the next year. Ten years later, in 1881, the Congregation was disbanded.

Maps, photos, and a brief history of the small community were found in an eighth-grade geography project done in 1980 by Sharon Schroeder. According to Schroeder's report, the small community also had a small store and a halfway house (hotel). The namesake tree is now gone and the town site is a farm and agricultural land.

Cottonwood County

Delft Pure Garage. (Courty of the Cottonwood County Historical Society)

One of Delft's garages. (Courtesy of the Cottonwood County Historical Society)

DELFT

1906 – 1993

CLASS D

APPROXIMATE LOCATION:
12 Miles Northwest of Mountain Lake

On the day that Barba Best visited Delft, several area women were canning cherries at the Carson Fellowship Hall. Children were riding their bikes through the clean, neat streets where many original Delft buildings still stand, though no longer operating or open for business.

Delft had several long-lasting businesses, the creamery operated for fifty-seven years, the post office was in existence for eighty-seven years. The Mennonite Church lasted the entirety of Delft village and then some. Perhaps most long lasting are the memories.

Barba grew up in the 1950s near Delft. She was a farmer's daughter and remembers her father selling his crops to the Delft Elevator. She attended the two-room Delft School where students were served hot lunches in the basement.

Delft, the village, was settled by Mennonite farmers from South Russia. Their original homeland was Delft, Holland, thus the naming of Delft Station. Ten years before a rail station was established, a skimming statin was built. When the rail station became a reality in 1892, the community of Delft developed. It is said Delft was a direct result of the Currie Line, a branch of the Chicago, St. Paul, Minneapolis, and Omaha Railroad. The line ran from Bingham Lake in Cottonwood County to Currie in central Murray County. Ten years after the station was established, Delft was platted.

Once the village was created, the rural skimming station was closed and a creamery was built in the burgeoning community in 1905. The creamery operated for fifty-seven years. It later affiliated with New Ulm, sold in 1958 and closed permanently in 1962. It is said the creamery, without a doubt, was Delft's most important industry.

A post office (first called Wilhelmine) was established in 1906. Delft Minnesota is the only post office in the United States to be named Delft. Throughout its history, the post office received some mail that was meant for the Dutch Delft, not the Minnesota Delft. Except for a brief interruption from 1906 to 1918, the post office operated until 1990, when its last postmark was issued.

Housed in a small fourteen-by-twenty-two-foot building, without running water or a restroom, the post office was the

Early Delft Store. (Courty of the Cottonwood County Historical Society)

Delft railroad warehouse. (Courtesy of Barba K. Best)

Delft Post Office. (Courtesy of the Cottonwood County Historical Society)

Delft street, 1980s. (Courtesy of the Cottonwood County Historical Society)

Carson Meeting House, 2015. (Courtesy of Barba K. Best)

Delft Elevator, 2015. The original elevator portion burned in 1975. (Courtesy of Barba K. Best)

Delft Creamery, 2015. (Courtesy of Barba K. Best)

movies, no dances, no tobacco, and no alcohol were ever available in the community. The reporter marveled at how clean and neat the community was. The stores had no signs on their exterior. One Delft store was still active and was filled with canned goods and other staples, but no clothing was on the store shelves. A small lunch counter in the rear of the store served hamburgers and cold meat sandwiches.

In 1975 the Coop Elevator burned to the ground. Plans to rebuild were implemented, and a concrete pad was poured but financial issues prevailed, and the elevator was never rebuilt. Delft was on the decline.

If the creamery was Delft's most important industry, the churches were, and still are, the heart of the community. Both churches—the Emanuel Mennonite (built in 1917) and the Carson Mennonite Brethren Church, which had originally been located in the rural areas of Delft, were major influences. The rural Carson church closed in 1948 and a new building was erected in the village. While it was uncommon to have two churches of the same faith and denomination in one community, both were more similar than different. Both had similar theological beliefs. One believed in baptism by immersion, the other sprinkled water during baptism. Both were centers of faith and were communal meeting places. The Carson church was, in fact, first called, the Carson Meeting Place. The Carson church, distinctively shaped in the letter "M" closed its doors in 2005. The building sat vacant for five years.

In 2009, five area couples, many of them former church members, worked to re-open the basement fellowship hall. Local residents joined together to build a stage, made tables, brought chairs in and converted the kitchen to a lunch-style coffee counter. Dubbed "The Underground," it was a fitting name because of the coffee grounds and it was underground. Aptly it was officially called the Carson Meeting Place as it was in its earliest days.

People of all ages come together, especially on Saturday nights, for fellowship, coffee, snacks, pizza, and community. The upper levels of the church are used for other events and get-togethers.

Delft, as a village, may no longer exists, but Delft the community continues.

community meeting place, especially after other businesses began to close. The last postmaster, Arlene Bartosh, recalls getting "live" deliveries. In the spring it was common to get shipments that "chirped and peeped" as the chicks arrived. One time she took receipt of a screened box filled with bees. A few had managed to escape the screening and were perched on the outside of the box. She hurriedly contacted the recipient and had them come and pick up the parcel as quickly as possible.

The last mail was postmarked November 2, 1990. The building was later moved to the nearby Heritage Village.

In the early years, Delft was a thriving village. The business district included two grocery stores, five gas stations/garages, the creamery, an elevator, a lumberyard, a hardware store, a feed mill, a two-room school, the State Bank of Delft, two churches, and the train depot among others. In 1925 the Interstate Power Company built a power line through Delft. $1,200.00 was donated to the village for the access and that greatly boosted the business section.

Delft was on the decline by 1968. A *St. Paul Pioneer Press* article highlighted the community. Stating that the Mennonite influence was strongly evident, the reporter told that no

Dodge County

Cheney overlay map. (Courtesy of Dan West http://www.west2k.com/misc/ghosttowns.htm)

ASHLAND

1856 - 1872

CLASS B

APPROXIMATE LOCATION:
160th Avenue 640th Street

Split along township lines, part of Ashland was in Ashland Township. The other part, twenty platted acres, was in Ripley Township. Businesses were established in both portions and both townships and included two blacksmiths, a wagon shop, a hotel, three stores, a steam mill, a Sabbath School, and a school.

Church services were held in the school as well as other town locations. The reverend walked nine miles every Sunday, no matter the weather or the season, to conduct services also in the Wasioja Church.

A Seventh Day Baptist Church was organized in 1855, as well as a small cemetery and the Ashland Town Hall were located two miles west of the village. A Presbyterian church was also part of the community.

Some old foundations are still visible.

AVON

1856 - 1866

CLASS A

APPROXIMATE LOCATION:
165th Avenue & 595th Street

Other than dates of post office operation, 1856 to 1860 and 1862 to 1866, little is known about Avon located in Section 7 of Wasioja Township.

CANISTEO

1876 - 1885

CLASS A

APPROXIMATE LOCATION:
South of Kasson - 250th Avenue & 685th Street

Mail was delivered semi-weekly to the small community named for the early settler's home village along the Canisteo River in Steuben County New York.

CHENEY (EDEN)

1886 – 1920s

CLASS C

APPROXIMATE LOCATION:
North of Dodge Center, West of Wasioja

A large property owner in the area, with land adjoining the proposed site of the village, donated part of his farm for the village. According to the Dodge County Historical Society, he stated that they could have their Cheney Post Office but he wanted the Eden Depot as his "Garden of Eden."

Former Cheney Livery. (Courtesy of Dan West http://www.west2k.com/misc/ghosttowns.htm)

Former livery building. (Courtesy of Dan West http://www.west2k.com/misc/ghosttowns.htm)

Former Cheney business, the blacksmith shop. (Courtesy of Dan West http://www.west2k.com/misc/ghosttowns.htm)

Former Cheney mainstreet business building, the blacksmith shop. (Courtesy of Dan West http://www.west2k.com/misc/ghosttowns.htm)

The village included a blacksmith shop, two stores, a barbershop, a creamery, the depot and stockyard, and a post office that operated from 1886 until 1924.

Early settlers were from the New England, New York area.

Most records seem to use Cheney and Eden interchangeably. Post office records show only Cheney as an established post office. There is no record of a post office operating under the Eden name.

The cheese factory was later converted to a barn. The Depot was demolished in 1940. The school building was sold to the Dodge Center Rod and Gun Club and moved. The church was moved and dismantled.

Cheney's main street is now a farm driveway. Other buildings, in ruins, are also on the farm.

CLAREMONT STREET

1850s - 1870s

CLASS A

APPROXIMATE LOCATION:
Intersection of 595th Street and 124th Avenue

Most of the early settlers traveled from the region of Claremont, New Hampshire, thus the naming of the community. The first settler, in May of 1854, chose his claim and marked his name and date on a tree. Later that summer others arrived and began putting up hay for the expected arrival of livestock set to arrive that fall.

For a time, Claremont Street was a bustling village. It was home to a general store, two hotels, a stage stop, a blacksmith shop, and a cheese factory.

When the railroad chose to lay its lines just south of Claremont Street, residents and businesses moved to the new railroad location, establishing the present day community of Claremont.

Today a private home sits on the former town site along with a Dodge County Historical Society Marker. Dodge County has over two dozen long-ago towns and have placed markers to commemorate the locations.

CONCORD

1856 - 1906

CLASS C

APPROXIMATE LOCATION:
9 Miles from Mantorville, along Highway #22 and #24

Once home to over two hundred residents, the village of Concord was first known as Sumner's Grove. The first settlers arrived in 1855 and soon after established the Eagle Flour Mill, using water power readily available from the Zumbro River.

A daily stage ran from Dodge Center with a semi-weekly run to Zumbrota. Concord included two general stores, two doctors, two blacksmith shops, a wagon shop, a milliner, a hotel, a justice of the peace, and a creamery. Two churches were also part of the community as was a school.

The school building still stands and is used as the town hall. The Baptist Church was moved to West Concord.

EAGLE VALLEY

1860 - 1960s

CLASS C

APPROXIMATE LOCATION:
190th Avenue & 540th Street

Built nearly 150 years ago, the Eagle Valley School still stands amongst the rolling hills of the countryside. In 1860 classes were conducted in the original log school building. In 1870/1880 the present standing school was built. The school closed in the 1950s.

In addition to the school, Eagle Valley was home to a store, a church, a dam, and a flour mill. Remains of the dam and mill can be found on York Creek near the school.

EAST CLAREMONT STREET

1874 - 1879

CLASS A

APPROXIMATE LOCATION:
150th Avenue & 595th Street

Old building foundations mark the location of the town of East Claremont Street. A post office operated only five years, from 1874 to 1879. Little else is known about the community.

HALLOWELL

1857 - 1860

CLASS A

APPROXIMATE LOCATION:
West of Dodge Center, 175th Avenue & 635th Avenue

Platted before the railroad line was determined, Hallowell had a sawmill, a store, and other necessary businesses so many towns have. A post office operated from 1857 to 1860. When the rail line routed through Dodge Center and Claremont, and not through Hallowell, the community died away.

HOBSON

1898 - 1925

CLASS A

APPROXIMATE LOCATION:
100th Avenue and 580th Street

Lasting just twenty-five years, the community of Hobson included a creamery and store. The store burned in 1925, and what was left of Hobson moved across the street, to Steele County.

MILTON

1865 - 1867 (1950s)

CLASS C

APPROXIMATE LOCATION:
North of Mantorville at 245th Avenue and 565th Street

Marked by a beautiful grove of pine trees, the community of Milton's school building still stands. The building of the former creamery, which operated until 1957, is also still standing. The lower floor of the creamery building is now a private home. A short-lived post office operated from 1865 until 1867.

OSLO

1879 - 1902

CLASS C

APPROXIMATE LOCATION:
MN #30, 250th Avenue & 730th Street

From the few records found, it is apparent the store was the impetus for the community and was the longest lasting of the settlement's businesses. A Norwegian bookseller opened the store in 1875. A succession of store owners operated the store until its permanent closing in the early 1940s. A post office operated a short time from 1879 to 1902.

Southern Minnesota backroads traveler Roger Langseth writes that in recent years, a gas station, an old store, a handful of homes, and the Vernon Township Hall remain at the location.

PUMPKIN HALLOW

Early 1900s

CLASS A

APPROXIMATE LOCATION:
265th Avenue and 535th Street, East of Berne

Little is known about the Swiss settlement just east of Berne. The original limestone school was destroyed in 1909 and a replacement school was built. It operated until consolidation with Pine Island Schools in 1956. In the days before a cheese factory was built, settlers made cheese in their homes. There are no physical remains of the settlement.

RICE LAKE

1857 - 1903

CLASS C/F

APPROXIMATE LOCATION:
MN #20, North edge of Rice Lake State Park

Even before Dodge County was established, the lakeside settlement of Rice Lake was going strong. Its location along the stage coach line made it an early travel center. The Tiffany Lodge was a stopping place for the stage and offered meals and overnight lodging to travelers. Horses (four of them were used to pull the coach) were rested or exchanged at the lodge as well.

When the railroad bypassed Rice Lake, the businesses and the population moved south to be near the newly established rail center of Claremont.

Rice Lake Church - "RiceLakeChurchMN" by McGhiever - Own work. Licensed under CC BY-SA 2.5 via Commons - https://commons.wikimedia.org/wiki/File:RiceLakeChurchMN.jpg#/media/File:RiceLakeChurchMN.jpg

In 1963, Rice Lake as designated as a state park. The original, now vacant, Methodist Church stands at what is now the northern border of the state park along Highway #20. The cemetery is still maintained and used.

RIPLEY

1890s - 1993

CLASS A

APPROXIMATE LOCATION:
130TH Avenue and 670th Street

Records of the small community are sparse and include no postal history. According to the Dodge County Historical Society, the town hall still stands. The first floor of the building once served as the District #65 school room.

SACRAMENTO

1856 - 1870s

CLASS A

APPROXIMATE LOCATION:
221ST Avenue & 605th Street

After gold was discovered at Sutter's Mill in 1849, gold fever was rampant all across the country. Even in Minnesota. Hoping to prey upon the frenzy, two men planted nuggets of gold around the Sacremento area, between Mantorville and Wasioja.

After spreading the word that gold had been found, a rush of people flocked to the area. Soon a bustling settlement arose and included a hotel, a small store, a stone quarry, a flour mill, a stage coach stop, several saloons, a dance hall, and a number of homes. One of the hotels, built in 1856 was later sold and moved to Kasson. The larger two-story hotel was in ruins though still standing in 1979. The roof collapsed and the building has since been demolished.

STEAM MILL HILL

MID 1800s

CLASS A

APPROXIMATE LOCATION:
East of Berne on Highway #24, 250th Avenue & 542nd Street

As one could imagine from the name, a community called Steam Mill Hill had to have had a mill and be situated on a hill. That it did. A steam mill operated near a small stream at the top of the hill. The picturesque area is hills, ravines, and valley. According to the Dodge County Historical Society, the district school building still stands above the road. The nearby town hall, built years ago is still used. Two sets of farm buildings remain at the top of the hill. For a short time, a small grocery store, "Do Drop Inn" was in operation.

UNION SPRINGS

1858 - 1873

CLASS A

APPROXIMATE LOCATION:
South of Kasson on 270th Avenue and 655th Street

The small community of Union Spings once had a tavern, a store, a blacksmith shop, a skimming station, and a school. A post office operated from 1858 to 1873.

VENTURE

1899 - 1906

CLASS G

APPROXIMATE LOCATION:
South of Claremont, 140th Avenue & 690th Street

Home to several businesses including a store, creamery and blacksmith, a school and several homes were also part of the community. The school building remains and is in a nearby farmyard used as an outbuilding. No other signs of the village remain.

VERNON

1867 - 1882

CLASS A

APPROXIMATE LOCATION:
North of Oslo, 250th Avenue & 710th Street

Best known for its cheese factory and creamery, Vernon was a thriving community until the railroad line bypassed it. The rail line spurred the growth of nearby Kasson and Hayfield. Vernon became history.

VLASATY

1896 - 1906

CLASS A

APPROXIMATE LOCATION:
South of Dodge Center, 200th Avenue and 680th Street

Spelled a variety of ways, the post office records officially recognize Vlasaty as the correct spelling. The community was located on the Chicago and Northwestern Railroad, and the railroad played a major role in the settlement's postal history. Early residents recall that the mail was delivered in canvas bags, which were thrown from passenger trains. This practice often damaged the mail bags as well as the mail inside

them and sometimes left mail strewn all over the place. The outgoing mail was similarly bagged and hung on a large arm on a pole near the tracks. As the train sped by, a special arm on the train picked up the bag dropping it in the rail car. Residents would pick up their mail at the store/post office which operated from 1896 until 1906.

Vlasaty included an elevator, a depot, a general store/post office combination, and a few other establishments. The second floor of the store was living quarters for the store owner.

According to the Dodge County Historical Society, after several years, Vlasaty was lost to time because of a "bad deal."

Today, there are no physical remains of the village. The area where the town once stood is dotted with wind generators.

WASIOJA

1856 - 1911

CLASS C

APPROXIMATE LOCATION:
4 Miles from Mantorville, 210th Avenue & 600th Street

Heartbreakingly tragic, the story of Wasioja illustrates the effect national events have on local history and how personal history can be. The Civil War, a changing economy, and the railroad all contributed to the demise of the once-thriving community of Wasioja.

Wasioja grew rapidly. The first building in the community was built in 1855, and by 1861 nearly one thousand people

The Doig house. (Wasioja Historic District, National Register of Historic Places, Mantorville, Dodge County, Minnesota. 75000977)

lived in the immediate vicinity. Being a stop on the stage coach line helped increase population. Soon the Wasioja business district included two hotels, a bank, a newspaper, a flour mill, a stone quarry & lime kiln, five churches, a hardware store, a furniture store, a farm machinery dealer, a dry goods store, several general merchandise stores, two doctors offices, a post office, a half dozen lodging places, a lawyer's office, and the seminary.

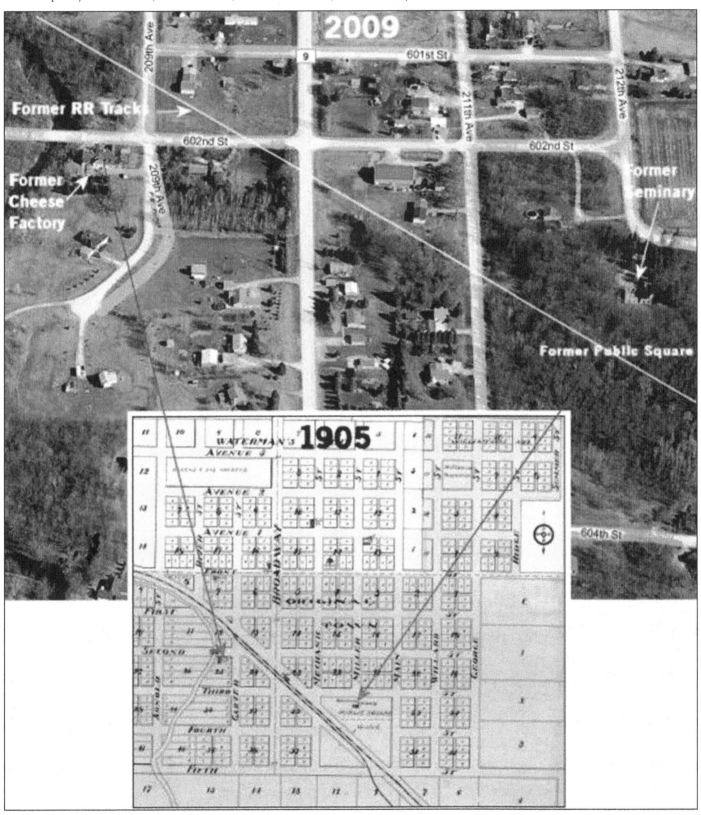

Wasioja overlay map. (Courtesy of Dan West)

Baptist church. (Wasioja Historic District, National Register of Historic Places, Mantorville, Dodge County, Minnesota. 75000977)

Civil War recruiting station. (Wasioja Historic District, National Register of Historic Places, Mantorville, Dodge County, Minnesota. 75000977)

Lime kiln ruins. (Wasioja Historic District, National Register of Historic Places, Mantorville, Dodge County, Minnesota. 75000977)

School house. (Courtesy of Wasioja Historic District, National Register of Historic Places, Mantorville, Dodge County, Minnesota. 75000977)

Current seminary walls. (Courtesy of: Dan West)

Historic District Collage: "2010-1025-WasiojaHD" by Bobak Ha'Eri - Own work. Licensed under CC BY 3.0 via Commons - https://commons.wikimedia.org/wiki/File:2010-1025-WasiojaHD.jpg#/media/File:2010-1025-WasiojaHD.jpg.

Cheese factory. (Courtesy of Dan West)

Wasioja Seminary entrance block. (Courtesy of Dan West)

Wasioja Seminary ruins. (Courtesy of Dan West)

Wasioja Seminary walls, 2015. (Courtesy of Dan West)

In 1860 the limestone seminary was built in the hopes it too would promote growth for the newly established village. Named the Minnesota Seminary, the school boasted an enrollment of more than 300 students in the first year. In 1861, the school became the Northwestern College, and classes were from primary grades to the collegiate level.

In 1862 the Civil War was at its peak, and patriotism was rampant across the county. Minnesota was no exception. In fact, Minnesota's involvement and participation ranks among the highest in the nation. Minnesotans volunteered in great numbers and served valiantly. It was said the Minnesota regiments earned great reputations throughout the war. Micheal Eckers, author of *The Boys of Wasioja*, wrote that "Minnesota boys could shoot, were tough, and they were used to the elements."

After a rousing talk from the seminary president, approximately one dozen students walked out of the school and went straight to the law office, which also served as the Civil War recruitment office. They enlisted and served as Company C of the Second Minnesota Regiment. In total sixty-eight men from Dodge County would serve in the Civil War. The enlistees included the students and a seminary professor. Freelance writer Loren Else writes that Company C saw battles at Mill Springs, Corinth, Missionary Ridge, and would march with General Sherman. It is also recorded that Company C stopped the Confederates near Chickamauga and suffered heavy losses.

When the war was over, Else writes that only twelve of the Dodge County enlistees would be present at final muster. Seventeen died of disease, seven were killed or mortally wounded, and twenty-one were wounded. Only one of the men who survived the war would return to Wasioja.

The community was devastated. With so few returning, heartbreak, the shortage of labor, and loss of markets, business after business closed. The lime kilns and quarry closed. Churches moved elsewhere. A fall cloudburst destroyed the dam and all milling ceased. The seminary continued on, but enrollment had been cut in half. Stage coach travel was giving way to railroad transportation. In 1866 the Winona and St. Peter Railroad ran its line four miles south of Wasioja, creating the new communities of Kasson and Dodge Center. Wasioja never recovered from the losses.

The Baptists stopped sponsorship of the seminary, and it reopened as the Groveland Seminary. It closed in 1875 but was again reopened later that year by the Wesleyan Methodist Conference. The school closed permanently in 1894.

A 1905 fire, speculated to be started by a group of young men having fun, destroyed the seminary building, leaving the ruins that remain today. A graduate and instructor, Reverend Gould preserved the ruins. After his death his heirs donated the site to Dodge County.

The former law office turned recruitment center, the two-story limestone school, the lime kilns, the Baptist church, and the Doig House as well as the Seminary ruins remain today. They are all now listed on the National Register of Historic Places. Memorial services and re-enactments are held at the historic site.

WESTFIELD CENTRE

1875 - 1893

CLASS C

APPROXIMATE LOCATION:
145th Avenue & 700th Street

Most of the early settlers were Norwegian with a few Irish. Twenty years after the first settlers arrived, a post office was established and operated until 1893. The Westfield Centre Norwegian Lutheran Evangelical Church was organized. Until 1919, when a church building was built on an acre of land donated by an area couple, services were held in the school. The church and cemetery remain.

Faribault County

Former Brush Creek Motel. (Courtesy of Tom McLaughlin)

BANKS

1864 – 1920s

CLASS A/B

APPROXIMATE LOCATION:
Northwest and Southeast Shore of Rice Lake, near US #90 and #22

Faribault County historians estimate that there are at least sixty-two lost towns within its county's borders. The majority were primarily postal stations, oftentimes located in early postmaster's homes. Others became small villages that served as rural social centers. Others developed into trade centers, at least for a time. Equally disparate is the amount of information and details preserved and available for research. Information ranges from nothing at all, to post office operating dates to full histories. Most lost towns fall into the former categories with minimal data available.

Banks is one Faribault County town we know a bit about. Records tell that Banks, during its history, was located at two different sites. The first was on the northwest corner of Rice Lake. The second was on the southeast shore of the lake. Banks was first known as Rice Lake, and for a short time was also known as Paynsburg (after an early hotel owner). From the mid 1850s until the early 1900s, Banks was a stage coach mail stop. The stages and four horses would overnight at the settlement. Nightly dances were held for the entertainment of stage passengers and were held on the second floor of the hotel.

Settling the area was hard work, made even more so by environmental conditions. Early settler A.J. Kiester said that the primary occupations were killing mosquitoes and trapping muskrats.

The first location included a hotel, general store, and post office, all under one roof. Other establishments were a blacksmith shop, a church, a bank, a school, and several homes. First housed in a log building, the school later consolidated with Kiester schools.

The railroad's decision to route their new rail line through Wells, sealed the demise of Banks. A modern farmhouse and church (originally organized as the Rice Lake Evangelical Church in 1861) are all that remained at the site in recent years.

Bank's second location included the Foster Cooperative Dairy Association Creamery (1874 to 1926) and a general store. The post office, originally located at the northwest site, later moved to the southeast site and operated there until it was discontinued in 1904. Facing financial problems, the creamery closed in 1926, and the store followed suit shortly after. There is no trace of the second location.

Historians note that Banks might have had a different development path had the railroad followed the stage coach line. However, the railroad routed through Wells, and that effectively sealed Banks's fate.

BRUSH CREEK

1873 – 1882

CLASS B

APPROXIMATE LOCATION:

We know that the town of Brush Creek had a post office for approximately nine years. Recent photos show a one-time, now abandoned motel. There is also a Brush Creek Township.

Brush Creek Town Hall. (Courtesy of Tom McLaughlin)

CLAYTON

1860 - 1899

CLASS G

APPROXIMATE LOCATION:
2 Miles South of Bricelyn

Eventually established as Clayton, the community was first named Prattsville, after an early settler and the first postmaster. The hamlet was a busy trade center for over thirty years and included a post office, store, creamery, Baptist church, newspaper office, and school. Clayton also had its own doctor. Faribault County's first telephone message was sent over the wires in Clayton. In 1899 and just two miles away, Bricelyn was established, causing the eventual demise of Clayton.

GUCKEEN

1901 - 1973

CLASS C

APPROXIMATE LOCATION:
½ mile south of I-90

Just one year after celebrating the Centennial Anniversary of their church, the members of Our Lady of Mercy Catholic Church made the painful decision to close. Several options were discussed and the result was to entrust the church to a Catholic Religious Society known as "The Confraternity of the Traditional Mass." The group, which had been organized six years earlier, designated the church as a Traditional Mass facility. Mass would be offered in Latin only. It was also sanctioned as a place where any faithful could fulfill their Sunday obligations.

Guckeen post office. (Courtesy of the PMCC – Post Mark Collectors Club)

Guckeen store. (Courtesy of Tom McLaughlin)

Early Guckeen postcard. (Author's Collection)

Our Lady of Mercy, Guckeen. (Courtesy of Tom McLaughlin)

Guckeen church. (Courtesy of Tom McLaughlin)

Guckeen Garage. (Courtesy of Tom McLaughlin)

Guckeen, originally known as Derby, was established in 1901, with the church being established the following year. A post office operated for nearly three-quarters of a century, from 1901 until 1973. The original post office building is on display at the Faribault County Fair.

Available records tell little about Guckeen's seventy-five-year history or its demise. The old store building was demolished in 2015, but several vintage buildings still stand.

HOMEDAHL

1877 - 1904

CLASS A

APPROXIMATE LOCATION:
5 Miles southwest of Bricelyn

Homedahl's close proximity to the newly established community of Bricelyn would prove to be its demise. Named for a Norwegian town, Homedahl included a creamery, blacksmith, jeweler, general store and post office. No church was ever built in the community but a traveling minister provided spiritual guidance.

MARNA

1901 - Mid-1900s

CLASS A

APPROXIMATE LOCATION:
Halfway between Frost and Blue Earth

Though the post office lasted just ten years (1901 to 1911) the community of Marna was a busy center for over fifty years. Marna also served as the site for the annual sugar beet dump. Marna's location and name were chosen by the Iowa, Minnesota, and Northwestern Railroad. The first lots were auctioned off in 1899. The community included elevators, a depot, stockyards, and a general store that operated from 1922 to 1972. The elevator is now owned and operated by Cargill.

VERONA

1856 - 1880s

CLASS A

APPROXIMATE LOCATION:
3 miles south of Winnebago

The town site was staked out in 1855 and two possible name choices were considered, Dewey and Verona. Verona, after Shakespeare's *The Two Gentlemen of Verona* was chosen. Growing quickly, Verona was at one time Faribault County's third largest town. A post office operated from 1856 to 1865. Over the years, nearby Winnebago drew trade, and Verona faded away.

WALNUT LAKE

1860 - 1880s

CLASS A

APPROXIMATE LOCATION:
5½ miles south of Wells

Located on the northwest side of the Walnut Lake, the town of Walnut Lake served as an early tourist destination. Several hotels, a few stores, a blacksmith shop, a short-lived post office, and a school constituted the community. Nearly all of the businesses were heavily mortgaged, and the owners eventually abandoned their establishments.

Today the area is still a recreational destination. The Walnut Lake State Wildlife Management Area occupies the region.

Fillmore County

Overland House, Bratsberg. (Unknown)

Birds eye view of Carimona, postcard. (Author's Collection)

Cherry Grove vintage building (Courtessy of Bernard H. Pietenpol - Pietenpol Aircraft Company)

AMHERST VILLAGE

1870/1902

CLASS A

APPROXIMATE LOCATION:
Cr #23

Early residents say the store in Amherst didn't look like much from the outside, but on the inside, oh the scents and smells. The aromatic spices, the scent of fresh ground coffee, the sweet-smelling penny candy—it was enough to make one heady. The large coffee grinder sat on the counter and invited one and all. It is no wonder the store was considered the area's social center.

The first settlers all built their homesteads along the road in the ravine. For that reason, the settlement was first called "strung out town," which was later shortened to Stringtown.

The store opened in 1860 and soon a blacksmith, a telephone exchange, a post office, a shoe repair business, a creamery, and a school were established in the small village. For a while the creamery thrived, but mismanagement caused its closure in the 1920s. After the creamery closed the building served as a dance hall.

Little remains of the village, and in recent years one occupied and a few abandoned homes sat at the old town site.

BIG SPRINGS

Mid-1860s

CLASS A

APPROXIMATE LOCATION:
County #22

Turning 160 acres into lots, the settlement was platted into business lots, parks, and church lots. Most sold for $25.00 up to $150.00 for corner lots. Records tell of two women from Pennsylvania who bought a corner lot hoping to establish a millinery shop. Upon their arrival they were dismayed to find their lot a mile from the nearest house and located in a slough. They promptly returned back East.

Today a few homes and St. Paul's Lutheran Church are in the area.

BRATSBERG

1862 - 1909

CLASS A

APPROXIMATE LOCATION:
CR #10 east of Whalen

Originally selling beer and alcohol, the Bratsberg Store disposed of the liquor trade after the first few years. A post office was established in 1860 and operated until 1909. At various times, Bratsberg included a blacksmith, a post offce and store, a wagon shop, a creamery, a garage, and three other stores. A town band also existed for several years.

Most if not all of the early immigrants to the region were from Norway, thus the name of the township. The Overland House, now on the National Register of Historic Places, was significant to early settlement.

Today there are about ten to twelve homes and the Norway Town Hall in the vicinity.

CARIMONA

1855 - 1902

CLASS A

APPROXIMATE LOCATION:
South side of Root River (West of Preston)

Thinking that a thriving village would attract a railroad and in turn status as the county seat, Carimona was platted in 1854. After all, the town site was along the stage coach route from St. Paul, Minnesota, to Dubuque, Iowa, so it was only natural the railroad line would follow the same route.

Soon Carimona included a flour mill, a tinsmith, a blacksmith, a cooper shop, a sawmill, a post office (1855 to 1902) and a for a short time, a printer. A nearby church and a brick school, which at one time had sixty students enrolled, completed the community.

Carimona's dreams of a railroad never materialized and the town faded away. In recent years all that remains is a handful of rural homes and large cemetery in the area.

CHERRY GROVE

1857/1903 - 1940s

CLASS D

APPROXIMATE LOCATION:
9 miles south of Wykoff, near County #5 and 160th Street

James Colby carried his prized nursery stock with him as he traveled from Vermont to Minnesota. Upon his arrival, he planted his cherry orchard just north of his homestead, thus giving the fledgling settlement its name—Cherry Grove.

Cherry Grove's post office was one of the first in Fillmore County. The first mail delivery was every other week and was brought by a bareback horse rider from Decorah, Iowa. When the stage coach line was established from Lime, Iowa, to

Spring Valley, Minnesota, through Cherry Grove, mail delivery was every day. Rural Free Delivery was established in 1899, and in 1915 Cherry Grove was a rural route, since then discontinued.

A school was established in 1895 and operated until 1958 when the school was consolidated with Wykoff and Spring Valley. The school building was later used as a commercial building.

Two stores, an East and a West, were the heart of the village. The community also included a barbershop, a grist mill, a blacksmith shop, and a cheese factory. A telephone exchange was established in the West store in 1903.

No history of Cherry Grove would be complete without including the Pietenpol family. In Cherry Grove's earliest days, Christopher Pietenpol operated the village's grocery and dry goods store (the store still stands today). He also served as postmaster. Another family member, Mike Munson operated the

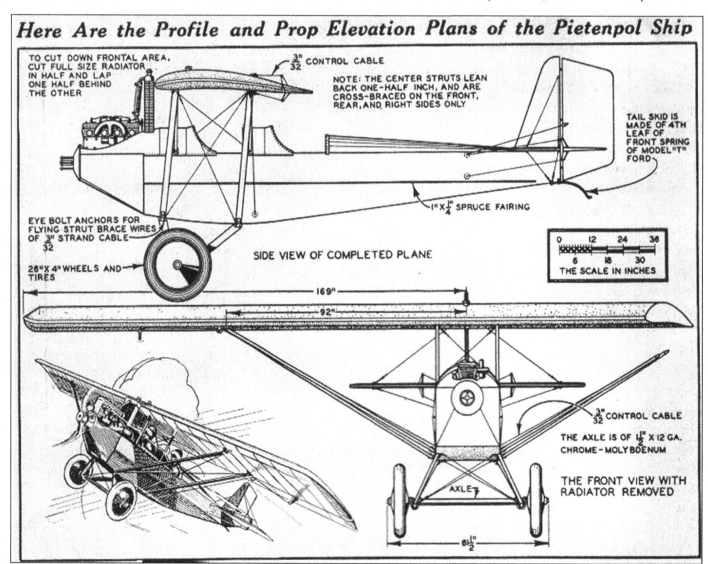

Original Pietenpol plans (Bernard H. Pietenpol - Pietenpol Aircraft Company)

The 1962 Bernard with a 1946 Piper and Corvair engine. (Bernard H. Pietenpol - Pietenpol Aircraft Company)

The 2012 Vitalis built. (Bernard H. Pietenpol - Pietenpol Aircraft Company)

The 1966 Air Camper. (Bernard H. Pietenpol - Pietenpol Aircraft Company)

Pietenpol Workshop and Garage. (National Register of Historic Places, Pietenpol, Bernard H. Workshop and Garage. Cherry Grove, Dodge County, Minnesota. 82002949)

Dash of 2012 Vitalis built. (Bernard H. Pietenpol - Pietenpol Aircraft Company)

filling station. Christopher's great-grandson, Andrew tells that his great aunt, Olive Munson, was known simply as "The Avon Lady." Andrew recalls that every year for Christmas, from the age of seven until his high school graduation, he received Avon aftershave in a decorative container from his great aunt.

It was Andrew's grandfather, Bernard Pietenpol, who is the best known Cherry Grove resident. Considered a "mechanical genius," Bernard is also considered the "father of the home-built aircraft movement in the United States."

From his youngest days, Bernard had an aptitude for all things mechanical. He could repair anything and also modified, designed and built powered lawn mowers, tractors, wheelchairs, and even a gas-powered electric generator. All with an eighth-grade education. He also built many motorcycles and automobiles. At different points in his life he ran a motorcycle repair shop, a Ford Motor repair shop, and a radio and television repair shop, as well as the town airport, all in Cherry Grove. But it was flying that captured his interest and his imagination.

As the Pietenpol website tells, flying was expensive and still is today. Average folks interested in flying could rarely come up with the money to maintain a plane let alone buy one. Bernard wasn't deterred and took it upon himself to build an airplane and learn how to fly it. He was convinced airplanes

Pietenpol air camper, 1930s. (Bernard H. Pietenpol - Pietenpol Aircraft Company)

Mounted Ford motor. (Bernard H. Pietenpol - Pietenpol Aircraft Company)

Pietenpol Air Camper. (Bernard H. Pietenpol - Pietenpol Aircraft Company)

The 1964 Air Camper, the first to be powered with a Chevrolet Corvair engine, the twenty-second to be made by Bernard. (Bernard H. Pietenpol - Pietenpol Aircraft Company)

could be powered by cheaper and more readily available automobile engines. His first plane was a bi-plane with a Ford Model T engine bolted on. His next attempt was a bi-plane powered by a rotary Gnome engine. After much testing, Bernard discarded the Gnome engine and went back to his original idea of making aviation affordable for the common man using an automobile engine. Bernard adjusted his design and with help from his wood-working father-in-law built the newly designed plane called the ACE.

Bernard moved his workshop into an abandoned Lutheran Church in Cherry Grove. By this time, Henry Ford had equipped his automobiles with forty-horsepower, four-cylinder engines. Since the engine had been on the market for several years, it was relatively easy to find them in junkyards. Bernard began to convert the Model A engine for his new monoplane design, the Air Camper. It was a huge success. Bernard drew up detailed blueprints and clear, detailed instructions in his building manual. He also offered parts for sale to builders who did not have the skills or equipment to make the necessary conversions. A completed Model A-powered Air Camper could be bought for $750.00.

In the 1960s, Chevrolet introduced the six-cylinder, air-cooled Corvair engine. It was the last engine Bernard would modify and work with. By that time Pietenpol's plans had been sold the world over, including Canada, England, Europe, Australia, and Africa.

Bernard died in 1984. In 1991 he was inducted into Minnesota's Aviation Hall of Fame. He is also recognized as the "Father of the Homebuilt Aircraft."

Bernard's first workshop still stands in Cherry Grove and is listed on the National Register of Historic Places. The two orginal hangars have been moved to historic sites. One is at the Fillmore County History Center in Fountain, Minnesota, and the other is at the Experimental Aircraft Association's Whitman Field in Oshkosh, Wisconsin.

Bernard's legacy continues. His grandson, Andrew, provides the Air Camper and Sky Scout plans and building manuals, sales and tech support for those who want to build their own aircraft. You can learn more at http://community.pressenter.net/~apietenp/

Be sure to check out the vintage and current photographs.

CHOICE

1887 - 1905

CLASS C

APPROXIMATE LOCATION:
Cty Road #43/#13, 11 miles south of Rushford, 11 miles north of Mabel

The picturesque valley near the area with the "cabbage rocks" was clearly the choice for early settlers, in location and in name. The five unique formations look like heads of cabbage and are on a bluff overlooking the South Fork of the Root River. Today, they are nearly inaccessible due to the growth of trees.

Choice creamery. (Richard Bruce Larson Photo Collection)

Choice school, early 1900s. (Richard Bruce Larson Photo Collection)

Choice store and creamery, 1906 (Richard Bruce Larson Photo Collection)

As far back as 1897 the community celebrated Independence Day with flair. At least on one occasion a band-operated merry-go-round was brought in from Rushford, and at other times a traveling medicine show made extended stops.

A Methodist Church was established and a church building was constructed. Regular services were held until 1952 when the chapel was razed.

A large creamery operated in the community and was known for its buttermaking.

Just a few days before Christmas in 1945, the Choice Store burned to the ground. An oil company serviceman overestimated the capacity of an underground gasoline tank and overfilled it. The excess gas seeped into a wood furnace which exploded. Four people were inside the building, but they escaped without injury. Two large storage buildings were moved to the site and served as the store until its closing in 1964. The buildings later, and still are, used for storage.

Following the church's exit in 1953, the school followed suit with the store closing in 1964. Today the storage buildings/old store and some vintage buildings still stand near the town site. A mile west of Choice the ruins of a flour and grist mill are hidden. Some of the old millstones can be seen in the surrounding area.

CLEAR GRIT

1878 - 1882

CLASS B

APPROXIMATE LOCATION:
Northeast of Preston on Heron Road - Old Barn Resort

Clear Grit's location at the heart of things was key. Located along the river and creek the readily available water power and supply provided for the construction of a mill and dam in 1869. Its close proximity to three towns—Preston, Fountain, and Lanesboro—also helped in the early development years. With a branch of the Southern Minnesota Railroad, Clear Grit seemed destined to be a thriving village, and for a while it was. The business district included a general store, a post office (1878 to 1882), a hotel, a wagon shop, a barrel factory, a hardware store, and a dance hall that was said to be very busy on Saturday nights.

Farming was the major livelihood, but four years of wheat disease (wheat smut) wreaked havoc. No crop rotation and a bad economy combined to hasten Clear Grit's demise. Businesses closed and people left. By 1882 Clear Grit was doomed.

Allis barn before restoration. (Courtesy of the Old Barn Resort, Preston Minnesota)

Allis barn. (Courtesy of the Old Barn Resort, Preston Minnesota)

Interior of Allis barn. (Courtesy of the Old Barn Resort, Preston Minnesota)

Edward Allis had a mechanic's lien on the mill and became the sole owner. Sensing an opportunity, Allis purchased the rest of the holdings, all 900 acres. Allis, of the Allis (Chalmers) tractor company renamed the property "The Reliance Stock Farm" and went into the dairy business with his son. No expense was spared in building up the farm. A three- (some say

Restored Allis barn. (Courtesy of the Old Barn Resort, Preston Minnesota)

four-) story dairy barn was 100 by fifty feet. It was framed in Milwaukee and shipped in sections to Minnesota. Holstein cattle were imported. Allis hoped his "playboy" son would take interest in the farm and would stay "down on the farm." Nine men, including a full-time veterinarian were hired to care for the prized herd. One of the bulls was said to weigh over 4,000 pounds. Two rooms in front of the barn were sleeping quarters. Another room was set aside for the churning of butter, which was shipped to Eastern markets.

Edward's son, Jere Allis, was interested in race horses and built up his stock to include twenty horses. The farm also had two race tracks. One of the horses, "Tommy Britton" was sold for $150,000. During the race year, the farm became the social center for the surrounding area. Dances, box socials, ball games, and ice skating were just some of the activities hosted by the farm. Pursuing her interests, Jere's first wife loved flowers. She had two gardeners, and they even built terraced and sloped gardens.

Jere and his first wife were divorced. After the death of Edward Allis, Jere's second wife gained control of the land and farm. In what would become known as the biggest land bargain in Fillmore County history, the farm was sold for $15,000 in 1906.

The farm was sold many times over and was in deteriorating condition when, in 1988, Vernon Michel purchased the farm. Michel hoped to restore the barn and develop a campground on the site. With restoration, the farm became known as the Old Barn Resort. In 1996, Doug Brenna and Shirley Endres purchased the business and have expanded it to a "resort" feel-

ing. Expansion and improvements have made the Old Barn Resort an area destination. Amenities include a 276-site campground, hostel, restaurant and bar, eighteen-hole golf course, pool and patio, fishing, tubing, and much more. The Old Barn Resort is the site of many special events including golf tournaments, weddings, family reunions, anniversaries, and more. Set amidst the natural scenic beauty of the Root River and along the Root River Trail, there is something to do for everyone. The Allis Barn is still the area's social center and still hosts many special events and activities. Check it out at www.oldbarnresort.com.

ELLIOTA

1854 - 1882

CLASS A/G

APPROXIMATE LOCATION:
Present City of Canton (2 miles north)

Elliota was once a busy stop along the Walker Stage Coach route from Dubuque, Iowa, to St. Paul, Minnesota. Elliota was established in 1853. Captain Elliot, for whom the village was named, gave away lots to all who would improve upon them. A post office was established in 1854, and soon a store and hotel were also part of the community. In 1855, both the store and hotel burned. By the early 1880s Elliota included four stores, a hotel, and other businesses. When the new rail line was routed just two miles from Elliota the decision was made to move the town there. Thus Elliota ceased to exist and the new village location became known as Canton.

ETNA

1856 - 1901

CLASS A

APPROXIMATE LOCATION:
County Road #14 in Bloomfield Township

Starting slowly in 1857, Etna, first called Tifton, developed into a settlement of over thirty buildings by 1882. Those buildings included a store, blacksmith shop, several sawmills, and a dozen homes. For many years, Etna had its own doctor.

A school was built in the 1880s and was in operation for nearly eighty years. A succession of many different teachers served the school. No teacher stayed longer than three years because the school board believed a change did students good. The last school term was in 1962/1963 with four students enrolled. After that year, the school consolidated with Spring Valley.

The Etna Union Church was established in the 1890s. Sunday School started in spring and ended at Christmas, due to the scarcity of heating wood. The church ceased to exist in 1971, and the building was removed by 1978. In its long tenure only two weddings were performed in the church, the first was unknown, the last one in 1941.

Without a railroad the town grew smaller and smaller, eventually fading. Today only a few homes and farms are in the area.

FILLMORE VILLAGE

1855 - 1905

CLASS A

APPROXIMATE LOCATION:
North of Wykoff

Once home to over one hundred residents, Fillmore Village was established in 1853 in the hills north of Wykoff. One church and several businesses, includ-

ing a general store, a drug store, a furniture store, two blacksmith shops, one hotel, a grist mill, a stave factory, and a school comprised the community. In 1882, the school had sixty five students enrolled.

The first church services were conducted in a room over the store. A dedicated church building was constructed in 1915 with a parsonage added in 1919/1920. In 1954, the church known as the Free Methodist Church, celebrated its 101st anniversary.

FORESTVILLE

1855 - 1902

CLASS F

APPROXIMATE LOCATION:
Southeast of Wykoff, Forestville State Park

As far as lost and long-ago towns go, Forestville is in a class by itself. Most Minnesota towns fall into the barren-land category, Forestville however, reaches the upper echelon of classifications, that of special status/historic site/state park designation.

Forestville was originally known as Watertown, named in honor of the early settler, Levi Waterman, who had first registered the claim in 1852. The claim was sold to Robert Foster shortly after its filing. Felix Meighan soon joined his friend Foster and Forestville took off from there. Meighan decided that a general store was sorely needed, so he decided to establish one

Forestville marker. (Courtesty of Seth Hardmeyer, highwayhighlights.com)

Forestville bridge. (Public domain)

of his own. He built a double pen log building that he used as his home and the store. According to the Minnesota Historical Society, which manages the site today, Foster and Meighan, with two hired hands, traveled to Galena, Illinois, for stock for the new store. The journey was long and included travel by ox cart and stagecoach.

The store, though crudely built, was a bustling success. Others coming to the region started their businesses near the store. Soon Forestville included a blacksmith shop, a cabinet shop, sawmills, a grist mill, a hotel, and a few other establishments. A new store was built in 1857. This building was more substantial. It was also the home for Meighan, his wife, and their seven children.

One of those children, Thomas, would figure prominently not only in the history of Forestville, but also in regional and state history. By age thirteen, Thomas left school to work in was when the Southern Minnesota Railroad bypassed the community in 1868. Many area residents left the fading village for bigger and better locations. The poor post-Civil War economy aided in Forestville's decline. As the Minnesota Historical Society states, Forestville's population in 1860 was 100, by 1870 it was sixty-eight and by 1880 it was down to fifty-five.

Meighan store. (Courtesy the National Register of Historical Places)

his father's store. He literally managed the store, and by age fifteen Thomas was traveling to Milwaukee and Chicago on buying trips. The Minnesota Historical Society reports that on one of his trips to Chicago, young Thomas witnessed the Great Chicago Fire of 1871.

The store and Forestville flourished for years, until the rush of settlers coming through the area dwindled and died down. The Civil War also took its toll. The final blow to Forestville

Meighan barn today. (Courtesy of Seth Hardmeyer, highwayhighlights.com)

Interior of Meighan store. (Courtesy of Seth Hardmeyer, highwayhighlights.com)

Meighan store marker. (Courtesty of Seth Hardmeyer, highwayhighlights.com)

Forestville 2014. (Courtesty of Seth Hardmeyer, highwayhighlights.com)

Forestville today. (Courtesty of Seth Hardmeyer, highwayhighlights.com)

The early 1880s saw Forestville's hotels close. Only the store and a few other businesses remained operating. Though the railroad had bypassed the community years earlier, many held out hope that some railroad would eventually come to the village. A few railroad lines did come to Fillmore County but not to Forestville. One went north of the village, another west.

The Meighans however, were doing very well, at least financially. For many years, the Meighans had offered the struggling residents credit. Thus they held many notes and options, all with high interest rates. When the farm economy went bust, the Meighans foreclosed, gaining large amounts of property and land. By 1889, the Meighans owned over one-thousand acres, including the entire town of Forestville. Managing such large pieces of property and the industries that went with it, the Meighans became the area's largest employer. Area men were hired to work the farms, and the women worked in the house. Wages were paid in store script and credit.

Thomas became politically active. Upon his appointment as president of the Preston bank, Thomas and his family moved, in 1910, to Preston and closed the store, lock, stock, and barrel. The store, at that time, was Forestville's last remaining business. With its closure, Forestville was history. Thomas died at his daughter's home in Pittsburg in 1936. Thomas had long hoped that Forestville would become a state park.

In 1963, Meighan's wish of turning his home into a park became reality. In 1971, the Minnesota Department of Natural Resources gave ownership of the land, the store, the house and outbuildings and barn to the Minnesota Historical Society. The DNR owns and operates the Forestville State Park while the Minnesota Historical Society manages the former village and its buildings.

In 1981, the Meighan Store was restored. It was sandblasted and new mortar was put into the cracks.

Historic Forestville offers visitors a step back in history. Journey to the past and experience life as it was in frontier Minnesota and in many long-ago towns. The store is just as it was when it was closed in 1910, including all of the original contents. Walk across the bridge into the village, tour the vintage and historic buildings and experience life as it was in the late 1800s. There are few places where history still lives as it does in Forestville. It is a unique opportunity to learn and discover life as it was over one hundred years ago, in a different time than today.

GRANGER

1857 - 1992

CLASS D

APPROXIMATE LOCATION:
County #16 just north of Iowa/Minnesota border

Street scene in Granger. (Courtesy of Georgia Rosendahl)

It's about as far south as one can go and still be in Minnesota. The Iowa/Minnesota state line runs through the heart of the twin communities of Granger, Minnesota, and Florenceville, Iowa. Both communities were established in the same year, 1857.

Granger was platted by early engineers Lewis and Granger from Massachusetts. The plat contained all but eighty acres of Section 34 of Bristol Township but included eight acres of Section 35. The lots were platted fifty by 100 feet (except for those along the irregular river front). The eighty-foot wide main street attracted businesses and soon the two communities were thriving. Early Granger included a blacksmith shop, a hotel, a wagon shop, and a drug store. A post office operated out of the drug store. At one time, the post office was the only one in Fillmore County not located at a railroad point.

A distillery and a brewery were also part of early Granger. The distillery was built in 1865 on the West bank of the Upper Iowa River, which ran north and south on Granger's west side. For some reason the distillery was closed by federal revenue agents. It later operated as a vinegar plant. A brewery began in 1871 but was later remodeled into a creamery and was rented by the Beatrice Creamery Company. Later in 1911 the Granger Cooperative Creamery was established and it would operate well into the twenty-first century. It is said that when the creamery closed in 2007 it was the last in Minnesota to accept milk in cans. Changes in the way area farmers, primarily Amish, marketed their milk affected the creamery's business line and hastened its demise. The dairy industry was changing and small-town creameries were greatly affected.

Blue Bottle Garden. (Courtesy of Georgia Rosendahl)

61

State Line Trail. (Courtesy of Georgia Rosendahl)

The Granger Creamery was for sale in early 2015. (Courtesy of Zillow.com)

A two-story school was built in 1874. It operated until consolidation with Harmony schools. During early Granger, the school was also the area's social center.

Granger was always an inland village. There were hopes for a railroad to come through the village, providing growth, but the railroad bypassed the community.

St. Matthew's Lutheran Church's first congregation was formed in 1873. A church was built, and in 1897 a parish school was added. A new church building was erected in 1955. It was damaged by fire in 1967 and a new interior was completed. The church is still active today.

In the 1980s Granger had about sixty residents. The Granger State Bank (1917), the post office, the creamery, a garage, a grocery store, an antique shop, a gas station, and a tavern were still operating. By 2007, when the creamery ceased operating, the *LaCrosse Tribune* reported that it was the latest decline for Granger, which had lost its doctor and the only store closed in recent years.

Presently the old creamery building was listed as for sale. Perhaps it will once again be used. Granger still has a community feel and is a small hamlet along with Florenceville as it has since the two began.

GREENLEAFTON

1874 – 1905 (1990s)

CLASS D

APPROXIMATE LOCATION:
County Roads #9 and #20 near Preston

The small settlement was named Greenleafton in honor of Mary Greenleafton, who donated $3,500.00 for the construction of the Dutch Reformed Church. The community once had two stores, a post office, a blacksmith shop, and the still-active church. Majestic and historic, the Greenleafton Reformed Church is the center of the small hamlet. Today, the church and a few homes remain.

HAMILTON

1863 – 1904

CLASS A

APPROXIMATE LOCATION:
Just east of Racine on Mower Fillmore Road

Traveling by covered wagon in 1852 from Ohio to Minnesota, the fourteen settlers crossed the Mississippi River at Dubuque, Iowa, and ferried on to Minnesota. Deciding to settle along the best waterpower in the region, they built their first house in 1853. Unknown to them, the land they chose was Dakota hunting ground. Over the years relationships with the Natives would be problematic and tense. One record tells that one settler's daughter, twelve years old, was kidnapped and never found.

Farnsworth home, 1890s (Courtesy of Dave Farnsworth)

Farnsworth home, 1943. (Courtesy of Dave Farnsworth)

The 1890 Farnsworth barn and granery. (Courtesy of Dave Farnsworth)

Bear Creek, May 2003. (Courtesy of Dave Farnsworth)

63

A post office was established in 1856 (under the name Elkhorn). Fifty acres were platted and the community was renamed Hamilton, after the home place of some of the settlers, Hamilton, Ontario, Canada.

By 1858, Hamilton consisted of over thirty buildings and included two stores, a blacksmith shop, a harness shop, a wagon shop, a hotel, several sawmills, a grist mill, a schoolhouse, and over twenty residences. A former Civil War surgeon served as the area's doctor.

The school building was constructed in 1860 was a one-room school. A new school building was constructed in 1935. In 1954 the school consolidated with Spring Valley, and the building was later converted into a private home.

Several organizations were active in Hamilton including the Good Templars. Two churches, a Methodist and a Baptist, served the spiritual needs of the community. Every year a Memorial Day event was held. There was a churchyard service, a parade, and residents placed flags on the soldiers' graves.

In 1890, the railroad bypassed Hamilton and the village faded away. Today the area is rolling farmland with only a few nearby homes.

HENRYTOWN

1890s - 1993

CLASS C

APPROXIMATE LOCATION:
5 miles west of Canton

For over 173 years the Henrytown Lutheran Church stood as a local and historic landmark. Over six generations of members attended the church as well as remodeled and updated it over the years. When the church burned in April of 2015, many said it was like losing an old friend, a part of the family.

Local news reports stated that a neighbor noticed flames in the church and called 911. By the time fire departments from Harmony and Canton arrived in mere minutes, it was too late. The church was engulfed in flames. The centuries-old wood spread the fire quickly.

The church office was near the front of the building. Firefighters were able to save some church records and the cornerstone. Church paintings by Norwegian artist Herbjorn Gauston were unable to be saved. A wood statue of Jesus was recovered but was charred beyond recognition. It is believed the fire started in the basement.

The church was a living remnant of the long-ago community of Henrytown. Established in the mid-1850s residents hoped Henrytown would become the county seat. The community included a blacksmith shop, a general store, a post office (1883 to 1902), a broom factory, a sorghum mill, a school and several residences. The school housed grades one through eight and operated until 1963 when it consolidated with Harmony.

The Fillmore County Poor Farm built in 1868 and operating until 1943 was located nearby. The facility was closed and sold.

A few rural homes remain and there are plans to rebuild the church.

HIGHLAND

1857 - 1902

CLASS A

APPROXIMATE LOCATION:
11 miles southeast of Lanesboro, CR #10

Aptly named, Highland's rolling hills gave the community broad views of the valley. The ridge just to the north of Highland was Fillmore County's second highest point.

At its peak in the mid-1860s, Highland included a blacksmith shop, a store and post office, a church, and a school. The school was established in 1857 and closed upon consolidation with Lanesboro in 1966.

Highland had a village water pump in 1872, located on a public street. The well was sixty feet deep and records tell that the last several feet had to be drilled through solid rock. Prior to the village pump, residents depended on cisterns, ponds and creeks for their water. There are ten to twelve homes in the area, a store, and café (1894) and a brick church (1921) near the old town site.

Highland street scene, postcard. (Author's Collection)

ISINOUR'S (JUNCTION)

1872 - 1970s

CLASS A

APPROXIMATE LOCATION:
3 miles borth of Preston, West of County #17

Historic Lenora church. (Courtesy of Ernie Balcueva)

For nearly seventy years, Isinour's Junction was in important rail depot on the Southern Minnesota Division of the Chicago, Milwaukee Railroad. During its heyday, six passenger trains and two freight trains, as well as many unscheduled trains, stopped in Isinour's each day.

In addition to the depot, Isinour's included a stockyard, a depot agent's home, a school, a sixteen-by-forty-foot counter-type lunchroom, and other businesses. The lunch counter was famous for its owner's homemade pies, doughnuts, beans, and sandwiches, all cooked on a wood cookstove. The owner's son recalled that his mother made over thirty-five pies every day.

As railroad services and importance declined, train stops became fewer and fewer. By 1970 train traffic was down to one train a day. In 1978 the railroad bed was abandoned, and the Minnesota Department of Revenue removed the tracks, creating a public recreation trail. The area is still referred to as Isinour's. There is parking for the bike trail, an old cabin, and a picnic and camping area near the old site.

LENORA

1856 - 1905 (1950s)

CLASS C

APPROXIMATE LOCATION:
5 miles east of Canton, near County #23 & #24

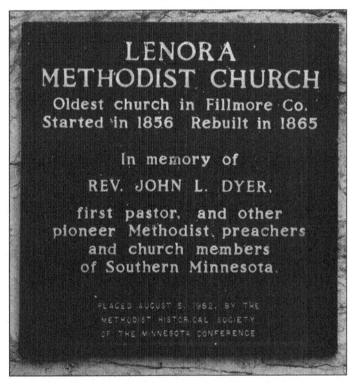

Lenora church historic plaque. (Courtesy of Ernie Balcueva)

Hoping to finance a church for the burgeoning community of Lenora, Reverend Dyer platted forty acres of land into lots. Proceeds from the sale of the lots would be used to build a large stone Methodist Church, with a school or academy in the basement.

Lenora, just two years old, was already home to a post office, a hotel, a livery stable, two stores, a broom factory, a community hall, a sawmill, and Fillmore County's first school. The school sat on high, rolling land and was pleasant in the summer, but during Fillmore County's long harsh winters it was desolate. To guard against children getting disoriented and lost while traveling to and from school, some plowed furrows from their homesteads to the school. The school house also served as the area social center. Several groups and organizations, included the Archean Society (a literary group), held regular meetings in the school building. The school was closed in 1962 upon consolidation with Canton Schools.

In 1908, a community hall was built and it quickly became the center of activity. Weekly dances, oyster stew dinners, pie socials, and many community suppers were held at the hall. Independence Day celebrations were grand affairs and included parades, fireworks, band concerts, picnics, speakers, races, ice cream stands, and even dances late into the evening.

Lenora's first store burned in 1933. It was rebuilt and operated until its closure in 1954.

As for the church, funds were raised for construction. Walls were being built when the Financial Panic of 1857 struck and construction was halted. A new pastor arrived in 1865 and a new structure was built within the walls of the old building. The church was Fillmore County's first church building. Sunday School and services were monthly and were presided over by a traveling minister from Lanesboro. Over the years membership waned, and the building fell into disrepair. The Lenora Cemetery Association took over the restoration and maintenance of the historic building. In 1984 annual services (usually at Christmas) were held. In mid-2015 regular monthly services, in addition to the annual services, were being scheduled.

NEWBURG

1855/1902

CLASS D

APPROXIMATE LOCATION:
12 miles east of Harmony County #24

Newburg Methodist Church. (Credit)

Newburg was settled in 1853 by homesteaders from LaSalle, Illinois. In 1854 a post office was established and soon a store, blacksmith shop, and a hotel joined the community. An early settler's home served as a tavern from the settlements beginning. In 1858 a new house and barn were built and was known as the Newburg House. Today the old store front, the Newburg Methodist Church and about ten homes remain in the area.

Newburg, Minnesota. (Credit)

PILOT MOUND

1856 - 1895

CLASS A

APPROXIMATE LOCATION:
Southeast of Chatfield

Pilot Mound Church. (Courtesy of Jim Dunn)

Also known as Pekin, a school was built in Pilot Mound in 1867. In 1930 the school building was destroyed by fire. Classes were held in the town hall until a new school could be built in 1931. In later years the school consolidated with Chatfield, and the building was used as a home.

Immensely talented, critically acclaimed local artist Karl Unnasch is preserving Pilot Mound's idyllic ten-acre setting. The 1800s Mercantile is now his art studio. He is turning his century-old home into a one-of-a-kind sanctuary (The Artists

Birds Eye View of Pilot Mound. (Courtesy of Karl Unnasch (Nicole Huss) www. http://karlunnasch.com/)

Panoramic Pilot Mound. (Courtesy of Karl Unnasch (Nicole Huss) www. http://karlunnasch.com/)

Pilot Mound Design, former Merchentile. (Courtesy of Karl Unnasch (Nicole Huss) www. http://karlunnasch.com/)

Pilot Mound Mercantile. (Courtesy of Karl Unnasch (Nicole Huss) www. http://karlunnasch.com/)

Pilot Mound Town Hall. (Courtesy of Karl Unnasch (Nicole Huss) www. http://karlunnasch.com/)

Pilot Mound. (Courtesy of Karl Unnasch (Nicole Huss) www. http://karlunnasch.com/)

Haven) open to all, especially fellow artists. Karl's artistic enterprise, Pilot Mound graphics is based in the community.

Karl creates stunning, creative works of art amid the historic setting. Many of his works (many instantly notable) are on display at prominent locations including educational facilities,

Pilot Mound street scene. (Courtesy of Karl Unnasch (Nicole Huss) www. http://karlunnasch.com/)

banks, medical centers, and other public gateways. He has taught at the collegiate level and works in a variety of mediums including stained glass. Check out his site at www.karlunnasch.com. Stop in while in Pilot Mound.

PROSPER

1866 - 1979

CLASS C

APPROXIMATE LOCATION:
On the Iowa/Minnesota border

Prosper sits on the Iowa/Minnesota border. A post office was established in 1866 and operated over 110 years. Records indicate that over the 110 years of its existence, the post office moved at least eleven times between the two states. Location depended on the postmaster appointment.

In July of 1913 a fire nearly destroyed the village. At 3:30 p.m. on July 24, 1913, a young boy noticed flames at the lumberyard. He ran through town sounding the alarm. The tele-

phone operator also put out the call for help. The *La Crosse Tribune* reported that over 300 area men (all of the town's residents) as well as many others from the surrounding communities of Mabel, Canton, Decorah, Preston, and Harmony came to assist in the firefighting efforts. The men came but none of the communities had firefighting equipment. The lumberyard was destroyed, but the bucket brigade saved the community from total destruction.

Prosper, Minnesota, 2014. (Courtesy of Ted Sherats)

TAWNEY

1898 - 1905

CLASS A

APPROXIMATE LOCATION:
7½ miles north of Mabel

Once along a Pony Express route, Tawney was a local social and trade center. It is said it never grew to full-fledged "town" status, but it most certainly was a "living community." As the historical marker goes on to tell, the Tawney Store was the town.

A post office was established in 1898 and was named after area Congressman James Tawney.

In 1986 when Minnesota #43 was reconstructed, the store was torn down. A historical plaque marks the old site.

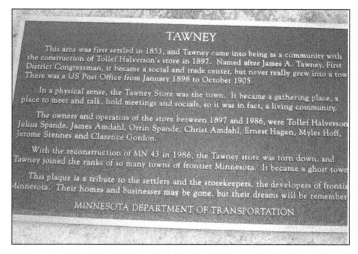

Tawney Marker. (Author's Collection)

Freeborn County

ARMSTRONG VILLAGE

1878 - 1958

CLASS C

APPROXIMATE LOCATION:
County Road #14 NW of Albert Lea

Once the elevator was built in 1878, the growth of a village was sparked. The village took the name of the owner of the first elevator, Thomas Armstrong. A post office was established in 1878 and lasted eighty years. For such a long post office tenure, relatively little is known about Armstrong. In 1882, the settlement included a blacksmith (for one year), a railroad depot, a creamery, and for many years a store. Several houses were also in the hamlet. Today, a large family farm is in the vicinity.

BANCROFT

1857/1902

CLASS A/G

APPROXIMATE LOCATION:
Present site of Good Samaritan Center, Albert Lea

When the Dakota Land Company of St. Paul first platted and settled the community in 1855, they chose to name it after the former Secretary of the Navy George Bancroft. Bancroft was also the founder of the U.S. Naval Academy at Annapolis. Why Bancroft was chosen as the namesake is unknown. There seems to be no connection between Bancroft and the community and no evidence the former secretary ever visited the community. One thing that is known is the community was established with the intent of its becoming the county seat. In fact, there was a clause in the legislative bill that organized Freeborn County that Bancroft would be the county seat. The clause was later repealed.

The first building put up on the townsite was a shanty built just before the store was. Within a short time Bancroft was home to a hotel, a store, a sawmill, a saloon, a post office, a blacksmith shop, and even a newspaper.

Albert Lea was chosen as the county seat in 1857. The loss of the anticipated designation spurred Bancroft's decline. Residents left, buildings were moved or torn down and according to sources, Bancroft was a ghost town by 1864.

Records indicate that "Old Bancroft" lasted from 1856 to 1860. Some sources indicate Bancroft had resurgence in 1890. The newer settlement had the Bancroft Creamery, the Bancroft Store, and the township hall. A historical marker was places at the site, County Road #22 and #14 in 1973. Today, the Good Samaritan Center stands near the site.

BATH

1877 - 1904

CLASS C

APPROXIMATE LOCATION:
County Roads #20/35

Even though Bath was a community well into the mid-twentieth century, it is considered a pioneer village because of its early tenure as a village (1857 to 1863). Sue Jorgenson, who lived in the area as a child, recalls her mother telling her that, as a baby, Sue and her family would go to Bath for movies. Blankets were spread on the ground and a movie was broadcast outside.

As a village, Bath, existed for just a short time frame. First known as Porter, Bath included a store, a creamery, a school, a Catholic Church (St. Alden's), and a cemetery. The creamery was known as the "North Star Creamery" and was later called Poplar Grove. The creamery went out of business in 1957 as did the store. Both buildings were still standing in the early 2000s. There are conflicting reports on the status of the church building. One record states the building was moved to Ellendale and another says the church was destroyed in 1958.

The Bath Township Board placed a historical marker at the site in 1973. In recent years, a farm equipment salvage yard was in the area as was the remaining cemetery.

CLOVER

1895/1908

CLASS A

APPROXIMATE LOCATION:
Pickeral Lake Township

Due to its early time frame, the small community of Clover is considered a pioneer village. The post office first operated as Adair. For a short time the village was also known as Clover Valley. A creamery and the store/post office combination constituted the bulk of the settlement. A nearby German Lutheran Church and a school were also considered part of Clover. The village faded after the creamery stopped operating. The creamery building was used as a machine shed until it blew down in 1962. The store building was moved to Conger where it was remodeled into a private home.

A historical marker was placed at the town site in 1973 by the Pickeral Lake Town Board.

CRAYON PARK

1890 – 1910s

CLASS A

APPROXIMATE LOCATION:
One-half mile east of County #30

Crayon Park was shown on plat maps in 1895, 1900, and 1913. After that it no longer appears on maps. Today Highway #46 goes directly over the area of Crayon Park.

DEER CREEK

Mid 1800s

CLASS C

APPROXIMATE LOCATION:
County #32

Prior to 1875, Deer Creek's first settlers arrived by prairie schooners or covered wagons as some call them. One of the first things settlers did was to build a school and a church with a cemetery. According to a Freeborn County history website, early settlers decided that the first person who died would be the first person buried in the new cemetery and a pastor would dedicate the cemetery. Unexpectedly, a passing "tramp" died and was the first buried in the cemetery. However, the cemetery was not dedicated until a resident died.

The London Norwegian Evangelical Church was built and, shortly after, another church, the Conference Church was constructed. In 1917 the two churches alternated services. Eventually it was decided to use only one church, and the people called the merged congregations the Deer Creek Valley Church.

The community of Deer Creek was right on the Iowa/Minnesota state line and parts of the community were actually in Iowa. A store came in 1895 with a creamery following in 1901. In 1906 the creamery burned, and a new building was erected. It later became a cheese factory. For a time a harnesss and repair shop was also located in the village. A town band existed in the early 1900s.

The church is all that remains at the site today. I could not locate any information on the demise of Deer Creek.

DORWART

Early 1900s

CLASS A

APPROXIMATE LOCATION:
1 mile from Clarks Grove

As with most "paper towns" Dorwart had a legal description, a map, platted streets and alleys, and residential and business lots drawn out, on paper. In reality, that is the only place "paper towns" existed. Kathy Jensen in her history of Clark's Grove wrote that not one lot was sold. Another source states that Dorwart had the shortest life of any Freeborn County locations.

Dorwart, or the vision of Dorwart, was created by the Burlington, Cedar Rapids & Northern Railroad in 1900. Dorwart was planned as a depot and rail siding. In 1902, the Chicago, Rock Island and Pacific Railroad took over the rail line, closed the Dorwart depot and made Clark's Grove the railroad's main stop.

Today, the golf course south of Clark's Grove now occupies part of the area platted to be Dorwart.

FAIRFIELD

1850s

CLASS A

APPROXIMATE LOCATION:
Nine miles east of Albert Lea

Discrepancies exist between the plans, the hype, the hopes, and the reality. In 1857, an early newspaper reported that Fairfield had been laid out and, supposedly, a drug store had been built, but it had no other improvements. Another newspaper, *The Freeborn County Eagle*, in 1859, reported that a pleasure trip traveler had visited the area and found "considerable disappointment" in what he found. He saw one house and that one being of poor quality and construction. The sawmill was gone leaving behind over 150 logs.

In response to the unflattering accounts, a C.W. Brackett responded with a letter to the editor. The letter touted Fairfield's amenities and planned progress. Stating that a steam sawmill would be making lumber within the week, a store with a large stock, over $4,500.00 worth, and other businesses such as a hotel, cabinet shop, and brickyard were under contract to be built. Lumber shortages appear to have been an issue with building plans. Brackett assured readers that by "the time the snow flies" Fairfield would be a bustling community.

Fairfield marker. (Author's Collection)

In 1973, the Riceland Township Board erected a historical marker at the site. It reads, "The Pioneer Village of Fairfield (1857-1860) consisted of a steam sawmill, post office, store, blacksmith shop and 4 homes."

GORDONSVILLE

1862 - 1969

CLASS D

APPROXIMATE LOCATION:
Highway 65 at Iowa Border

Gordonsville, still a roadside settlement, lies at the end of the Minnesota section of the historic Jefferson Highway. Immediately after traveling through the village, you are in Iowa.

Gordonsville Highway Marker. (Andrew Munsch www.deadpioneer.com)

Minnesota/Iowa state line near Gordonsville. (Courtesy of Andrew Munsch)

Gordonsville. (Courtesy of Andrew Munsch Sorry)

Gordonsville Depot. (www.west2k.com)

Until the 1930s, Gordonsville was a thriving village. Businesses included a creamery, a tile plant, several stores, a bank, a lumberyard, a community hall (on the top floor of the bank), a post office which operated over 100 years, a Methodist Church, a dray (freight) line, and several other businesses including a meat market that butchered and sold meat by buggy. The butcher later added a confectionary and sold ice cream.

A Methodist Church was built in 1883. Many revivals were held in the early days. A new church was built in 1955.

An early three-room schoolhouse was located near the church. The original school building burned in 1916, and a one-room school was built as a replacement. At one time enrollment was at forty-nine students, all under one teacher. Area schools later consolidated.

ITASCA

1857 - 1861

CLASS A

APPROXIMATE LOCATION:
Site of former Wedge Nursery near Albert Lea

Considered one of Freeborn County's earliest and largest communities, Itasca, or as the post office was known, Freeborn Springs, was a strong contender for the county seat designation.

The village was settled and platted in the mid-1850s. By 1860, Itasca included a hotel, a general store, a dry goods store, a blacksmith shop, a shoemaker's shop, a post office, a photographer, a dentist, a newspaper office, and approximately fifteen homes. When nearby Bancroft became abandoned, many of the buildings, including the sawmill, were moved to Itasca. The town was booming until November of 1860 when Albert Lea was designated the Freeborn County seat. Some sources report that the designation was decided by a horse race held in Itasca. The community of Itasca faded quickly.

The Bancroft Township Board erected a historical marker at the town site in 1973. The former Wedge Nursery occupied part of the former townsite.

MOSCOW

1859/1903

CLASS C

APPROXIMATE LOCATION:
County #25/34

In 1986, hoping that he would want to visit Minnesota's Moscow, the Township Board invited Soviet President Mikhail Gorbachev to visit them while he was visiting Minnesota. After all, the community had been named, in sorts, for Russia. It's said that when the area's dense forest was ablaze one year, it resembled Napoleon's burning of Russia. Thus the newly platted (1857) village was named Moscow.

The community had a flour mill, a post office, a general store, a blacksmithy, a schoolhouse, a sawmill, a creamery, and a hotel.

In 2012, all that remained was the former store building, the abandoned creamery, and a few houses. A small park and the Moscow Town Hall are also near the old town site.

KNATVOLD

1899 - 1905

CLASS A

APPROXIMATE LOCATION:
Near Freeman Town Hall, Freeman Township

The town was first called Oslo, then known as Freeman in 1890, and lastly changed to Knatvold in 1900, in honor of Senator T. Knatvold. Never large, the community included a town hall, a small creamery, and a general store. The creamery closed in 1914, and the post office was discontinued that same year.

A historical marker was placed at the former town site by the Freeman Township Board in 1977. Today all that remains of Knatvold is the Freeman Town Hall.

LERDAL

1892 - 1908

CLASS C

APPROXIMATE LOCATION:
County #25 and 800th Avenue, Richland Township

Still considered a village in 1988, the population at that time was twenty-five. In its early days, Lerdal was home to a general store, a telephone exchange, a town hall, a harness shp, a shoe shop, a blacksmith shop, and a post office (1892 to 1908). A creamery was also part of the community. Known as the Riceland Creamery, it was the first to make "sweet cream" butter.

In 1909 the post office was discontinued, the general store was struck by lightning and burned to the ground and all of the businesses except for the creamery and telephone exchange were out of business and gone. The telephone exchange was later sold (1962) to the Continental Telephone Company. The creamery closed in 1958. The creamery building still stands as do several of the residences.

SIGSBEE

1890s - 1940s

CLASS A

APPROXIMATE LOCATION:
Near County #115/118

Sigsbee was named in honor of Dwight Sigsbee, the commander of the battleship *Maine* at the time of its explosion in 1898 in Havana Harbor.

The small community had a creamery, a post office (which was discontinued in 1900), and a store.

Poor roads made it difficult to get dairy products to nearby Lerdal, Hayward, or Moscow, so Sigsbee area farmers established a creamery in 1893. The creamery burned to the ground in 1927. With transportation improvements, especially the automobile, rebuilding the creamery was not practical and was unnecessary. The loss of the creamery signaled the rapid decline of the hamlet.

The store, built in 1898, had a succession of owners and operated until 1937. The store building was moved to Hayward and converted into a private home. The store owner was Sigsbee's last resident, and the store was the villages last building.

SUMNER

1857 - 1872

CLASS G

APPROXIMATE LOCATION:

Not too far from Sigsbee was the early pioneer village of Sumner. A post office operated from 1857 until 1872. Hopes were high for the community and its location along the stage coach line from Albert Lea to Austin. The village never realized its promise and potential and the village reverted back to farmland.

ST. NICHOLAS

1850s

CLASS A

APPROXIMATE LOCATION:
Borders Albert Lea Lake

Home to many of Freeborn County firsts, St. Nicholas was located on the south shore of Albert Lea Lake. The early community was the site of Freeborn County's first blacksmith shop, the first post office (1856 to 1858), the first hotel, and the first general store. It is said the town site was the area's most scenic with a broad view of the water, a sand beach and a distant shore lined with trees.

From the beginning, St. Nicholas was groomed to be the county seat. Every effort was made to gain the designation. When Albert Lea was chosen, St. Nicholas began its decline, buildings removed, and the former town site became farm land.

A regenerated St. Nicholas was created in the 1950s. Primarily a tourist stop, the new St. Nicholas was approximately six miles to the north of Highway 16 and included a pioneer village and a small museum. With the construction of Interstate 90, the settlement was quickly abandoned. Most of the artifacts were sold at auction, and many of the buildings stand along Highway 46. The city limits of Albert Lea have since expanded to the edge of what was once the pioneer village.

Some sources speculate that counterfeiting activities took place at the original St. Nicholas site. After being abandoned for years, the Old Store was sold, dismantled and moved to a nearby farm. While tearing down the building, a set of counterfeiting tools (bits and pieces of a crucible, bars of metal and dies that could be used to make fifty cent pieces) were found.

TRENTON

1857 - 1901

CLASS A

APPROXIMATE LOCATION:

Though a historical marker has been placed at the town site, nothing remains of Trenton. After the creamery closed, most of Trenton's other buildings were moved to other locations. The village included a creamery, two stores, a blacksmith shop, and a school. Records state that the village had no homes, though the store had upstairs living quarters.

Goodhue County

Bombay Depot. (www.west2k.com)

Claybank Marker. (Courtesy of Heather Monthei)

Claybank. (www.west2k.com)

ASPELUND

1872 - 1905

CLASS C

APPROXIMATE LOCATION:

Consisting of a store and post office, Aspelund was a trade center in the 1880s and 1890s. The post office was discontinued in 1905. Today all that remains is a nearby church, a township hall, and three houses.

BOMBAY

1903 – 1932 (1990)

CLASS C

APPROXIMATE LOCATION:
Minnesota #60

Created in 1903, Bombay was the only entirely "new" village created in Goodhue County in the twentieth century. Early settlers didn't like the name and would have preferred a more "Norwegian" sounding name. Reaching its peak in 1917, the World War I years, the village began its decline shortly after. The village and its businesses, especially the store, suffered economically when the state highway was rerouted in 1932. The store that had prospered earlier, finally closed in 1992.

In recent years, the elevator is the only remaining business. The former store and a few houses mark the location. Bombay never had a post office, a church, a school, or a town hall.

CASCADE

1882 - 1901

CLASS A

APPROXIMATE LOCATION:

Even though Cascade was a mill company town, it did develop an identity of its own. The school was the cultural center of the community. Cascade's decline began as early as 1885 when the Minnesota and Northwestern Railroad bypassed the settlement. The final blow was on October 2, 1894, when fire destroyed the mill and cooper shop. They were never rebuilt. By 1942 Cascade was a ghost town. Today little remains.

CLAYBANK

1890 - 1904

CLASS A

APPROXIMATE LOCATION:
Near Junction of County #6 Boulevard and 350th street, near Highway #58

Rich deposits of clay were located in northern Goodhue County. In 1861 a German potter began making crocks, jugs, bowls, and other items. He operated until 1871, but he wasn't the last to make use of the clay deposits. In 1877 the Red Wing Stoneware Company came to the region. Others followed, including Minnesota Stoneware and North Star Stoneware. After merging, the two became known as the Red Wing Union Stoneware Company and in 1936 as Red Wing Pottery. They ceased manufacturing stone ware in 1967. Red Wing Pottery remains a Minnesota icon.

With the completion of the Duluth, Red Wing, and Southern Railroad in 1889 digging expanded. A store was built and a post office was established in 1892.

For many years, Claybank was a bustling community. Two large boarding houses primarily for the clay workers, and two grain elevators were later part of the settlement. The post office was discontinued in 1904. The store operated until the 1950s. A 1958 auction sold off the store, signaling the end of the Claybank. The rail line was abandoned in 1965 and the tracks were removed the next year.

Claybank Pits. (Author's Collection)

EGGLESTON

1875 - 1934

CLASS C

APPROXIMATE LOCATION:
Neighborhood of Red Wing

Goodhue County's northernmost post office location, Eggleston, was an early railroad town. Primarily a trade center for the area, Eggleston was also known as Prairie Island. The settlement included a grain elevator, two stores, a post office, a creamery, and later a radio shop. The Kinney Store operated for years and was at one time a popular fish fry eating establishment. The store/restaurant operated until 1985. The building still stands and is used as a residence and trailer court office. Historian Roy W. Meyer tells that, with today's trailer park residents, Eggleston has a larger population today than it did in its heyday.

Eggleston Depot. (www.west2k.com)

FAIR POINT (FAIRPOINT)

1857 - 1902

CLASS A

APPROXIMATE LOCATION:
County #1 and 515th Street

For many years, Fair Point (later Fairpoint) was a thriving crossroads community. Platted in 1857, a post office was established that same year. The community had a suc-

cession of postmasters, and as area historian Roy W. Meyer wrote, the turnover in postmasters was indicative of Fair Point's business turnovers.

Several businesses tried and several failed. The longest lasting one was the Fair Point Cooperative Creamery, which made cheese until 1946. Meyer writes that once the cheese factory closed, the Goodhue County Electric Cooperative cut power to the building and Fair Point ceased to be.

A German Evangelical Free Church was moved two miles south where it operated as a community center for years. The church and the cheese factory are long gone. A nearby house and cemetery marked the site in recent years.

FOREST MILLS

1879 - 1898

CLASS C

APPROXIMATE LOCATION:
Near junction of County #48 & County #10

Long the subject of historian Roy W. Meyer, Forest Mills was an early mill town. A typical company town, the settlement included many mill town standard businesses including a cooper shop, a store, a warehouse, and eventually a post office. Population peaked at 100 residents, many of them mill workers.

The milling company declared insolvency in 1894, and the settlement's decline followed. The post office closed in 1898. The feed mill and elevator were dismantled in 1917-1918. The cheese factory crumbled away. The school was rather long-lived, built in 1871 and closed in 1945. The building was later sold. In 1948 several new homes were built at the site. Today it's a small hamlet.

HADER

1857/1903

CLASS C

APPROXIMATE LOCATION:
U.S. #52 and County #8

When the stage coach line changed its route between Cannon Falls and Zumbrota, the intersection of that with the Red Wing-Kenyon Road was

Minneola Lutheran Church. (minfamilien)

An Old West Saloon and a campground operated in recent years.

Hay Creek Campground and Old West Saloon. (Courtesy of Hay Creek Campground and Old West Saloon0

Hay Creek Depot. (www.west2k.com)

a natural location for a town. Thus Hader was established in 1857. Platted with high hopes and expectations, even that of the potential county seat designation. Falling short, Hader still became a busy trade center for a time. Its failure to secure at least a railroad would prove to be its downfall.

Still along a major travel route, Hader is today a hamlet with two former stores serving as homes, the former cheese factory turned repair shop, and a handful of other homes.

When U.S. #52 was widened to a four-lane, much of Hader was lost to the expansion.

HAY CREEK

1874 - 1895

CLASS C

APPROXIMATE LOCATION:
Junction of State Highway 58, Hay Creek Trail, and 315th Street

By 1870 a German settlement developed near the flour mill, and it grew quickly. By 1878 the population peaked at 150 , the village included the mill, a general store/post office, three blacksmiths, three stone masons, a doctor, and two churches. A saloon later joined the community, and a brewery lasted for a short time.

Hay Creek was a busy trade center for years but by 1900 had seen its best days, having only three listings in its business community.

OXFORD MILLS

Late 1800s - 1903

CLASS B

APPROXIMATE LOCATION:
Southwest of Cannon Falls on Oxford Mill Road

Developing around the Oxford Mill, the small settlement called Oxford Mills never had a post office. Consisting of a half dozen homes and a Methodist Church, the settlement's mill remained profitable long after many other mills had gone out of business. In 1903, the mill burned, however, and with the loss of the mill there was no longer a reason for the settlement to exist.

REST ISLAND

1890s

CLASS A

APPROXIMATE LOCATION:
Along the shores of Lake Pepin

Quite possibly the only community ever established for inebriates, Rest Island was just that. Established by John Woolley, a one-time alcoholic and later candidate for president on the Prohibitionist Party ticket, the colony was located along the shores of Lake Pepin. Supported by a few substantial donors, several cottages were built as was a farm, which, it was hoped, would self-support the endeavor. At its peak in 1892-1893, a large hotel was built and a post office was established.

For a time things seemed to be going well. However, persistent flooding, which covered the island, and lack of continuing contributions due to the Financial Panic of 1893, support was declining. Adding to the matters, John Woolley was accused of mismanagement of funds. Investigations showed a discrepancy of just over $3,000. Woolley made up the difference with his personal funds. Deep in debt, Woolley turned over the property. It was promptly vacated. The post office was discontinued in 1893, and Woolley's great experiment was over.

SEVASTOPOL

CLASS A

APPROXIMATE LOCATION:

Little more than a paper town, Sevastopol was located in a hollow surrounded by high bluffs. Area historian Roy W. Meyer wrote that the settlement had few characteristics of a true village, it was chiefly a collection of taverns.

SKYBERG

1859 - 1951

CLASS C

APPROXIMATE LOCATION:
Southeast of Minnesota #56 and County #11

It wasn't until the railroad arrived that Skyberg began to develop as a village. With rail service established, Skyberg (sometimes spelled Skyburg) soon had a growing business

Skyberg (Skyburg) Depot. (www.west2k.com)

sector, which included a milk station, a grain warehouse, a hotel, an eating place, a dressmaker, a co-op creamery, a store, a livery, and a post office. The post office was rather long lived lasting nearly one hundred years.

The community later had a bank, and when it closed in 1919, Skyberg began to decline. The Great Depression further accelerated the decline and soon Skyberg was a roadside hamlet.

SOGN

1892 - 1903

CLASS A

APPROXIMATE LOCATION:
County #9 and #14

The Goodhue County Historical Society has undertaken and completed quite a task. They have placed brown historic road markers at the sites of their long

Sogn marker. (Courtesy of Andrew Filer)

Top: Sogn country; bottom: Sogn today. (Courtesy of Andrew Filer)

ago towns (for an example see the Sogn photos). Now it is possible to easily visit Goodhue County's long ago towns and places. Take a driving tour and see for yourself the beautiful countryside and visit the sites of long ago history.

Sogn is considered a late-comer to Goodhue County's post office system. The post office was established in 1892 and lasted just over a decade. Reaching its peak in the early 1900s, the several businesses declined after the post office closure. The store and cheese factory continued for many years. The creamery, despite valiant and varied efforts, closed in 1959. Six months later the store went out of business. A filling station operated from 1944 to 1978.

Today the former cheese factory and a handful of homes occupy the site.

A school was built a mile east of the village in the 1950s. After consolidation, the building became the Goodhue County Education District offices.

Wastedo today. (Courtesy of Andrew Filer)

WASTEDO

1857 - 1903

CLASS A

APPROXIMATE LOCATION:
U.S. Highway 52, 380th Street, and 90th Avenue

Lasting nearly fifty years, Wastedo had a post office, a creamery, a mill, and a few other small businesses. Two houses remain, and the Wastedo name lives on.

WHITE ROCK

1871 - 1895

CLASS D

APPROXIMATE LOCATION:
County #1 & County #8

Never platted, White Rock developed "haphazardly." Getting off to a slow start with only one business in 1873, five years later the settlement had two black-

Goodhue County Education District offices, Wastedo. (Courtesy of Andrew Filer)

smiths, a shoemaker, a tailor, and a general store/post office. In later years, a saloon, a feed mill, and a creamery were part of the village. After 1900 a Woodmen of America Hall was built. When the bank opened in 1915, a boom of sorts took place. Area historian Roy W. Meyer wrote that the bank survived the Depression and, in fact, was thriving at the end of the twentieth century. The bank even expanded, with branches in Cannon Falls and Bellechester.

WHITE WILLOW

1876 - 1894

CLASS A

APPROXIMATE LOCATION:
County #6 south of Junction with 400th Street

Originally along the stage coach line, White Willow later moved to be near the railroad to an already thriving village known as Rice. Roundabout mail delivery had the mail delivered by train to Rice, then taken to White Willow to be sorted. Unusual to have mail transported to a post office two miles away, the post office later relocated.

The community of White Willow, according to Roy W. Meyer, thrived after the loss of the post office for a short time. The growth of nearby Goodhue caused White Willow to decline.

The depot closed in 1919 and was removed in 1930. In 1956 the rail line was abandoned and the rails later pulled up. Meyer writes that one by one the houses and building were gone. The store was auctioned off in the 1910s and the building moved in the 1940s.

White Willow Depot. (www.west2k.com)

Houston County

Faith Lutheran Church and Cemetery, Black Hammer, above. (Courtesy of Pastor Liptack)

At left, Faith Lutheran Church, Black Hammer. (Courtesy of Bob and Sandi Hamilton)

BEE (BERGEN)

1891 - 1905

CLASS C

APPROXIMATE LOCATION:
T-7 on Iowa/Minnesota State Line

Store in Bee, half in Minnesota, half in Iowa. (Courtesy of Travis Cleveland)

State lines can on occasion run through a community, but seldom do they run through a building the way it does in Bee, Minnesota. When I first read that the Iowa/Minnesota border ran through the Bee Store, I was fascinated and knew there was a story to be heard.

I imagined walking through the front door in one state and exiting through the back door in another state. I saw the fun and quirky side of it and never gave much thought to the logistics of it. With further reading and research, I began to see just how problematic having a state line run through a business could be.

According to a Houston County history publication the first storekeeper, Joseph Swartzkop, didn't have any issues running his store, at first, even with the fact that some of his stock was in Iowa and some in Minnesota. It was when he opened a saloon that things got complicated.

Iowa was a dry state (no alcohol sales). The laws started being strictly enforced in the mid-1880s. No problem, the alcohol was moved to the Minnesota side of the building. A note was made of the advantages of operating in two states was that if someone wanted to avoid arrest in Iowa, they simply stepped over the state line and law enforcement had no jurisdiction in the other state. The same applied to Minnesotans wanting to avoid arrest—step over the line into Iowa.

A later owner recalled that sales tax was an issue. Iowa had enacted a sales tax long before Minnesota did. To keep prices consistent, the storekeeper paid the sales tax out of his own pocket. Both Minnesota and Iowa had a cigarette tax. Iowa's tax was higher, so cigarettes were kept and sold in the Minnesota half of the store. Two cash registers were required, one to ring up the purchases in each state. Property taxes were paid to both states.

In its heyday, Bee had a store, a mill, a post office, a creamery, and a blacksmith shop. The community was primarily Norwegian and had been settled in the 1860s. History of the village is sparse. At one time Bee was also known as Bergen. Bee was also known for its high quality butter, which had been awarded the National Creamery and Buttermakers Award.

Today, Bee has the look of a long-ago town. The store, now a home, still straddles the state line.

BLACK HAMMER

1871 - 1902

CLASS C

APPROXIMATE LOCATION:
County Road #4

Probably the only "Black Hammer" in all of the United States, this Houston community's name is Norwegian in origin. According to a Houston County history pub-

Bee, Minnesota, village. (Courtesy of Errin Wilker, http://iagenweb.org/allamakee/history4/bee.htm)

Black Hammer Village. (Author's Collection)

lication, the name is derived from "sort" "hammer," which means black hammer. The term usually refers to a hand tool for pounding but sometimes refers to a hill shaped like a hammer. Early settler Knud Berjo saw the charred look of the hill. It reminded him of a hill in his homeland, Slidre Valdres, Norway. The name stuck.

The hill offers a panoramic view of the surrounding countryside. A unique landmark, a rock formation, built in the likeness of a woman and known as the "lady on the hill" was said to have been constructed in 1878 by an early settler who owned the land at the time.

The Houston County Historical Society tells that the hill has long been the location of many celebrations, the biggest being the Fourth of July.

An early mill was operating by 1857 but by 1866 it had been destroyed by a flood. A few residences had also been built near the mill. One of the early settlers was given the nickname "Mathias with the Fork." According to the Houston County history, he was given the name because he never went out after dark without a pitchfork.

The fledgling community was struck by tragedy on August 6, 1866, when the most devastating flood to hit the area struck. The mill and all the homes, except for one, were swept away. The mill and the homes were never rebuilt.

Black Hammer, the village, continued on. By 1871 there was a store and a blacksmith shop. The Houston-Decorah Mail Stage began delivery tri-weekly. A post office was established that same year. It operated until 1902.

Growth was slow but by the 1890s a wagon shop and a second store was opened. Operating under a succession of owners, the store would stay open until the late 1950s. The store building was later sold. After Black Hammer's school consolidated with Spring Grove Schools, the Black Hammer Swift Scooters 4-H club purchased the brick school building. The

4-H club meetings were held in the building, and in 1977 they celebrated their fiftieth anniversary.

The heart of the community was (and is) the Faith Lutheran Church. A frame church was built by the Norwegian settlers in 1868, it wasn't long before the church was too small so it was torn down, and a bigger church was constructed. Services were held in the Norwegian language until the mid-1930s. In 1958, the congregation celebrated its centennial anniversary and its 125th in 1983.

In recent years the majestic church and adjoining cemetery are at the old town site, as are a handful of homes.

FREEBURG

1858 - 1947

CLASS A

APPROXIMATE LOCATION:
County #249 and Crazy Corners Road

Prosperous in the 1920s, natural disasters, a changing economy, and changes in transportation would see Freeburg decline. Dating back to the 1850s, Freeburg was named after a village in the Black Forest of Germany, Freiburg. The Minnesota community faded away by the 1940s to 1950s.

In the 1920s Freeburg was home to a bank, a creamery, a shipping association/stockyard, a railroad depot, a post office (1858 to 1947), two stores, two blacksmith shops, a barbershop, three taverns, and a flour/grist mill.

The Reno-Preston Railroad, now defunct, was the artery of the village as well as the surrounding area. As automobile traffic increased, rail service declined. Early residents recall that as passenger service was slowing down, the few remaining passengers rode with the conductor in the caboose. The fare from Freeburg to Caledonia was twenty-five cents. The train would pick up and leave off people wherever they wanted.

The Great Depression of the 1930s also took its toll on the small community. Stock was being shipped by truck, so the shipping association/stockyard ceased to operate in the 1930s. The creamery was remodeled into a tavern, complete with a swimming pool with a flowing well. It was dubbed "Little Miami." The stores, east and west, operated until the 1960s. One of the stores was later remodeled into a garage/repair shop. Because of modern methods and less dependence on horses, the blacksmith shops closed.

Not only did the Depression and new technology affect life in Freeburg, the most devastating of all was the "Big

Flood of '46." According to a Houston County history publication, on the night of June 16, 1946, a devastating flood swept down the North and South forks of the Crooked Creek. Eleven inches of rain fell in a cloudburst over the region. Fields were covered. The force of the water washed out the railroad tracks of the Reno-Preston branch of the Chicago, Milwaukee, and St. Paul Railroad. Power lines snapped, and residents were without power for over a week. Roads were washed out. Bridges were submerged or swept away, falling into the creek. Huge gaping sink holes were gouged out of the land. The Freeburg Depot floated off its foundation and collapsed one-half mile downstream. The post office and store had three and one-half feet of water, which caused severe damage. Some residents had to be rescued through second floor windows.

Area historian and resident Lucille Pohlman writes in a Houston County history that nine sows and their baby pigs were swept away. The next day, eight sows and their piglets came walking home, exhausted but alive. Pohlman also writes that the carcass of a cow was found high in a cottonwood tree. Many lost their autos.

The pool at "Little Miami" was filled in with mud. The "Little Miami" would continue to operate for years and was said to be one of the cleanest establishments in southeastern Minnesota. Reviews were glowing. In early 2015, the business was for sale.

Freeburg was home to Peace United Church of Christ and St. Nicholas Catholic Church. Peace UCC celebrated their 100th anniversary in 1985. The original church was built in 1885, with a new building constructed in 1895. In 1968, Freeburg's St. Nicholas Church celebrated its 100th anniversary. The last Mass was held in 1978. I understand the building was razed in 2006.

The Freeburg School was built in 1858 and a Houston County history tells that it was still standing in 1985.

Little Miami. (LOOP NET)

JEFFERSON

1860s – 1940s

CLASS C

APPROXIMATE LOCATION:
Far southeastern Minnesota, one mile from New Albin, Iowa

Jefferson holds the distinction of being the farthest southeastern town in Minnesota. Jefferson would also become an Iowa Town (New Albin). How did a Minnesota town become an Iowa town? All it took was the Mississippi River to change its course.

The early settlement, first called New Landing, was situated in a natural harbor. There was good fishing, and the river was wide enough for steamboats to visit. Steamboat traffic helped spur the growth of the village as well. Homes were built, businesses were established, and a three-story stone warehouse was constructed to handle the river boat cargo.

Things looked good for Jefferson. In just a few short years the Mississippi River changed its course and Jefferson's livelihood. Steamboats could no longer get close enough to the harbor. So early settlers and businesses moved the town one and one-half miles south and became New Albin in Iowa.

One of the advantages of New Albin was that it was a larger town site. It wasn't confined to the small area between the high

Jefferson Warehouse. (National Register of Historic Places, Jefferson Grain Warehouse, Jefferson, Houston County, Minnesota #94001386)

Jefferson Warehouse. (National Register of Historic Places, Jefferson Grain Warehouse, Jefferson, Houston County, Minnesota #94001386)

Jefferson Warehouse. (National Register of Historic Places, Jefferson Grain Warehouse, Jefferson, Houston County, Minnesota #94001386)

bluffs and the river as Jefferson was. Soon only a handful of homes were left in Jefferson. A Houston County history publication states that the homes and former area of Jefferson remained known as Jefferson, but the town itself became New Albin.

Jefferson continued on but was dealt a fatal blow in 1940. Before 1940 a narrow dirt road connected New Albin, Iowa, to La Crescent, Minnesota. A new highway was built and in so doing the remaining seven houses in Jefferson were torn down or moved.

Today the stone warehouse still stands and is on the National Register of Historic Places.

LOONEYVILLE

1855 - 1870

CLASS A

APPROXIMATE LOCATION:

Two years before the village was surveyed and platted, a post office had been established. The year 1855 also saw the establishment of a small store. According to the Houston County Historical Society, the store was stocked with "a wheelbarrow full of goods." The next owner increased the stock and also built a larger, log store building. He later built a frame structure. The business closed in 1858. For a short time, the only visible remnants of the settlement were the corner stakes. There is no evidence of the village remaining today.

LORETTE

1856 - 1871

CLASS A

APPROXIMATE LOCATION:
County Highway #25

One of the characteristics of a "boom and bust" town is that the town was heavily dependent on one industry, one economic base. Most often it was a natural resources such as timber or mining, but it could also be a transportation access point. Countless towns lived and died because of the railroad. For Lorette, it was the stage coach access. Everything in Lorette came about because of the stage coach. The community was born of the stage coach and the stage line's demise was Lorette's curtain call.

According to area historian Donna Huegel, stage coaches followed ridges rather than valleys. This was meant to diminish the threat of Native American attack or ambush. The route's location was along the B&Y (Black and Yellow) Territorial Road. Another historian, Tom van der Linden, writes that ten miles was the distance a coach could travel with one team of horses. Lorette's location fit the bill in those ways and more.

The early Territorial Road ran from La Crosse to St. Paul, passing through Lorette, which was the first stage coach stop west of La Crosse. It was on the South Ridge, eight miles distance following what is now County Highway #25. The two-story log building was an early landmark and was constructed in 1856 by landowner Seth Lore. According to Huegel, the building had an immense fireplace that extended along half of the side of the building. There were three sleeping rooms on the first floor with one upstairs chamber. A cook room was an extension off the back of the building. A two-story twenty-by-thirty-foot addition was built in 1859. A blacksmith shop, a livery barn, and other buildings were part of the complex. A post office was established in 1859 and was discontinued in 1869. A frame school was built in in 1876.

But it was the stage that defined Lorette. Records show that passengers unloaded for three different stage lines. It is said that it was common to feed seventy passengers at dinnertime. At times over one hundred were served.

A cemetery was established, which, in recent times, is maintained but seldom used. If you visit the cemetery, take note of the large Norway spruce tree. The tree was planted 150 years ago. Infant Florence Carpenter died in Lorette in 1876, as she and her family were traveling through the area. The spruce seedling was planted to mark her grave and is now huge. A memorial stone also marks her grave.

Today farms sit at the T junction that marks the village site. Several years ago a historian/resident, Ed Schumacher, created a historical sign. Made from old red cedar boards mounted on a recent metal building it reads "Lorette House." Underneath is a black and yellow painted sign that reads "B&Y Trail." It also has a carved outline of a bison.

The Lorette House no longer stands, nor are there any remains of the settlement. The only known remnant of the community is its sign at the Houston County Historical Society Museum.

MONEY CREEK

1856 - 1907

CLASS A

APPROXIMATE LOCATION:
Just off Highway #76 not far from Houston

With a name like Money Creek there has to be a story or two. There are. Most likely more folklore than fact, the stories run from a man drying the bills in his pocketbook. A gust of wind came up, blowing the money in the water and downstream. Another tells of a man who put his money into his hat brim so it wouldn't get wet as he forded the stream. While crossing the creek a tree snagged his hat and downstream the money went. Thus the township and the village (first named Hamilton) were renamed Money Creek.

Both the village and the township were bustling and included a post office (1856 to 1907), doctor, machinery dealer, sawmills, feed mills, a dance pavilion, a race track, a gun shop, hotels, dressmakers, a blacksmith shop, a stage coach stop, a creamery, a ferry, a tonsorial artist, a dentist, a tannery, a wagon shop, a nursery, a Woodsman Lodge, taverns, a Baptist Church a garage/filling station, a stockyard, and more. The community also had a baseball team.

When the creamery and school closed, the village began to lose other stores and businesses. By 1982, there was only a manufacturing plant operating in the old school building.

The last classes were in 1969/1970. Students were then bussed to Houston or Rushford.

NEWHOUSE

1890 - 1933

CLASS A

APPROXIMATE LOCATION:
Half-way between Spring Grove and Mabel. One and one-half mile north of the Iowa State Line, Newhouse Road

Even though Newhouse was established in 1879, when the Caledonia, Minnesota, and Western Railroad built a station and elevator, it didn't reach its peak until the 1890s. The village was first called Newport, but the name was later changed to Newhouse after Tollef Newhouse, the landowner on which the settlement sat.

A post office was established in 1880 and was discontinued in 1903. It was reopened in 1904 and closed permanently in 1933.

Newhouse was home to two stores, two restaurants, a combination restaurant/barber shop, a shoe repair shop, and a farm implement/blacksmith place. The Farmer's Alliance, a political movement that established cooperative stores, elevators and a shipping association, was also active in the settlement. Another farmer's group, the Farmer's Equity Company was also active and operated until the 1930s. The well-stocked mercantile lasted until 1946. Later a tavern would operate.

Today the area has a few farms.

RENO

1880 - 1935

CLASS A

APPROXIMATE LOCATION:
#26 And Hillside Road - near Reno Recreation Area

Life in Reno was based on the railroad. In the early days, Reno consisted of an engine house, coal shed, ice house, depot, assorted buildings, and a railroad car scale. Two sections of four to six men were stationed at Freeburg to serve the line.

The elevator was another early component of Reno. It operated from 1912 to the 1920s. Because the mill was located across a slough, access was limited. A walkway was built and later a larger bridge to serve teams, wagons, and autos was constructed. The site was located a short distance from the more recent government dam. At one time, the mill employed a twenty-two-man crew.

A hotel operated until the mid-1920s. It was destroyed by fire but was rebuilt. After the repeal of Prohibition, the lower floor was operated as a tavern. It was again destroyed by fire in the 1940s. Again it was rebuilt. It 1985 it was still a tavern.

A store and post office was in business until the 1930s. A school house was also part of the community.

Declining railroad traffic by the 1940s saw Reno losing its railroad facilities. The "Big Flood of '46" wreaked havoc with railroad lines. The depot was moved to St. Albin, Iowa, in 1950. Reno became just another siding. Operating on a limited basis, including one year of closure, rail service closed permanently in 1981.

The area is now a recreation area. The RJD Memorial Hardwood State Forest offers seventeen miles of riding and hiking trails in the summer and cross-country ski and snowmobile trails in the winter. There are five campsites and six horse campsites. A spectacular view of the Mississippi is also part of the recreation area.

RICEFORD

1856 - 1871

CLASS A

APPROXIMATE LOCATION:
County #8/29

Once on a pace to be Houston County's largest village, it is said that over four hundred people lived in the settlement of Riceford. There are a few versions as to how Riceford was named. The most likely was that it derived its name from its stream crossing, ferries, and landings. Henry Mower Rice once had a trading collection depot near the site of the creek in 1810. Records indicate he and his agents used the ford regularly while collecting furs in the region. Known as Rice's Ford, the name became Riceford. One source states that Rice's Ford was used before Houston County was established.

Heavily advertised, many settlers were attracted to the region. Stage coach access was also key to settlement. Development plans were ambitious. The plat of Riceford showed several streets running north/south and east/west. In anticipation of the hordes of settlers that would arrive, a Riceford suburb was platted with the original layout. As a Houston County history publication states, the population of Riceford never reached expectations, and the few houses built in the suburb, known as South Riceford, were soon abandoned and razed. By year's end 1856, approximately twelve business lots had been sold. The following year a mill and two stores were built.

With continued stage coach travel through Riceford a hotel was soon built as was a blacksmith shop and a farm implement dealership. The village even had a canvasser of books and stationary. Also in operation were lime kilns and stone quarries, a school, and approximately one dozen homes.

Brown's Mill, better known as the Upper Mill was a three-story structure. The adjoining pond stretched a half mile in length. It was designed and built by prominent area millwright Luther Preston. Preston had designed and built several regional mills as well as the woolen mill in Preston (which was named after Luther). After changing ownership multiple times, and switching from water power to steam power, the mill was destroyed by fire in the late 1890s.

The 1860s saw a second mill begun in Riceford, the Crystal Mill, near the juncture of Crystal and Rice creeks, just north of the village. A foundary was also operating, as were several other professional and skilled services, including a lawyer, doctor, stone masons, and carpenters.

A restaurant, pool hall, and photography shop were established. Another hotel, a few boarding houses, and a saloon were also added to Riceford as was a shoe shop, harness/saddle maker, and even a watch repair shop. According to the Houston County Historical Society, the saloon was short-lived as the innkeeper converted at a revival meeting and never again sold a drop of liquor.

In 1878, a Doctor Nye joined the community. A Houston County history publication tells that "what he lacked in medical proficiency he made up for in the formality of his attire." It's said he was never seen without his frock coat and high silk hat. He was nicknamed "The Pill Doctor" as his medical knowledge did not go beyond the dispensing of pills and herbs.

Riceford was heavily invested in the milling of wheat so any issues affecting the wheat crop had serious impact on the livelihood of Riceford. After years of growing wheat without crop rotation, the soil was depleted. Add in cinch bugs and poor weather, and the wheat-growing years came to an end.

Another devastating blow to Riceford was the coming of the railroad. The Reno-Preston Railroad came to the area in 1879 and bypassed Riceford. Many businesses closed up, packed up and moved on.

A side effect of the railroad transportation was that it signaled the end of stage coach travel. Riceford had always had stage coach service, and many of its businesses were dependent on the traffic.

By the turn of the century, Riceford had only two stores and one mill operating. One of the stores continued on until 1956 when competition from nearby towns made it impossible to stay in business.

There was religious activity in Riceford, but references and records are sporadic. At different times in Ricefod, there were Methodist missionaries, Quakers, Seventh Day Adventists, Catholics, Lutherans, and varied Revivalists. Only one church was built in Riceford. In 1877, area Lutherans formed a congregation of their own.

Today the Lutheran Church still stands and a few homes are in the area.

SHELDON VILLAGE

1856 - 1903

CLASS A

APPROXIMATE LOCATION:
County #10/11

Back in the mid-1800s, Sheldon was a thriving community with two mills, a Presbyterian Church, a cobbler, a cabinet maker, a blacksmith, a sorghum mill, a cream-

ery, an implement dealer, many stores, and several saloons. An apothecary operated and dispensed all types of medicines. It also carried a good supply of rock candy for the children. The community even had its own doctor who would often deliver sermons for the pastor when needed.

One area resident, a horse lover, owned many fine trotters and even had a race track just east of the village. Another early resident had a large workshop of which the second floor was used as a dance hall.

A brick kiln operated near the mill. It is said that the region's clay and sand mixture made the best bricks near and far. Early residents recall that as the clay was removed from the ground, a pond was formed. It made for great ice skating.

Mail was first brought by stage coach. A post office was established in 1857 and was discontinued in 1903.

The community also had a school house. At one time enrollment was at an all-time high of seventy students. The school was later closed with consolidation with Houston Schools. The school building was later used as a community center. Many area groups and organizations held their meetings there. The hall also hosted anniversary parties, baby and wedding showers, graduation parties, and more Annual potluck meals were held in the hall.

Area resident Ethel Johnson wrote that in 1982 all Sheldon's businesses were gone. Still Sheldon was a tranquil place to live. Today the Sheldon Town Hall and several homes are near the old town site.

WILMINGTON (GROVE)

1861 - 1950s

CLASS C

APPROXIMATE LOCATION:
Off County #28 on gravel

Water availability was of the utmost importance to early settlers. It was often the most important deciding factor when determining homestead and settlement locations. The water source was imperative to survival for the people, their stock, their farming and their businesses. So it was with Wilmington (Grove).

Founded in 1860 the community was first known as Nitterdal. It wasn't until 1888 that records tell of Wilmington's first business, the Crystal Springs Creamery. It was a private enterprise until 1904 when it was sold to local farmers and operated as a cooperative effort. A new building was erected

Church Marker. (Courtesy of Jo Walsh)

Wilmington Church. (Courtesy of Cyndi Gipp)

in 1924 and was used until the creamery closed in 1950. The building still stood in 1982.

A store was established in 1889. Wilmington's buttermaker built a second store, and it was so successful, the first store was bought out, and the building was moved and adjoined to the second store, making for a roomy business. The store building burned to the ground during an intense lightning and thunderstorm. A replacement was promptly built. It closed in 1935. It was later reopened but just for one year.

Other businesses included a feed mill, a blacksmith shop, a shoe repair shop, a sawmill, a garage, and a poultry dressing plant. Both the feel mill and poultry business used steam from the creamery for their power and their hot water.

The Wilmington Mutual Insurance Company was established by thirty area farmers in 1876 and is still going strong.

Wilmington's first church was built in 1868 on a two-acre plot donated by an area resident. It was next to the log school. It served the community until 1908 when the present standing building was built in a more centrally located area of the community.

The church and adjacent cemetery are all that remains of the early community. There is a wooden historical marker at the site.

WINNEBAGO VALLEY

1858 - 1906

CLASS B

APPROXIMATE LOCATION:
County Road #5 near Eitzen

Oftentimes early long-ago towns were not compact with clearly defined borders, boundaries or even town limits. Village homes, businesses, schools, and churches could and often were spread out in a wide geographical area. Winnebago Valley, or Watertown as it was originally known was one such town, being located in two geographic areas approximately one-half mile apart. Confusing the matter were the terms "Upper" and "Lower." Both referred to Winnebago Valley, the Upper part of the town was to the west, and the Lower part to the east.

Historian Barbara Scottston and Terry Atherton explained that the terminology came from distinguishing between the two mills and their location on the Winnebago Creek. One was upstream and the other was further downstream.

Seems the two locations each required their own businesses. According to Scottston and Atherton, in addition to the mills, there were two blacksmith shops and two stores, one in each location. Sharing other businesses, there was a school (Upper), a hotel/tavern (Lower), and later on an auto repair garage and numerous houses. The post office migrated between the Upper and Lower sites, occupying several dwellings and buildings.

Today the Johnson Mill still stands and is on the National Register of Historic Places. The Upper Mill is still standing

Johnson's Mill. (National Register of Historic Places, Johnson's Mill, Winnebago, Houston County, Minnesota #8200296)

and has been converted into an event venue. The mill, built in 1860, is now a tavern on the first floor with living quarters on the second and third floors. It can be rented for special events.

YUCATAN

1856 - 1905

CLASS C

APPROXIMATE LOCATION:
County #4, ten miles off State Highway #76, between Houston and Caledonia

Why Yucatan? The naming of the small community and of the township remains unclear, even a mystery as early historian and reporter Burr F. Griswold wrote.

Burr, in writing of Yucatan, tells that the first stake holder in the area was Edwin Stevens in 1856. He built five log cabins, sold them the first year, and promptly left the area for Worth City, Iowa. Later he moved to Washington State, never to return to Yucatan. Stevens also built a flour mill and was in the process of building a sawmill before he departed. The mill was completed in 1856 by Edmund McIntire from Dedham, Massachusetts. The village of Yucatan was actually located on McIntire's claim, and Dedham was the village's first postal name. McIntire would later serve in the state legislature as the Yucatan area's first representative.

Once thriving, Yucatan included a blacksmith shop, a dance hall, a store, a creamery, a school, a mill, a post office

Yucatan Cemetery, (Courtesy of Duane St. Mary)

and a number of homes. By 1967, the population had dwindled to a dozen people.

A later article by Robert Gehl tells that an addition to the mill, constructed in 1859, housed a still for making whiskey. Corn for the still was acquired as toll for work done in the grist mill. It is said that the still had a 100-gallon-a-day capacity.

The Dedham Mill was swept away during the flood of 1866. It was a never rebuilt.

A log school was built in 1857. During the Civil War a frame building was erected. Since consolidation, area students have attended class in Houston.

One of Yucatan's earliest businesses operated well into the twentieth century. According to the article written by Gehl, the store had once been two stories, the top floor being a dance hall. A tornado damaged the building and it was rebuilt as a one-story structure.

Area backroads travel enthusiast, Roger Langseth, writes that the old school building, the store front and approximately four homes were at the site in recent years.

Jackson County

Bergen Kimball Korner. (Courtesy of Tom McLaughlin)

Bergen street scene. (Courtesy of Jason Smith)

BERGEN

1889 – 1900 (2000s)

CLASS D

APPROXIMATE LOCATION:
County #30 & #21

Shortly after its founding in 1895 by Norwegian immigrants, a creamery and a store were established in the German-named community. According to former area resident and historian, Jason Smith, the creamery operated for forty years. The store however, lasted much longer. For years, the store was the center of the community. It sold food and clothing and in later years it included a gas station and post office. In recent years, the only Bergen store-front sold antiques. The social center of Bergen was, and is, the Bergen Bar and Grill, still operating today, offering some of the best food around.

Another local landmark just a few miles from Bergen was the Kimball Korners Tavern. The store, located one mile west of the Martin County line and four miles south of the Cottonwood County line was at the intersection of #29 and #85. Originally further into Jackson County, the store was moved two miles closer to Martin County in 1962. According to a *Fairmont Sentinel* newspaper article by Jenn Brookens in 2012, the store burned to the ground in 1963 as a result of arson.

The Bergen Store. (Courtesy of Jason Smith)

Someone set the curtains on fire. It was rebuilt that same year. The store sold mainly groceries in the early years but moved to sandwiches in later years. It is said they had the best burgers in the area. The property was closed and sold to Jackson County in 2012.

A short distance away, Jason Smith writes, is the Bethany Lutheran Church. The community was once home to three churches, but in 1920 the three combined into one congregation. The church is the social and spiritual center of the area.

Bergen church. (Courtesy of Jason Smith)

Bergen sign. (Courtesy of Jason Smith)

Elm Creek south of Bergen. (Courtesy of Jason Smith)

MILOMA

1906 - 1930

CLASS A

APPROXIMATE LOCATION:
County #7, southeast of MN #60

Truly a lost town, a historical marker at the site is the only remnant of the one-time rail station. Actually the depot in Miloma was shared by two railroads, the Milwaukee and the Omaha. The name Miloma combines the first three letters of each railroad name. For twenty-five years the small settlement was known as Prairie Junction, but it was later changed to Miloma. A post office operated under the name Miloma from 1906 to 1930. The community also included two elevators and a hotel.

PETERSBURG

1893/1967

CLASS C

APPROXIMATE LOCATION:
County Road #4

The community had a post office until relatively recent times, from 1893 to 1967. The community also had a school (razed in approximately 1995), a creamery, a post office, store, bank (for a short time), a blacksmith shop, and a few churches, including the Union State Line Church. In recent years there were a handful of homes, a farm implement dealership and the church in the area.

Union State Line Church, Petersburg. (Courtesy of Tom McLaughlin)

Petersburg, Minnesota, building. (Courtesy of Tom McLaughlin)

Petersburg, Minnesota. (Courtesy of Tom McLaughlin)

Sioux Valley store. (Courtesy of Tom McLaughlin)

SIOUX VALLEY

1879 - 1906 (2000s)

CLASS C

APPROXIMATE LOCATION:
#4 and 400th Avenue

Perhaps the most enduring part of Sioux Valley is the legacy of the Sioux Valley School. The school was built in 1918 and operated until its dissolution in 2000. It was then purchased for use as the Sioux Valley Lutheran School which has since ceased operation.

Sitting on twelve acres of land, the school is a 35,000-square-foot, two-story structure. The second story included a large library, three classrooms, and three offices if needed in future expansion. A 1953 addition included the gymnasium, the stage, a youth room, shop, and classrooms. Throughout the years, the school consolidated with nearby school districts until its purchase and use as the Sioux Valley Lutheran School. The building is still used for community events.

The community also had a post office from 1879 to 1906, a creamery and a store.

Sioux Valley School. (Courtesy of Tom McLaughlin)

SPAFFORD

1894 - 1903

CLASS C

APPROXIMATE LOCATION:
Highway #16 – Now County #34

Known as Spafford, the post office operated under Spofford. It was in operation from 1894 to 1903. It had a well-known store/gas station that lasted into the late twentieth century. At one time a hotel also operated in the community. The nearby Grace Lutheran Church is still active. A few buildings/homes were in the area in recent years.

Grace Lutheran, Spafford. (Courtesy of Tom McLaughlin)

Le Sueur County

Immaculte Conception church and congregation in Marysburg's early days. (Courtesy of Immaculate Conception Church, Marysburg MN http://www.maryschurches.com/index.php/marysburg)

Immaculte Conception church, Marysburg. (Courtesy of Immaculate Conception Church, Marysburg MN http://www.maryschurches.com/index.php/marysburg)

Marysburg Church 1899. (Courtesy of Larry Korteum)

CAROLINE

1876 - 1893

CLASS A

APPROXIMATE LOCATION:
Old Highway #5, between Kasota and Mankato

Long ago towns do fade away and disappear but rarely are the buildings stolen away.

According to an article in the Fall 2008 Blue Earth County Historical Society newsletter and referring to an earlier 1982 article, it was claimed that the church in Carline was stolen. It seems an agitated reader wrote a letter to the editor of the *Mankato Review* in 1889. He asserted that the 1876 church building was literally stolen. A response was posted by the Reverend William Coop stating that the church, in decrepit condition after several years of neglect and vandalism, had been acquired by legal but quiet negotiations.

Caroline was located on Old Highway #5 between Kasota and Mankato. The community was named for the eldest daughter of the landowner who granted the railroad the right-of-way and building rights. The town site of Caroline had early been the site of Chief Sleepy Eye's main village.

Conrad Smith, the landowner, constructed a stone house which he operated as a general store. A lime kiln, with a railroad spur, was also built. The railroad station had passengers boarding on the first floor with a signal tower on the second floor. A post office, a dance pavilion, and a few homes were also part of the small community.

The Milwaukee Road Railroad line was rerouted and Carline faded away.

CORDOVA

1887 – 1907

CLASS A

APPROXIMATE LOCATION:
County #2 near junction of County #5 at Gorman Lake

Even though Cordova was incorporated in 1878, it never acted independently of the township and its government. Platted and located on the south shore of Gorman Lake, Cordova, at its peak included three general stores, one hardware store , two blacksmith shops, one wagon shop, two hotels, two sawmills, a school, two churches, and a post office, which operated from 1887 until 1907.

LEXINGTON

1856 - 1907

CLASS A

APPROXIMATE LOCATION:
County #26 near the junction of Countys' #5 and #32

Lexington's first years were harsh. Platted in 1857 on a two-hundred-acre parcel of land, Lexington developed quickly. That first year, twenty students attended school, held in a private home. A general store operated for two years. A sawmill was built but burned in 1860. It was rebuilt that same year albeit on the opposite side of Clear Lake and much larger. It was also coupled with a grist mill that operated until the 1880s.

Even with all that development the years of 1857 and 1958 were hard. That first winter many families went hungry and survived by grinding corn on the home coffee mills. A land hunter was murdered and the murderer captured and hung by an angry mob.

According to the Le Sueur County Historical Society, in 1882 Lexington had a post office/general store, a flour and grist mill, and the only steam amber cane refinery in the county. The refinery had a capacity of 5,000 gallons of syrup per season.

The founding of Le Sueur Center ended Lexington's growth and if fact hastened the small settlements decline and demise.

Today the Lake Front Bar and Grill is located in the area.

MARYSBURG

1894 - 1903

CLASS C

APPROXIMATE LOCATION:
Junction of County #16 and John Street

Lasting less than ten years and with a population of less than 100 at its peak, Marysburg was a small trading center. A post office, a store, and a few other structures operated. The post office was discontinued in 1903.

The Immaculate Conception Catholic Church still stands and is very active in the region.

Immaculte Conception church, Marysburg, today. (Courtesy of Immaculate Conception Church, Marysburg MN http://www.maryschurches.com/index.php/marysburg)

OTTAWA

1856 - 1954

CLASS D/F

APPROXIMATE LOCATION:
County #23 and #26, the Minnesota River, and Cherry Creek meet in Ottawa

First known as Minnewashta, Ottawa was platted in 1856. A post office was also established that same year. The first years brought a great rush to Ottawa but the community never developed as expected. Part of the reason for that may have been that an early land developer stipulated in the land deeds that no liquor of any kind would be allowed.

Ottawa remains. (Courtesy of A. Filer)

Ottawa Depot and creamery, postcard. (Author's Collection)

Charles Swartz house and barn. (National Register of Historic Places, Ottawa Stone Buildings, Ottawa, Le Sueur County, Minnesota, 82004705

Methodist Church. (Courtesy of Amy Rubey Lencowski)

Purchasers objected and many backed out of their purchases. This further decreased the growth of the community. Lots that had once been sold for $500 were now being sold for ten dollars.

With time, the village did develop, and several large hotels were built. By 1883, the village included a hardware store, a tin shop, a wagon shop, two blacksmith shops, a flour mill, a grain elevator, a post office/general store, and an Omaha Railroad depot.

Charles Swartz house and barn. (National Register of Historic Places, Ottawa Stone Buildings, Ottawa, Le Sueur County, Minnesota, 82004705

Vintage Ottawa Church. (Charles Swartz, National Register of Historic Places, Ottawa Stone Buildings, Ottawa, Le Sueur County, Minnesota, 82004705)

Vintage town hall. (Charles Swartz, National Register of Historic Places, Ottawa Stone Buildings, Ottawa, Le Sueur County, Minnesota, 82004705)

The community lasted well into the twentieth century. The post office operated nearly 100 years. After its life as a pioneer village, the community was a small town.

Today the village still has a community feel. There are seven stone buildings on the National Register of Historic Places and the Le Sueur County Historical Society is at work preserving the historic significance of the village. Take a step back in time and visit the quaint historic setting of Ottawa.

Ottawa Church Plaque. (Courtesy of Amy Rubey Lencowski)

PETTIS

1850s – 1970s

CLASS A

APPROXIMATE LOCATION:
Between Kasota and Cleveland

Sometimes you don't find lost towns; they find you. That's the way it was with Pettis. I had not heard of Pettis, and no mention was made of it in my research. It truly was lost, at least to me. So it was a surprise, a very pleasant surprise, when I learned of the long-ago Le Sueur County community.

An email from Ruth Pettis Collins first brought Pettis to my attention. She introduced herself and told me her grandfather grew up in the Pettis General Mercantile Store that her great-grandfather built. Pettis was a small community along the rail line between Kasota and Cleveland. Her great grandfather sold parcels of land for the rail line to be built through the countryside, connecting communities.

Over the course of more emails, Ruth generously shared photos, information, history, and tales. She brought Pettis alive,

Ottawa scene 2014. (Courtesy of A. Filer)

Pettis Train Station. (Courtesy of Emily Pettis/Ruth Pettis Collins)

and, through her, I was able to learn so much about one of Le Sueur County's long-ago towns. She also connected me with Connie Voight Giles, who had written the history of Pettis as a high school report in 1972. It is the most complete written record of the community. Relying heavily on the resources provided by Ruth and Connie, the tale of Pettis came to life.

The Pettis family had been in the area since 1856 when newlyweds Harlow and Sarah (Davis) Pettis set up a home on the shores of Lake Emily. The couple had five children, Alva, Alan, Alma, Adna and Amy.

When the Farmington Division of the Chicago, Milwaukee, and St. Paul Railroad extended their line into the area in 1902, the railroad came through Alva Pettis's farmland. (near

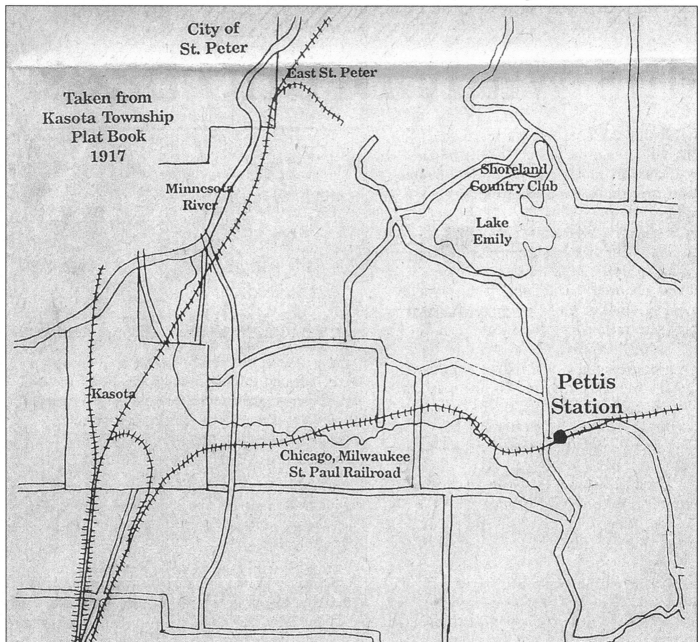

Pettis location map. (Courtesy of Ruth Pettis Collins)

Pettis and Davis Wooden Coins. (Courtesy of Lois Pettis)

Pettis Elevator. (Courtesy of Emily Pettis/Ruth Pettis Collins)

Le Sueur County highways #18 and #19 intersection). Being experienced in lumber yard management (he already owned a lumberyard in Mora, Minnesota), Alva built a lumberyard near the rail line. Lumber from this mill was used to build the other buildings in the settlement, which included a blacksmith shop, an elevator, and a stock yard. Since Alva owned the land upon which the settlement sat, it was named after him, Pettis.

Soon a two-story tin building with a porch joined the community as a store. The store carried a variety of goods. For a time, machinery was sold out of a lean to attached to the store.

Area farmers often sold eggs, butter, and other goods to the store. Payment was in the form of aluminum/tin coins. The aluminum/tin coins came in various denominations and were used as cash, redeemable only at the store. The store was also the community's social center. Young people would often gather at the store in the evenings and play cards and eat peanuts. During the day, the old-timers would sit around the potbellied stove and visit.

The railroad did travel through Pettis but only stopped when passengers or cargo was boarded or unloaded. If there was a passenger, Carl Pettis or his younger sister Ila, would hang out a flag, which signaled the train to stop. If it was after dark, Carl or Ila lit a lantern as a signal. Ila Pettis Davis recalled that no matter what the weather was like, rain, freezing cold, or too hot to walk, as a kid she had to run to the station and get the signal out for the train, as well as get the fire started or stoked in the potbellied stove. It was a service to the community. A twelve-by-twelve-foot building with a potbellied stove served as the depot. During the cold months, people would call Pettis Station and tell them they planned to be taking the train. Carl/Ila would go down to the depot and stoke up the stove, so the waiting passengers would be warm. The wait for the train could be a long one. Connie Voight Giles wrote that the train was never on time. The fare for the trip from Pettis to Mankato was twenty-five cents. Lois Stangler Pettis, wife to Carl Pettis Jr. recalls growing up on the shores of Lake Emily

Pettis Baseball Team. (Courtesy of Ruth Pettis Collins)

and hearing the train whistle at noon, daily, in the mid- to late 1930s. Her father, Hugo Stangler, was a farmer on the shores of Lake Emily, and he traded at Pettis, Minnesota.

The trains also picked up livestock, grain, produce, and other goods. Sugar beets were a major crop in the area so a separate loading dock was located along a siding rail. The general store also had a storage building down by the tracks, having a floor built of railroad ties, with a loading platform near the railroad.

Pettis also had a co-op grain elevator, a stockyard, and a sorghum press. The grain elevator was built by Alva Pettis near the tracks. It was used by local farmers to store and trade/sell their grain. It was known as the the Farmers Elevator, in Pettis, Minnesota. This structure was later sold to the farmers living near Traverse, Minnesota. Farmers settled and families grew. Area children attended school at the Lake Emily or Lake Washington schools.

At one time the store operated as a tavern. The store burned in 1937, and there were at least three versions as to the cause of the fire. One said that a spark from an oil burner started the fire. Another was that a too-wild party in the tavern caused the fire, and the other posseted , since it was Prohibition, the fire was deliberately set by someone not happy with it being a tavern.

Baseball was very popular in the early twentieth century and like many communities, Pettis had a town team. Pettis also had a horse racing track. Early resident Orange Louis Davis III recalled that on Sundays families would bring their horses and their full-meal picnic baskets and would spend the day watching the races and competing with each other.

A pea vinery was started in Pettis in the 1940s. Farmers brought their peas to the vinery where the peas and vines would be separated. Today that is done right in the fields.

Other than living quarters above the store, Pettis had no village homes. Most residents were nearby farmers, and Pettis served as the trade and social center. There were tenant's

Pettis Station. (Courtesy of Gerald Dobie)

apartments for rent at the Alva Pettis homestead/farm within walking distance of the mercantile store.

With less dependence on rail traffic and the increasing automobile travel, Pettis declined. Connie Voight Giles wrote that in 1972 only two buildings stood in the community, one being the depot and the other the storage building. The store foundation was dug up with road construction by the county. The elevator foundation still exists on the Dobie land. Current resident Gerald Dobie has dug up well tiles on his land where shallow wells provided water to the stockyards down by the railroad tracks. The road construction on Le Sueur County #18 destroyed the front porch steps of the mercantile store. Artifacts, such as some of the Pettis aluminum/tin coins, Pettis and Davis Store advertising plate and a few photos remain with descendants of early settlers. They also remain to tell us the history of a small rural community in Le Sueur County.

Advertising Plate. (Courtesy of Lois Pettis)

Lincoln County

Verdi School Bus. (Courtesy of Kathleen Keller Thiesen)

Vintage Verdi. (Courtesy of Kari Morford)

VERDI

1879 - 1997

CLASS C

APPROXIMATE LOCATION:
County #2 & #9

Longevity would be the hallmark of Verdi. Established in 1879, with a post office and store, Verdi would experience a growth spurt with the arrival of the Chicago and Dakota (later known as the Chicago & Northwestern Railroad) in 1879. The construction of a railroad turntable and the housing and living needs of three section crews created a busy and bustling community. Over the years, Verdi's business section and population would grow even more.

Named for the Italian composer Joseph Verdi, the name also means "greenness" and well defines the lush prairie area. Because of its long life, there were more resources and information available on Verdi than for the majority of lost towns.

Records show that, over the years, Verdi businesses included a two-story creamery, which burned in 1916; a blacksmith shop; the Verdi Hotel with twenty-six rooms (torn down in 1942 and moved to a nearby farm where it was repurposed as a home); a butcher shop; Enke's General Store (which had an upstairs hall with an outside stairway that hosted silent movies and other events as well as dances); a lumberyard; a small café; a tavern; a dance and pool hall; several groceries; the Verdi State Bank; and many others.

The bank was robbed in the 1930s by three armed men. Slightly over $1,000 dollars was taken. The three were later apprehended, two of the robbers received sentences of twenty years. The third man, who served as lookout, received an eight-year sentence. The bank later moved to Comfrey.

Several activities were popular in Verdi, including baseball, basketball, football, softball, and wrestling. The school was central to the community, and also hosted several events and programs. Verdi was one of the first school districts in Minnesota to use motorized school buses. The Verdi Crop Sale, an annual event, was held until the school's closure in 1969.

Built in 1889, the Verdi United Methodist Church was also considered a community treasure. In its history, it served as a town and school museum and houses remnants of the school trophy case, class photos, and seats from the school, which stands vacant just across the road.

The post office was established in 1879 and lasted nearly 120 years until 1997. Through its years, mail was delivered by horse-drawn vehicles, Model T Fords, motorcycles with side cars, homemade snowmobiles, by foot, and by auto. Oftentimes the closure of the post office signaled the official demise of a village. For Verdi, that wasn't so long ago.

Because of its rather late lifetime, there have been several articles written on Verdi as well as oral histories gathered from

Verdi Country Scene. (Courtesy of Cory Funk)

Verdi Today. (Creative Commons)

resident reunions and get-togehters. One autobiography enti-tled "The Box Man" was authored by early twentieth-century resident Walter Keller.

According to Walter, his parents came to farm in the Verdi area in 1907. He was born two years later. On the day of his birth, Verdi experienced a bad snowstorm. The attending physician had to stay on the Keller farm for two days before he was able to get home.

Walter recalled that during his school years, the school had ten to twelve students in grades one through eight. A pot-bel-lied stove dominated the classroom. One year Verdi experi-enced another bad snowstorm. The teacher, living quite a distance away, could not get back to the school for nearly a month. The students were ecstatic with the unexpected vaca-tion. Their joy was short-lived as they learned they would have to attend school a month longer in the spring.

National events affected the lives of Verdi residents. Walter remembered he had saved part of every pay check in 1929, nearly $300.00. He had it in the Verdi State Bank. When Pres-ident Roosevelt ordered the Bank Holiday, he lost $150.00, nearly six months' pay.

Music and dancing were popular. Verdi residents were pe-riodically treated to the music of the Lawrence Welk Band. Walter recalled that a person could dance all night for $1.00.

There are lots of memories of Verdi but perhaps the most universal one, the one that nearly everyone recalls, is that of Hero, the circus elephant. The circus visited Verdi in 1915. Circuses were always a popular attraction in any community and that was true in Verdi. The main attraction in 1915 was Hero the elephant, said to be the largest elephant in captivity.

According to several written resources and recollections, the day was rainy and cold, with a few snow flurries. Hero had been put to work pulling circus tent stakes. Hero's trainer was intoxicated and became increasingly abusive. Hero finally snapped, turning on his trainer, knocking him down and then chasing him around the grounds in a game of hide and seek.

The large animal, in his rage, tore a wagon apart, pushed bandwagons off the tracks as well as other vehicles, even top-pling a cage of lions. The scene turned into pandemonium. In their fear, crowd mentality had people begin shooting at Hero with every weapon they could find. Bullets rolled off Hero's hide, causing the enormous elephant to become con-fused and angered. The rampage continued for two hours until some had found high-caliber bullets, and Hero was fi-nally felled. Veterinary students were put in charge of exam-ining and disposing of the body. Over two hundred low-caliber and 100-high caliber bullets were found in Hero's hide. It is said that the hotel served elephant meat for weeks. The hotel owner purportedly had an elephant hide bag made. Hero's re-mains were put on display in a South Dakota museum, as was the hide bag.

Another oft-mentioned story is that of a hot-air balloon that landed in one of the Verdi farm fields. Sighted in 1918, the hot-air balloon was determined to be a U.S. Army balloon that was testing a device for dropping leaflets and circulars. The question might be, was this a prototype for the current drones used by the Army?

Verdi, as a village, slowly faded into history. There is still a community feel and several buildings still stand.

Lyon County

Amiret Building. (Courtesy of Tom McLaughlin)

You're on the Right
BURCHARD ELEVATOR
BURCHARD, MINN.

Burchard Elevator. (Courtesy of Lyon County Historical Society)

AMIRET

1878 - 1992

CLASS C

APPROXIMATE LOCATION:
Southeast of Marshall

The 1870s were pivotal years in the history of Amiret. In 1874 the area was first organized and named Madison. In 1874 the railroad moved its station a mile northwest, and the village was laid out as Amiret. Arthur P. Rose wrote that the township was also named Amiret by legislative enactment. (In 1872, a store and post office had operated as Coburg.)

The Congregational Society built a church in 1873, and it was later moved in 1875. The first school classes were taught in a board shanty in 1875.

Early predications said that Amiret would continue on to become a thriving village. Coburg had the distinction of being Lyon County's first town to be abandoned. During the 1870s grasshopper plagues, the town was moved a mile north, reestablished and renamed Amiret.

The post office operated until very recently, 1992.

BURCHARD

1886/1945

CLASS A

APPROXIMATE LOCATION:
6 Miles West of Balaton

Today a few houses stand where Buchard once was located. Begun in 1900 as a railway station, the settlement was named for H.M. Burchard, a Chicago and Northwestern land agent in Marshall. Considered more of a rail siding and grain-buying point than a true station town, Burchard was platted with only two blocks in 1885. A hotel was quickly built, as was a general store. A post office was later established, and a school was on the town plat map in 1889.

The Lyon County Historical Society writes that by 1912 Burchard was little more than a grain-buying and shipping point. Though the town had nearly vanished, the elevator was used for storage until the late 1970s.

In the fall of 2014 and 2015, the Lyon County Historical Society offered bus trips to visit the county's lost towns.

Burchard, 1900. (Courtesy of Lyon County Historical Society)

CAMDEN

1874 - 1900

CLASS A

APPROXIMATE LOCATION:
Near Lynd on Redwood River

Once home to a large grist mill and several businesses, the settlement of Camden declined when the Great Northern Railroads bypassed the community along with the establishment and growth of nearby Lynd. By 1912, the businesses were gone and only a few homes remained.

Camden was home to Lyon County's best known flour mill, the Camden Mill. It is said that remnants of the mill can still be found.

DUDLEY

1903/1907

CLASS A

APPROXIMATE LOCATION:
Clifton Township

Originally established as a rail station in 1901, the plat included just four blocks. Even that was too large as Dudley never developed. The railroad station closed in 1904. The post office continued for a few years. The Lyon

Dudley Depot. (Courtesy of the Lyon County Historical Society)

County Historical Society writes that the Dudley Co-op remained active for many years. In fact, the co-op earned sales of more than $300,000 in the 1960s.

HECKMAN

1901 - 1914

CLASS A

APPROXIMATE LOCATION:
5 Miles Southeast of Marshall

More of a rail siding along the Chicago Northwestern Railroad than a true station settlement, Heckman was named for a dining car supervisor. A post office operated for a few years.

Martin County

Center Chain Store. (Courtesy of the Martin County Historical Society)

CEDARVILLE

1868 - 1903

CLASS A

APPROXIMATE LOCATION:
215th Street and 65th Avenue

Bypassed by railroads not once but twice, Cedarville was a thriving trade center for over thirty years. Located on the north end of Cedar Lake, the community had a post office from 1868 until 1903. The village also had two stores, a hotel, a blacksmith shop, a wind grist mill, and several homes. A school was established in the earliest days of the settlement, 1867.

A Methodist Episcopal Church was established in 1880. A traveling minister served the congregation on a limited schedule. A church history tells that due to "exceptionally severe storms and unpredictable snowfall in the winter of 1880/1881, which made roads unpassable, the minister only reached Cedarville three times. Once in October 1880, again in June 1881, and lastly in September 1881.

In 1899 the Chicago and Northwestern Railroad and the Minneapolis and St. Louis Railroad both bypassed Cedarville, signaling the rapid decline and demise of the village.

A 1933 *Daily Sentinel* news article reported that over 1,000 cars and 4,000 people attend a picnic and history outing in "Old Cedarville." Early settlers, including the first white boy born in Martin County, were honored guests, and several speakers were part of the program.

The Martin County Historical Society has erected a marker at the old village site.

Cedarville Diamond Jubilee. (Courtesy of the Martin County Historical Society)

CENTER CHAIN

1858 - 1905

CLASS A

APPROXIMATE LOCATION:
Old highway #15 near Minnesota/Iowa border

Fairmont, in its earliest days, was said to be "a bachelor village" and a bit "on the seamy side." According to an early news article, Center Chain, located on the east bank of Iowa Lake, was considered "the cultural center of the county." Center Chain was also Martin County's first settlement. During the "Indian Scare" of 1857, according to a historical marker, the frightened residents of Fairmont fled to Center Chain for safety.

Center Chain included a post office (1858 to 1905) and general store combination. The top floor of the building housed a community hall and was the area's social center. A creamery operated for over two decades, from 1894 to 1908. Early church services were held in a nearby school. The First Community Church was dedicated in 1900. The store carried a bit of everything including groceries, smoked meat, candy, tobacco, and other staples. The store was located near the Minnesota/Iowa border.

In 2001 a historical marker was erected by the Martin County Historical Society.

DESOTO

1876 - 1903

CLASS A

APPROXIMATE LOCATION:
1¼ mile north of Dunnell on Highway #4

In 1899, sentiments ran high after the Spanish American War. So when the new Minneapolis & St. Louis rail station stop was named Desoto, folks didn't take kindly to the new station having a Spanish-sounding name. Even though explorer Hernando de Soto (1495-1542) had been credited with discovering the Mississippi River, the people didn't want the village named for a Spaniard. They raised $1,500 and moved the fledgling village further south, establishing the community of Dunnell. Desoto, with its new side track, a well and a tank lasted just three months. The Martin County Historical Society erected a marker at the Desoto site in 2002.

EAST CHAIN

1862 - 1906

CLASS D

APPROXIMATE LOCATION:
12 Miles Southeast of Fairmont

Over forty years ago a writer, Barbara Blanchard of the *Daily Sentinel*, referred to East Chain (shortened from East Chain Lake) as a "never-never village, a village that never was and probably always will be."

Laying claim to being one of Martin County's oldest communities, Blanchard wrote that East Chain isn't listed on Martin County's list of towns and villages, but it is on some maps. Even today, long past its heyday, Each Chain has the feel and the look of a community, and it doesn't take much to imagine the settlement at its peak.

That peak was in the late 1800s. According to Blanchard, the area was settled by various ethnic groups, the English first, then the Swedish, the Germans, and the Polish. All traded in the village but nationality kept many different religious denominations active.

At one time, the community business district include two general stores (both operated for over fifty years), a water powered mill, a real estate office and a post office (1862 to 1906), a meat market, a few blacksmith shops, a few cafes, a barbershop, a busy co-op creamery that operated for sixty-five years, an auto and machinery dealership, a shoe repair shop, a feed mill, three auto repair garages, a candy store, a tavern, and several homes.

Social activities were important and a Woodmans Hall and Royal Neighbor Lodge operated. Dances were so popular dancers had to wait their turns to get on the dance floor.

At least three area churches were active—a Catholic, a Lutheran and a Methodist.

East Chain was predicted to continue steady growth. As the automobile became the mode of transportation, the village of East Chain dwindled. Still, its location on the north shore of East Chain Lake is picturesque and popular.

Holy Family Catholic Church, East Chain. (Courtesy of Tom McLaughlin)

Methodist Church, East Chain. (Courtesy of Tom McLaughlin)

Store front, East Chain. (Courtesy of Tom McLaughlin)

After its peak days, several businesses and buildings were repurposed. Some were moved or torn down. The East Chain bank, across from the Methodist Church, closed in 1923 but was later a café, a barber shop, and a beauty shop. The East Chain Hotel (1871) rented two rooms to the county library for a time. It was remodeled into a home in the 1960s.

One of the stores closed in 1988 was later used as a coffee shop while the upstairs living quarters were remodeled into apartments. The barber shop, after closing in the 1970s was used for storage and torn down in 1988.

Several buildings still stand. Many new homes have been built in the area, and people still call East Chain home.

FOX LAKE

1872 – 1960s

CLASS C

APPROXIMATE LOCATION:
Main and Schley

At one time, Fox Lake was a station stop on the Iowa, Minnesota, and Northwestern Railroad. The village was on the east side of the lake and was established in the early 1870s.

First known as Walnut Grove in 1867, the town was then known as Bucephalia in 1873, then Fox Lake in late 1873. The post office, originally called Walnut Grove from 1874 to 1876, was discontinued only to be reopened in 1901 as Fox Lake. The area was a rural branch until 1965.

Several buildings and some homes remain in the area today.

Fox Lake, Minnesota. (Courtesy of Tom McLaughlin)

Fox Lake store front. (Courtesy of Tom McLaughlin)

IMOGENE (IMOGEN)

1901 - 2000s

CLASS C

APPROXIMATE LOCATION:
6 miles east of Fairmont, 2½ miles south of Granada

People are still gathering in Imogene (Imogen), Minnesota, just as they have for over 100 years. Now they congregate at the "Ghost Town Tavern" as most of Imogene, the village, has faded into history.

The community was settled in 1899 and was first known as Cardona. But the Spanish American War had just ended, and it was fresh in people's minds. Not liking the Spanish name of Cardona, the townspeople changed the post office name to Imogene, while the rail station continued to be known as Cardona. For the sake of conformity, the railroad then changed their station name to Imogene. However, the post office, spelled Imogene without the ending "e," Imogen, the train station with it.

Just where "Imogene" came from is speculation, and many versions have circulated. The tales tell of a love-lorn young man naming the nearby lake after his lost love, Emogene, to the version that it is named after a young girl who drowned in the lake.

Imogene became a bustling village. For a time it was an important shipping point for grain and livestock. Other early businesses included a stockyard, the rail depot, a blacksmith shop, a barber shop, a lumberyard, a saloon later turned store, a post office (1901 to 1913), and the elevator. Considered Imogene's longest running business, the elevator operated for ninety-nine years. For years it was known as the Garry Elevator and was owned by early resident Michael Garry and later his son. The Garry Elevator was sold to buyers in 1987 and was renamed the Imogene Elevator. It operated until 2000.

Population numbers fluctuated. Records indicate that in 1901, the population of Imogene was twenty-one. In 1939 it was up to one hundred. By 1945, 139 residents lived in Imogene. After the depot and school closed, the population dwindled to twenty-one residents.

Ghost Town Tavern, Imogene. (Courtesy of Tom McLaughlin)

A popular landmark in the area was Roy's Café, established in 1947. According to Mike and Liz Garry's *A Century of Memories* the café was especially busy when I-90 was being constructed. The road workers and crews would stop for lunch and dinner at the café. It later became known as the Cozy Inn.

A Century of Memories also tells of a 1950s event. Two young boys were playing in the backyard of an Imogene home. They discovered a large box. Boys being boys, they pushed the box aside and found a foot wide hole. One of the boys, just three years old, slipped and fell feet first into the hole. Trapped, the fire department was called. Oxygen was piped down to the boy via a rubber hose, but the hole was so tight, they could not reach the boy's head. A parallel hole was dug, nine feet down. Water began seeping in and it was feared the well would collapse, burying the young boy. After some tense moments, avoiding tragedy, the boy was rescued uninjured.

Today the elevator still stands, and the Ghost Town Tavern is a popular destination.

LONE CEDAR

1867 - 1879

CLASS A

APPROXIMATE LOCATION:
Halfway between Fairmont and Jackson

Imogene elevator. (Courtesy of Tom McLaughlin)

Halfway between Fairmont and Jackson sat the Lone Star Tavern and Halfway House named for its "halfway" location and for a large cedar tree growing in the area. Not just a rural post office, it was also important because it was a transfer station. Stage coaches would stop to refresh their horse teams, drivers, and passengers. Overnight lodgings, meals, and a refreshing drink could be had in the primitive sod house. The post office was later transferred to Sherburn when, in 1879, the Milwaukee Railroad arrived there. The Martin County Historical Society tells that over one hundred families had been served by the Lone Cedar Post Office in its twelve-year history.

Nothing remains of the site and, in fact, all had disappeared within years of the post office closure. In 2001, a historical marker was placed at the site by the Martin County Historical Society.

MANYASKA

1900 – 1908 (1960s)

CLASS A

APPROXIMATE LOCATION:
Between Welcome and Ceylon County Road #22

Once again farmland, no evidence remains that a town once existed on the prairieland. But, exist it did and for many years. Manyaska was a thriving station stop on the Chicago, Northwestern Railroad. The rail line ran from Eagle Grove to Fox Lake. At its peak, Manyaska had two lumberyards, a blacksmith shop, a creamery, a depot, a grain elevator, a general store, a hotel and a post office (1900 to 1908). The settlement was also a busy shipping point for livestock, grain, and other farm products.

In 1929 the first elevator burned to the ground. The next year a team of horses pulled the Fox Lake Elevator down the railroad tracks to Manyaska.

Through all of Manyasksa's years, the store was the mainstay of the community. The first store was built in 1899 and burned in 1918. Four years later, it was rebuilt and operated along with the elevator until 1945. The elevator burned in 1960 and was never replaced. The store was sold in 1951 but the new owners continued opperation until 1961, when they moved the building to Welcome and converted into a home.

Through the years, Manyaska declined slowly. One by one the buildings were sold to farmers and were moved to their farmsteads to be used as storage buildings. The store was the last building to leave the former town site.

Even after its heyday, Manyaska was a social center. Many a resident recalls free movies on Sunday nights as blankets were spread on the ground and families enjoyed the evenings feature.

Today a historical marker erected by the Martin County Historical Society marks the former town site.

NASHVILLE CENTER

1892 - 1904

CLASS A

APPROXIMATE LOCATION:
2833 240th Street

Stories of people and their times are what bring history alive. Former Nashville Center teacher and life-long Nashville Center resident Nora Boler Conklin knew that and shared tales of early Nashville Center, the village and the township, in a reading at a 1939 Martin County Historical Society meeting.

One of the stories she told was about the school district dividing into two districts. There was a dispute over which district the school house belonged to, so the school building was moved so many times that the children would have to get up on top of their sod houses every morning to see where the school house sat before they headed off for classes. Conklin also entertained her audience with tales of blizzards, grasshopper plagues, Fourth of July celebrations, and horse thieves.

Grasshopper plagues devastated much of the region in 1873 and for several years. All crops were ruined. Things got so bad that then Governor Pillsbury proclaimed a day of prayer.

Horse thieves also operated in the day, and were said to have come from far away, probably Fairmont. Cloth was sacred so men's pants were often made out of grain sacks. The grain sack pants were also stolen quite frequently. Farmers would paint their name on the sacks. Often a farmer would steal his neighbor's pants and have his wife sew a patch over the painted name, covering the original owner's name. One day a farmer's threshing machine tore off his patch exposing the original owner's name in big bright letters.

Conklin tells that Nashville Center had a garage, a church, and a school house. Records also show that a post office was established and operated from 1867 to 1904. Nashville Center had a creamery, a general store, millinery shop, a blacksmith shop, a livery, a hardware store, and a machinery shop. A Woodsman Hall was also active.

Hopes were high that the railroad would reach Nashville Center. In 1899 the railroad line was built from Madelia to Fairmont, bypassing Nashville Center. A new rail station community, Truman, was established. Truman's growth would hasten Nashville Center's demise. The creamery moved to Truman and, with time Nashville Center, would fade into history. A historical marker was erected by the Martin County Historical Society in 2000.

NORTH STAR

1875 - 1923

CLASS A

APPROXIMATE LOCATION:
Between Fairmont and Sherburn, between 150th Street and 160th Avenue, on 190th Street

North Star Church. (Courtesy of the Martin County Historical Society)

Even though the store closed in 1910, the North Star Church continued to serve area residents until 1923. The church building was torn down in 1937.

North Star, a small German settlement was founded in the late 1870s. A creamery was built in 1894, and a general store was established the following year. The post office was moved to the store in 1898. The community also included an ice house, a parsonage, a telephone company, and several homes. The post office was discontinued in 1904 when nearby Welcome began a rural mail route.

North Star was said to be a busy trade center. A historical marker was placed at the site by the Martin County Historical Society.

North Star Creamery and store. (Courtesy of the Martin County Historical Society)

North Star Church and parsonage. (Courtesy of the Martin County Historical Society)

PIXLEY

1876 - 1903

CLASS A

APPROXIMATE LOCATION:
Southeast of Fairmont on 280th Avenue

TENHASSEN

1862 – Early 1900s

CLASS A

APPROXIMATE LOCATION:
County #8 Near Ceylon

Said to have rivaled Fairmont in size and importance, Tenhassen, at one time, was a busy commercial center. In fact, in the 1870s it was considered the most important settlement in Martin County.

Originally called Tuttle's Grove (1855 to 1873) after an early settler, the community was later called Tenhassen, a Dakota word meaning "sugar maple." In its earliest years, the fur trade was the livelihood of the settlement. In 1875, it was hoped the Fort Dodge & Fort Ridgely Railroad would route their new line through the village. The rumors started a growth spurt, and soon a post office was established under the name Tenhassen. It operated until 1902. The village also included a blacksmith shop, a hotel, three stores, a steam sawmill, and a school. When the railroad line didn't materi-

alize, Tenhassen began its decline. Hastening the demise of the village was the arrival of the new railroad line in 1898. Running their line approximately one mile west of Tenhassen and creating the new village of Ceylon, the growth of the new railroad town was the finish of Tenhassen.

In its history, Tenhassen was the site of many of Martin County "firsts." The first corn grown in the county was grown by Calvin Tuttle. The first marriage in Martin County was in 1857 and was a Tuttle. The first bridge built across the inlet of Lake Okamanpeeden was built in 1858 by the Tuttles. The bridge was reportedly 160 feet in length and was built in only two weeks and did not have any nails or metal rods. Heavy rains washed the bridge away. A ferry service was established and lasted for many years, until the ferry boat sank in the middle of the inlet. A new wooden bridge was built, and it was recorded that the pilings for the new bridge were driven into the old boat. Ice and spring floods later carried that bridge away. A later bridge was built in 1959. Tenhassen also had the first hotel and the first store of record. Lester Carver was the first Martin County resident to lose his life in World War I.

According to a Martin County Historical Society record, there was a "famous" Carver-Tuttle fight. Samuel Carver, a direct descendent of the *Mayflower* settlers, settled in Tenhassen in 1862. For some reason Calvin Tuttle did not like that, and he told Carver and his family to move on. Moving a short dis-

Decker Tenhassen Store. (Courtesy of the Martin County Historical Society)

Tenhassen today. (Courtesy of Tom McLaughlin)

tance, the Carver family set up a homestead. A few days later, Carver was again told to move on. Carver stated he had already moved once and wasn't going to move again. Tuttle said that if a settler could beat him in a fight, he and his family would leave the area. The fight occurred in August of 1862, Tuttle lost and keeping his word; he and his family left the area for good.

Today an original building and a Martin County Historical Society marker are at the former village site.

WILBERT

1898 - 1907

CLASS D

APPROXIMATE LOCATION:

Home to St. John's Lutheran Church, Wilbert, the village, has faded with the years. The church was begun in 1890 and held its first services in the school build-ing, later the Baptist Church. Construction on the church began in 1891. In 2010 the church celebrated its 125th anniversary. The church also operated a school until the early 2000s. A post office operated from 1898 to 1907. The church is still active and the community feel is still very present.

Wilbert. (Courtesy of Russell Reimers/St. John's Lutheran Church, Wilbert)

St. Paul's Lutheran Church, Wilbert. (Courtesy of Russell Reimers/St. John's Lutheran Church, Wilbert)

Mower County

Freund Store NRHP. (Both photos are National Register of Historic Places, Freund Store, Johnsburg, Mower County, Minnesota 86000867)

CORNING

1884 - 1906

CLASS A

APPROXIMATE LOCATION:

Short lived Corning was settled in 1884 and organized in 1894. A post office operated from 1894 until 1906. The post office began in Freeborn County but later transferred to Mower County in 1902. It was discontinued in 1906, and for all intents and purposes Corning had nearly faded away by that same year.

FRANKFORD

1855 - 1900

CLASS A

APPROXIMATE LOCATION:
Frankford Township

Mower County's original county seat, Frankford, lost the designation in a hotly contested battle with Austin. The county records were stolen in an incident known as the "Tin Box Courthouse" (*see* High Forest in Olmsted County). Austin won the county seat in a later vote.

Frankford was platted in 1856 and was along Deer Creek. In its earliest days, Frankford was home to three stores, three blacksmith shops, a wagon shop, a grist mill, a chair and coffin factory, a shoe shop, a harness shop, one hotel (The Patchin), and a post office located in the hotel.

A limestone school was built in 1867 with the stone supplied by a nearby quarry. A Baptist Church stood across from the school. The church's cemetery is well maintained and still used. When the Southern Minnesota Railroad came though the region, several towns were created which made river settlements such as Frankford unnecessary.

HAMILTON

1855 - 1863

CLASS A

APPROXIMATE LOCATION:

Sharing its location with both Mower and Fillmore counties, the village existed in both counties. Hamilton existed for a brief time. The post office operated from 1855 to 1863.

JOHNSBURG

1891 - 1900

CLASS D

APPROXIMATE LOCATION:

½ a mile from the Iowa/Minnesota border

Lying less than one-half mile from the Iowa/Minnesota border, Johnsburg was a stout German village. Settled by immigrants from the Johnsburg, Illinois, region, the community was centered around the church. St. John the Baptist Lutheran Church is considered the first Catholic Church in Mower County. Services were first held in 1853 and presided over by a missionary priest. A log church was built in 1859, with living quarters for the priest added a few years later. A brick church building, still distinctive today, was constructed in 1908. The church is still going strong and is a local landmark.

Fruend Store today. (Courtesy of Creative Commons license)

St. John the Baptist Catholic Church, Johnsburg. (Courtesy of Creative Commons license)

MADISON

1857 - 1875

CLASS A

APPROXIMATE LOCATION:
Highway 218 and Milwaukee Road Railroad

Created when a general store was established, Madison had a post office from 1857 until 1875, a hotel, a livery stable, a sawmill, and a railroad station along the Chicago, Milwaukee, St. Paul and Pacific Railroad. After a short spurt of development, Madison did not grow as expected. By 1903 the town site was once again farmland.

OLD LEROY

1860s

CLASS A/G

APPROXIMATE LOCATION:
Now part of LeRoy

Today's city of Leroy was platted in 1867 along the newly laid track of the Iowa and Minnesota Division of the Chicago, Milwaukee, and St. Paul Railroad. But that Leroy predated today's Leroy and was in another location. It is now referred to as "Old Leroy," and was two miles north of the present municipality.

In 1865 a sawmill was built near an early settler's homestead. When the railroad arrived in 1867, two miles south, businesses chose to locate near the railroad line, and Old Leroy declined. The land upon which the original village once sat was donated to the village for use as a park and is today part of the Lake Louise State Park.

Freund's Store, established in 1880, was also a central component of Johnsburg. After several years in business, a larger store was erected, and the original building served as a saloon. According to a feature article in the May-June 2015, *Austin Living* supplement magazine, due to Prohibition in the 1920s, the saloon was closed. After Prohibition ended, a bar was added to the rear of the store. In later years, movies were shown on the side of the store building. The top floor of the building was used as a community center and many a dance, traveling theater group, school event, wedding, and more were held there. Lasting nearly ninety years, the store closed in 1967, but still stands and is on the National Register of Historic Places.

The community also included a blacksmith, who was known for his oyster stew.

RAMSEY

1874 - 1875

CLASS A

APPROXIMATE LOCATION:

A post office operated for just one year, 1874/1875. For a short time the settlement was a station on the Chicago, Milwaukee, and St. Paul and Pacific Railroad.

SUTTON

1886 - 1907

CLASS A

APPROXIMATE LOCATION:

A small settlement along the Chicago Northwestern Railroad, Sutton had a general store, a creamery, a blacksmith shop, and a post office that operated from 1886 until 1907.

VARCO

1875 - 1882

CLASS A

APPROXIMATE LOCATION:
4 miles south of Austin

Platted in 1875, Varco was a station along the Chicago, Northwestern Railroad. A post office operated from 1875 until 1882. The grain elevator operated for several years after the village's decline.

Murray County

Current Lake church. (Courtesy of Tom McLaughlin)

General store, Current Lake. (Courtesy of Tom McLaughlin)

CURRENT LAKE

1877/1900

CLASS C

APPROXIMATE LOCATION:
MN #91

Lime Creek Railroad Depot. (www.west2k.com)

Best known for its general store, the first structure in Current Lake was built in 1902. It carried general merchandise and a lean-to served as living quarters. The original store burned in 1905, was rebuilt and still stands today. The nearby church, Sillerud Swedish Lutheran Church, is still active today. The church recently made news when church members painted bales of hay as "Angry Birds" characters. According to the *Marshall Independent*, the church created six teams of members who took turns filling all the necessary roles needed to conduct Sunday services.

Current Lake store, Current Lake. (Courtesy of Tom McLaughlin)

LIME CREEK

1889/1971

CLASS C

APPROXIMATE LOCATION:
Near Westbrook

Early rough and unimproved roads made getting grain to market difficult, at best, so shipping terminals along the rail line were established. As the shipping points were established, small communities also arose. Lime Creek was one of those settlements.

Lime Creek was established in 1888 by two land owners. It was named for the creek that ran through the area. The town site was surveyed and registered in 1898. At the time it was customary to designate the streets and avenues as gifts to the community.

The railroad was built in 1889, and a depot was constructed. Two trains passed through the community every day. Since grain was the basis of the community, three elevators were built. The first one was a primitive structure that had to be filled by hand. Boxcars were also filled by hand using wheelbarrows. A grain warehouse was built in 1891 along the Omaha branch line. Records show that, at one time, more grain was shipped from Lime Creek than from any other town on the Black Hills Branch of the Chicago, St. Paul, Minneapolis and Omaha Railroad.

In its heyday, and by 1894, Lime Creek had a post office, a school, a blacksmith shop, a general store, a butcher shop, and a saloon.

Historians credit two main causes for Lime Creek's demise. The first was the loss of two of the elevators. One burned down, the other was torn down. Businesses declined with the loss of the elevators, and soon Lime Creek was just a whistle stop for the railroad.

The other factor was the founding of Westbrook. Before Westbrook, Lime Creek had served a fifteen-mile radius, after Westbrook, this range shrank to a five-mile radius. Lime Creek could no longer complete with the larger village.

Lime Creek, Minnesota, ("Lime Creek MN". Licensed under Public Domain via Wikipedia - https://en.wikipedia.org/wiki/File:Lime_Creek_MN.jpg#/media/File:Lime_Creek_MN.jpg)

WIROCK

1907/1934

CLASS A

APPROXIMATE LOCATION:
5 miles west-northwest of Fulda

Now on display at Noble County's Pioneer Village, the old Wirock train depot keeps the history of the times and the long-ago village alive.

Wirock is considered Murray County's last village to be established. In 1906, when the Chicago, Milwaukee, and St. Paul Railroad needed land for a side track, early settlers Herman and Amelia Weirauch deeded the railroad two acres of land. They also deeded an additional seven acres of land for a town site with the stipulation that, if the town didn't develop, the land would revert back to the Weirauchs. Plans were laid and filed, and the town was established. It was decided to name the settlement after the Weirauchs but deciding that the name was too hard to pronounce, and ended out being called Wirock.

An elevator was built in 1907. By 1909 a store had also been established. The store building was converted into a home and moved to Slayton. A second, larger store was built. It operated as a general store as well as a produce and cream station. The store had a succession of owners. About the same time as the second store was built, 1920, a depot and blacksmith shop were also established, as was a hardware store and a post office.

At one point the community knickname was Buttinksky, because the villagers thought the community was "butting" into Fulda.

Early Wirock Depot. (Courtesy of the Murray County Historical Society)

Early Wirock. (Courtesy of the Murray County Historical Society)

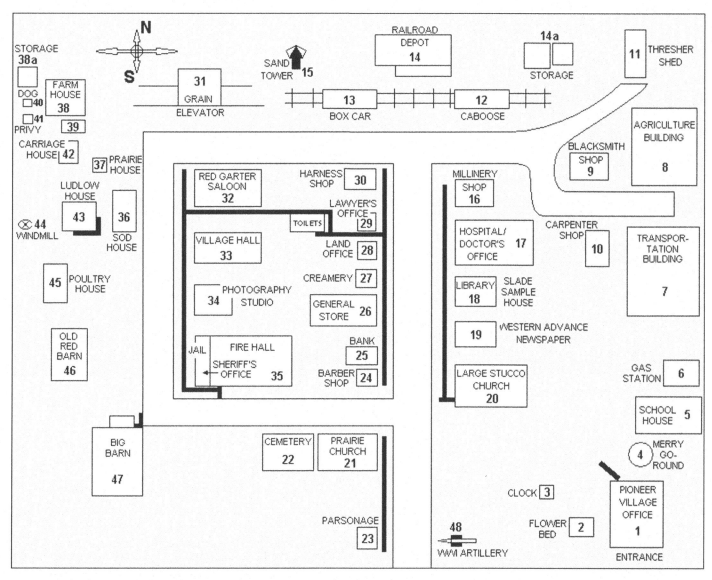

Pioneer Village Map. (Pioneer Village – Nobles County Historical Society)

With time, Wirock became a memory. The old depot was moved to the Pioneer Village in Nobles County. Pioneer Village got its start in 1958 when the Nobles County Historical Society purchased a school house that had been closed since 1944. The building was moved to the county fairgrounds and it was only open for display during the County Fair. In 1968, other buildings were acquired and the decision was made to create a historic site that would be open throughout the summer. Two and one-half acres of land was purchased. The school house was the first building to be located in Pioneer Village. There are now forty-six buildings, with thirty-six on display. Tours are self-guided. History abounds and the village is a perfect family outing. Learn more at http://www.nobles-pioneervillage.com/

Wirock Depot. (Pioneer Village, Nobles County Historical Society)

Village of Wirock. (WIKIWAND)

Nicollet County

Moo-seum (top) and Moo-seum tractor. (Courtesy of Ruth Klossner)

BERNADOTTE

1871 - 1904

CLASS D

APPROXIMATE LOCATION:
One mile north of Junction of Nicollet County #1 & #10

When I first contacted Ruth Klossner of Bernadotte, she told me Bernadotte had a population of about twelve people and three dogs. During the summer of 2015, it also became home to the Guinness World Record for largest collection of cow-related items, 15,144 pieces. That collection is housed in Ruth's home, known as the "Moo-seum." Ruth is commonly known around the area as the "Cow Lady" and has been featured in numerous newspaper articles, radio and television broadcasts, and agricultural magazines, locally and world-wide. The collection includes figurines, stuffed animals, tins, creamers, watches, clocks, prints, apparel, and so much more. The previous record holder was a woman in Australia who had 3,200 cows. Ruth has topped that by more than 12,000!

In June 2015, to satisfy the Guinness World Book's requirements, two people spent two days counting every cow in Ruth's collection. The numbers were staggering and included 3,264 figurines, 888 stuffed animals, 537 mugs and glassware, and over 605 pieces of apparel. Every cow in Ruth's collection is numbered, recorded on a computer spreadsheet and includes the description, size, price, how it was acquired and more.

Ruth began collecting in the late 1970s. She grew up on a dairy farm and has always "loved cows." Her first item was a cow and calf figurine she bought at an auction, paying perhaps eight dollars. Ruth says more than one quarter of her collection are gifts or free items picked up at dairy meetings and other places. Items come in surprising ways. One item was left at the church across the road with a note saying "Ruth, can I come home with you? I want to live at the Moo-seum." The

Moo-seum at Christmas. (Courtesy of Ruth Klossner)

Bernadotte creamery. (Courtesy of Ruth Klossner)

answer was, Yes! Ruth never did learn who left the cow. One piece in her collection, a silver cow creamer, was gifted to Ruth by Tippi Hedron, of Alfred Hitchcock's *The Birds* classic movie. Tippi was born in nearby Lafayette and spent some time with Ruth when she returned to the area to be grand marshal of the Lafayette Centennial Parade in 2000.

The largest item in Ruth's collection is her vintage 1950s Ford 8N tractor, which she drives in area parades. Ruth hosts an annual open house the first week in December and on special occasions. She also welcomes visitors by appointment.

The showcase of Bernadotte, however, is the stunningly beautiful Gothic Style church, Bernadotte Lutheran. The church has a long history, dating back to 1866, when the church was organized. In the early days, the congregation was served by a visiting pastor who conducted services in homes or in a school house as often as circumstances and weather permitted.

Early Bernadotte Lutheran Church exterior. (Courtesy of Ruth Klossner)

Early Bernadotte Lutheran Church. (Courtesy of Ruth Klossner)

Early interior of Bernadotte Lutheran. (Courtesy of Ruth Klossner)

Early Church gazebo. (Courtesy of Ruth Klossner)

Early parsonage of Bernadotte. (Courtesy of Ruth Klossner)

fisk Supper, served at the church, in 1927. In later years church organizations took over the supper, and it continued until 1994.

After the Lutefisk Supper was discontinued, an annual Swedefest has been hosted by the church each June. The event is held in the adjoining church park, which has a gazebo/bandstand and park shelter.

As a community, in its earliest days, Bernadotte had a general store, post office, and a creamery. The store closed in 1966 and was demolished in 1992. The creamery, first known as Riverside Creamery, opened in 1895. Its name was changed to Bernadotte Cooperative Creamery Association in 1944. A butter manufacturing plant, the creamery made up to 263,000 pounds of butter in a year. It closed in 1959 when state regulations made it impossible to continue.

Ten acres of land was donated and the congregation purchased forty acres of surrounding land from the railroad for five dollars an acre. A parsonage was built and the congregation's first thirty-eight-by-fifty-foot church was built in 1872. By the mid-1890s, a larger church was needed. Members hauled field stone in for the foundation. The Gothic style 106-by-fifty-foot church was completed in 1897. The Vogelpohl organ was completed and ready for use by February 1898. It was completely restored for its 100th birthday in 1998.

A 1929 parsonage fire destroyed many church records. Services were conducted in Swedish on the second and fourth Sundays of the month until 1943. At the church's seventy-fifth anniversary in 1941 it had 465 members and ninety-nine children. The church will celebrate its sesquicentennial May 1, 2016.

As early as 1890, the community had its own band, the Bernadotte Band. Though disbanded and reorganized several times, it continued until 1962. The band performed near and far It was featured as "The band without a town" in the *St. Paul Pioneer Press* in 1926. The band started the annual Lute-

Church gazebo. (Courtesy of Ruth Klossner)

Bernadotte Lutheran Church in the fall. (Courtesy of Ruth Klossner)

Bernadotte Lutheran Christmas interior. (Courtesy of Ruth Klossner)

The Bernadotte Cooperative Cold Storage Plant was established in 1938, next to the creamery, and continued in operation until 1997.

Some folks may remember the Bernadotte International Airport, as made famous by WCCO Radio's Roger Erickson. As the story grew through more than three decades, it grew to having not only the airport, but Lutfiska Airlines, Charlie's Cafe Mediocre, the Lutefisk Emporium, the Bernadotte Mall of America, a university, a marching band, and the Roger Erickson Open golf tournament. While the airport existed only in people's imagination, it had quite a following, and people drove out from the Twin Cities, looking for it!

Bernadotte may be a lost town, but it is a busy place and home to twelve people, three dogs, and a collection of over 15,000 cow-related items.

BRIGHTON

1879/1902

CLASS A

APPROXIMATE LOCATION:
6 miles south of Bernadotte

The community had a creamery, a blacksmith shop, a store, and post office.

HEBRON

1857 - 1885

CLASS A

APPROXIMATE LOCATION:
Just south of Junction of #25 and #161

Thank goodness for those folks who research, preserve and record local history. Without their work, their writings, their remembrances, their knowledge of long ago places, any local history would be lacking. In the case of Hebron, Dave Goodell and Ruth Klossner have worked hard to preserve the settlement's history. Goodell conducted years of research, and Klossner wrote the historical articles that so well preserved the past. According to Goodell, two

David Goodell at Hebron Memorial Day service, 2015. (Courtesy of Ruth Klossner)

Hebron Memorial Day service, 2015. (Courtesy of Ruth Klossner)

Brighton Marker. (minnemom.com)

159

settlements were laid out in the 1850s. One was Eureka, the other Dakota City. A post office was established in Dakota City and was officially called Hebron. Mail was delivered by steamboat. Hebron's post office was discontinued in 1885. Both the Eureka and Dakota City (Hebron) were casualties of the Panic of 1857.

Faith and education were a high priority in Hebron. Records tell that a school was established in 1865. Area farmers raised the money to build and supply the school. The one-room building also served as a community center and meeting place. According to Goodell, there were twenty-nine students in 1909 and sixteen in 1918, the school's last year. Upon consolidation, students traveled to Judson for classes.

Early church meetings were held in the Grange Hall. In 1880 the Methodist Episcopal Church purchased the hall and remodeled for use as its church. Services were presided over by traveling pastors. Regular services were held until 1906, with intermittent services conducted until 1921. At that time the church was dissolved. Both the church and the school buildings were later moved off site.

With the school's consolidation, the church's closure, and changing economic times, the coming of the automobile age, Hebron faded into history.

The Hebron Cemetery is all that remains of the village. It is very well maintained, and burials continue to be made there. An afternoon Memorial Day services is held at the cemetery each year, with the Nicollet American Legion and Auxiliary color guard and firing squad taking part. Past and present Hebron area residents, including Goodell, plan and put on the program. A new flagpole was installed and dedicated in memory of an area person buried there in 2015.

of grasshoppers caught and killed. During July of 1875, Belgrade Township alone paid bounties on 992 bushels.

Conveniently located halfway between New Ulm and Mankato, Kerns was established for that reason. It was named for the Kerns brothers, early settlers, though not the first in the area.

Over its lifetime, Kerns had a store, a post office (which only operated for three years), a creamery, a school, a tavern, and other businesses. The store housed the post office. It had living quarters on the top floor and was operated by a succession of owners.

Kern's first school was built in 1861. It was replaced by a brick building in 1876. The school had two separate entrances, one on the left for the boys and one on the right for the girls. Matching privies were out back. The building is now a private home.

A Congregational Church was established in 1862. Box socials were an important part of the church and was an annual event. The Congregation disbanded in 1940. The building was later moved to West Mankato where it is still being used as a church.

A baseball team and band were also active in Kerns. Another community feature was an ice skating rink. The community dammed up a creek to create the rink. A chicken coop was used as a warming house and as more space was needed, a granary was added to the warming house space. The rural electric cooperative provided power.

One of Kern's lasting community organization is the Kerns Birthday Club. The group was established by the women of the community in 1935. It began as a sewing club. They met the second Wednesday of the month and they still do.

The old creamery stack is the lone remnant of Kerns. A historical marker was erected at the old town site.

KERNS

1898 - 1902

CLASS C

APPROXIMATE LOCATION:
County #14 near 421st Avenue, near North Links Golf Course

Disaster struck the Kerns area often and hard, especially in those early years. Most of the settlement was destroyed by a prairie fire in 1860. A grasshopper plaque devastated a wide swath of southern Minnesota, including the Kerns area in 1874 and 1875. Grasshoppers were so abundant that a ten cents bounty was paid for each bushel

KLOSSNER

1876 - 1903

CLASS D

APPROXIMATE LOCATION:
At the junction of Old Fort Road (Nicollet County #5) and State Highway #15

Native resident and newspaper reporter Ruth Klossner has more than just a shared name with the Nicollet County village of Klossner. The settlement along the Minneapolis and St. Louis Railroad on the Winthrop to New Ulm line was named for Ruth's great-great uncle Jacob Klossner. Jacob owned the land upon which the railroad siding was

Klossner Depot. (www.west2k.com)

placed. Living to the age of ninety-seven, the local newspaper tells that upon his death in 1944 that Jacob had lived under twenty-one of the thirty-two US presidents. He saw five big wars as well as the Indian Wars. He was also a member of the state legislature, owner of a hardware store, was a banker in several area communities, and for a time was acting New Ulm mayor. Ruth has notes on the history of several Nicollet County communities and has graciously shared her history.

The first carload of wheat was shipped from Klossner in August of 1896. The railroad bed was removed in 1975.

Klossner's first businesses were a lumberyard and a blacksmith shop. A post office was soon added. In 1979 the post office moved to the bank, and bank employees were responsible for sorting the mail and putting it in boxes for pickup. Rather long-lived, the post office was discontinued in 1985. Throughout the post office's life, it was operated at several locations, including the general store, the community center, and the bank.

Over the years other businesses included a creamery that operated for over fifty years and was the largest creamery and milk plant in Nicollet County for many of those years. A general store operated for seventy-seven years. It was built in 1889. In later years the building was used as the post office and the community center, hosting many events, dances, meetings, and more. The building was lastly used as a beauty shop. It was later demolished.

Once home to two elevators, Klossner's current elevator merged with the Lafayette Farmers Co-op elevator in 1968.

The Klossner State Bank opened in 1919. A brazen daytime robbery took place in 1923. Three thousand dollars in currency, bills, and Liberty Bonds was stolen by five armed men who blew up the safe. The blast was so strong it shattered the bank's windows and even sent a piece or two of shrapnel through the window of a residence across the street. Newspaper reports stated that the robbers got away, but all later ended up in jail or dead.

Over the years additions were made to the bank. By 1976 deposits totaled more than seven million dollars, the highest deposits of any bank in Minnesota located in a community of less than one hundred. The bank later moved to New Ulm.

A very popular ballroom operated in Klossner for many years. Ruth estimates that it was built in 1911. The large building had a bar and pool table in the front and the ball-room in in the main portion of the building. Dances were held several times a week and a number of big-time bands played there. Known as the Golden Rule Ballroom, it also hosted roller-skating, with the old clamp-on skates, in the 1950s. Movies were shown on a screen projected onto the ball-room wall. The projector was placed on a car parked between the ballroom and general store.

In 1969 or thereabouts, the Klossner House began in the old ballroom building. The front of the building, and later part of the dance floor, was converted into dining space. The Klossner House operated until 2014 and had good food and featured old-time music. The building and all of its contents were sold at a 2015 auction.

During the 1980s, Klossner was the site for the West New-ton Antique Tractor Pull. All tractors had to be 1950 models or older.

There is a lot of history in Klossner, and, luckily for us, folks like Ruth Klossner are preserving it for future generations.

NEW SWEDEN

1884 - 1905

CLASS C

APPROXIMATE LOCATION:
Near Highway #22 and MN #11

How does a place get removed from official Minnesota highway maps? When I learned that New Sweden was removed from the maps in 1976, as were some towns in my home area, Crow Wing and Belle Prairie, I won-dered just how a town declines so much that the state didn't even recognize it as a place any longer. Things may have changed with the coming of the digital age, but back in 1977 it there was a system to determining how a town was removed.

According to a *Minneapolis Tribune* 1977 article, the decision to remove a place was not taken lightly. The superintendent of the cartographic unit of the Minnesota Department of Transportation says there are three main criteria. Requests for place name removal comes each fall from the traffic engineer in each of Minnesota's nine transportation districts.

Before removal, requests are investigated including "photo logging." MNDOT had (in 1977) a staggering amount of color slides taken every fifty feet on both sides of Minnesota's state trunk highways. (In 1977, that was over 12,000 miles). Road

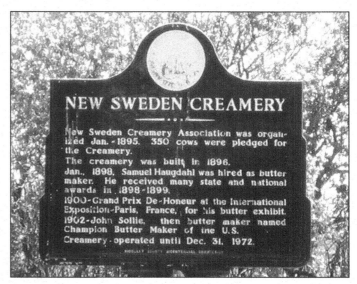
New Sweden Marker. (minnemom.com)

maps were then checked with roadside photos to make sure that there were no signs for a place not on a map and vice versa.

A name did not come off the map until they knew there was no longer a sign on the road. Removal was not permanent as a name that had been removed from a map could be put back on in future years.

In 1976, New Sweden was removed from official state maps.

New Sweden, named for many of the early settlers' home-land, had a store, a creamery, and a post office that operated from 1884 to 1905.

NORSELAND

1865 - 1905

CLASS C

APPROXIMATE LOCATION:
#22 Near #52

Land prices have gone up exponentially since 1851 when the Sisseton and Wahpeton Railroad sold their lands to the U.S. government for seven cents an acre. Once the Traverse de Sioux treaty was signed, the region was inun-dated with settlers. An early history reports that in 1850 Min-nesota had just 157 farms. Ten years later, in 1860, there were over 18,000 farms in Minnesota.

The first settlers in the Norseland area arrived in 1854. De-parting from Muskego, Wisconsin, the group, called the Nor-wegian Colony, traveled for seven weeks, eventually settling in near St. Peter.

Norseland Store NRHP (at right) and Norseland Store side view (above). (National Register of Historic Places, Norseland Store, Norseland, Nicollet County 83000918)

A Norseland Church Congregation was formed in 1858, and the first church building was constructed in 1866. An earlier parsonage had been built in 1864. It is said that the two-room parsonage had a leaky roof that let in snow and rain. It was later improved upon. One source states that the church housed one of the area's first pipe organs. The Scandian Grove Lutheran Church was also active. Both churches celebrated their Sesquicentennial in 2008.

The Norseland Store was also central to the community and is a last vestige of the settlement today. Built in 1858, it was later renovated; a wood clapboard structure was built around the original building. The store served as the community post office, the barber shop, a repair shop, which later became a Ford dealership and more. Groceries were housed on the first floor, and an elevator made moving items upstairs much easier. A tavern, though short-lived, also was part of the store for a time. In 2006 the store closed, but the egg business that had begun in the early days with farmers bringing their eggs to trade, continued on. One record tells that the tavern was destroyed by fire in 1945. The cause of the fire was believed to have been spontaneous combustion in the sawdust surrounding the ice house. It was never rebuilt.

A popular eatery was the Black Lantern Café, ca 1927. A small building was used for food preparation. Tables and

chairs were outdoors along stone paths. Lanterns lit the gate. They served light lunches, ice cream, and beer. One early resident recalled that Minnesota Governor Floyd B. Olson once

Norseland Marker. (minnemom)

163

visited the café and ordered an onion sandwich. Out of onions, the cook had to raid a neighbor's garden for the needed onions.

Camp Norseland, a Scout camp was located in the area. Fourth of July celebrations, with an ice cream social, were a tradition. However the high cost of fireworks forced the display to end in 1990.

ST. GEORGE

1894 - 1904

CLASS C

APPROXIMATE LOCATION:
County Roads #5 & #16

Standing for nearly one hundred and fifty years, the St. George Store was torn down in late 2010. Area historian Ruth Klossner wrote in a 2010 news article that the original structure was St. George's first store and saloon and was known as "Schwabenhalle." It was destroyed by fire during the Dakota Conflict. The owner was killed during the attack. A new store with living quarters was rebuilt. It was operated by a couple of owners. One could buy just about anything at the store. Ruth also told that fresh bakery was available on Sundays and after church, there was "standing room only." The store was put up for sale in 1977 but no buyers stepped forward. Klossner writes that the store closed its doors in 1979. An auction was held later that year to sell the store contents. Occasionally rented, the building stood vacant for most of the next thirty years.

St. George Church. (Unknown)

St. George is a roadside hamlet and has a church. The former church school now serves as a fellowship hall. The church itself is active and celebrated its 150th anniversary seven years ago. Several homes are in the area, and many still call St. George home.

TRAVESE des SIOUX

1876 - 1903

CLASS B/F

APPROXIMATE LOCATION:
Near St. Peter, Traverse des Sioux Park and Historical Site

One of the most significant historical sites in Minnesota is known as Traverse des Sioux. In 1851 it was a missionary outpost. Within a year of the historical treaty signing, it was a burgeoning village of 200. Blacksmith shops, hotels, seed stores, and others were soon part of the community that is said at one time had over seventy buildings.

Two quarter sections of land were purchased by Henry Rice, then president of the Traverse des Sioux Land Company. Several town plats were laid out—as many as seven in total— and some were overlapping each other. Several names for these town sites were proposed. In 1865, Henry Sibley made a plat that covered the area from the river to the prairie and called it Traverse des Sioux. Town sites establishment continued for years and included today's St. Peter. Some were started and died very quickly. Dakota City (Mills) in 1856 was one. Union City, Swan City, Hilo, and Eureka were just some of the others. All of them faded into history except St. Peter.

From all signs it seemed that Traverse des Sioux would become Nicollet County's most important city. Lot prices fluctuated at a roller coaster level. Some lots, purchased for $1.00,

Log cabin near treaty site. (National Register of Historic Places, Traverse des Sioux, St. Peter, Nicollet County Minnesota 73000990)

STORE

HERE STOOD MYRICKS' LARGE BRICK STORE, SAID TO BE THE FIRST SUCH BUILDING IN THE TOWN. IT WAS LATER DISMANTLED AND THE BRICKS WERE USED AGAIN IN ST. PETER.

Myrick's Store site (above) and from the east (bottom). (National Register of Historic Places, Traverse des Sioux, St. Peter, Nicollet County Minnesota 73000990)

sold later for $300 and later were back down to $1.00. Construction of buildings boomed. By 1857 over seventy buildings had been erected and included five stores, two hotels, churches, a school, and the community was home to over 300 people. So prosperous was the community that the village once served as the Nicollet County seat.

All that would come to an end with the Dakota Conflict of the 1860s. Fearing that the village couldn't offer ample

Fur post cellar depression. (National Register of Historic Places, Traverse des Sioux, St. Peter, Nicollet County Minnesota 73000990)

Overview of former town of Traverse des Sioux. (National Register of Historic Places, Traverse des Sioux, St. Peter, Nicollet County Minnesota 73000990)

protection, many residents fled to nearby St. Peter for safety in numbers. A housing shortage occurred in St. Peter, so Traverse des Sioux homes were loaded onto skids and pulled to St. Peter by oxen teams. Most of the residents that fled never returned to Traverse des Sioux. With time any and all remaining buildings were either moved to St. Peter or left to decay. The land reverted to pasture land. St. Peter was eventually named the Nicollet County seat.

Formerly a state park, today the site is a Minnesota Historic site managed by the Minnesota Historical Society. It is a state

Traverse des Sioux town marker. (Author's Collection)

historic site and a Minnesota State Monument. It is also listed on the National Register of Historic Places. Learn more at http://sites.mnhs.org/historic-sites/traverse-des-sioux

WEST NEWTON

1862 - 1901

CLASS D/F

APPROXIMATE LOCATION:
County Road #21, near New Ulm

Untouched for years, for decades, the Harkin Store in West Newton, Minnesota, remains as it was when the doors last closed for business in the early 1900s. Running along the top of the wall runs a U.S. flag border, but look closely, the U.S. flag only has thirty-nine stars. That is only one of the multitudes of history that permeates the old building. The store is one of the last vestiges of the once-thriving community that faded into history with the closing of the post office and the loss of population and customers. Better roads and improving transportation proved to be the major factor in the small settlements decline and demise.

Along the north bank of the river, a road led from Fort Snelling to Fort Ridgeley and on to Birch Cooley. The village of West Newton was laid out at the end of a day's journey along the road, either way. An influx of early settlers, finding the area had good land, West Newton developed rapidly. Soon the busy trade center included the Harkin Store, a post office, a saloon with a top floor dance hall, a mill, a blacksmith shop, a wagon shop, a livery/stable, and just down the river, a brew-

Harkin Store. (National Register of Historic Places, Harkin Store, West Newton, Nicollet County, Minnesota, 73000989)

ery. Perhaps the most popular and active was the Harkin Store and post office. People came from all around, by foot, by wagon and horseback to shop for supplies and to pick up their mail. The saloon and dance hall was especially busy in the early days. Entire families attended the dances, arriving in the

Harkin Store marker. (minnemom.com)

Harkin Store building. (National Register of Historic Places, Harkin Store, West Newton, Nicollet County, Minnesota, 73000989)

Harkin Store interior. (National Register of Historic Places, Harkin Store, West Newton, Nicollet County, Minnesota, 73000989)

early evening, dancing all night and returning home after sunup.

A school district was established, and three churches were founded, a Methodist, a Catholic and German Lutheran.

Disasters were common in the area. The Dakota Conflict was one. Grasshopper plagues were another. The grasshoppers were so plentiful they darkened the sky and destroyed everything. In 1876 a deadly tornado wreaked havoc and killed twelve people, including nine children. An ongoing struggle with persistent flooding played a key role in the demise of West Newton. Perhaps the deciding factor in the settlement's demise was the community's failure to secure a rail line. That, in conjunction with not securing an inter-county bridge

spelled doom. An early history tells that without improved roads and bridge, West Newton "was out of luck."

In a twist of fate, the roads that originally led people from West Newton are now highways bringing visitors and tourists to the historic site. The store's guest book tells of visitors from at least thirty-two states and several foreign countries, including Germany, New Zealand, Scotland, and Japan.

The Harkin Store is now managed by the Minnesota Historical Society. Its interior and contents remain as they were the day the business closed. The centerpiece of the store is the original pot-bellied stove sitting upon the original brick platform. Chairs and a cracker barrel are near at hand. The shelves are filled with old dishes, canisters, and other vintage nineteenth-century items. Throughout the summer, the Minnesota Historical Society hosts a wide range of events ranging from June Dairy Day, an Independence Day celebration, bluegrass concerts, costumed interpreters and several other special events. Learn more at http://sites.mnhs.org/historic-sites/harkin-store.

Nobles County

Org building. (Courtesy of Cory Funk)

Org depot. (Courtesy of the Nobles County Historical Society)

ORG

1895 - 1917

CLASS C

APPROXIMATE LOCATION:
4 miles southwest of Worthington

Org is not a common name and where it came from is unknown. What we do know is that the settlement was slated to be called Iselin after an early landowner. When the Worthington and Sioux Falls Railroad came through the region they called it Sioux Falls Junction. Putting those names aside, the general manager of the railroad dubbed the new settlement Org, and the name stuck.

The general consensus was that Org had a poor location from the get go. It was located between Bigelow and Worthington, and most agree Org never had a chance. Even so the settlement served area farmers for years.

Org is said to have been located on the highest point of land in Minnesota, at the top of the grade. Only one building was constructed in all of 1890. For ten years that building was the lone building in the settlement. The village wasn't platted until nine years later in 1899. In 1899 an elevator was built, as were a lumberyard and a coal yard. With the establishment of a general store and a post office, other improvements followed.

At one time Org included two stores, a blacksmith shop, a post office, a carpenter shop, an implement dealership, a lumberyard, a coal yard, two grain elevators, and large hay shed. In later years a filling station, a garage, and a restaurant were in the area.

Org had its moments of fame. Teddy Roosevelt spoke to a crowd of 150 for ten minutes from the rear platform of a railroad car in Org. William Bryan and Taft both had special train cars that made stops in the settlement.

Org's railroad shipping point was a settlement mainstay. One resident stated that more hay was shipped from Org than from any other place in the United States. Org was also one of the few places where one could turn a whole train around. Org was also noted for having women train dispatchers, depot agents, and telgraphers.

Some say that by the 1950s Org was little more than a name. In 1954 the railroad stockyards were removed. In 1976 Org was one of several Minnesota communities removed from the official highway map. In the 1970s only twenty-six people still lived in the settlement. In recent years new buildings have been constructed in the area.

Org remnants. (Courtesy of Cory Funk)

READING

1900 - 1985

CLASS D

APPROXIMATE LOCATION:
7½ miles northwest of Worthington

Early Reading. (Courtesy of the Nobles County Historical Society)

Reading may no longer have a post office but it still has its own zip code. Reading may no longer be a full-fledged village, but they are a complete community.

In October of 1899, the site was selected to be the first town along the new Burlington Northern rail line through the area. Since the site was on land owned by Harry Read, the settlement was named Reading. The first building constructed was a six-room residence. As soon as the track was laid, several businesses sprang up and included an elevator, a lumberyard, a stockyard, a hardware store, and a general store (with a restaurant on the top floor). A post office was established in 1900. Other buildings, including the Presbyterian Church and a school, were moved in. Over Readings long history, businesses would come and go—a bank, a garage, a telephone exchange, two churches, a consolidated high school, a supper club, a carpenter, a construction firm, a community center, a

grocery store, and a bus line. Many lasted until recent years, and some are still operating today. Even though Reading didn't grow as the Burlington Northern Railroad expected, it did develop into a lively trade center, a true community and a home to many.

The two-story school had grades one through three and four through six on the lower floor, and grades seven through ten on the top floor. Students rode on the district's three horse-drawn buses. A local history tells that the first gasoline-powered

Early Reading scene. (Courtesy of the Nobles County Historical Society)

Reading Grain Elevator, early days. (Courtesy of the Nobles County Historical Society)

Bird's-eye view of early Reading. (Courtesy of the Nobles County Historical Society)

Early Reading street scene. (Courtesy of the Nobles County Historical Society)

Church of the Bretheren, Reading. (Courtesy of Tom McLaughlin)

Bethel Church, Reading. (Courtesy of Tom McLaughlin)

Reading Depot. (www.west2k.com)

Reading school razed in 1996. (Courtesy of the Nobles County Historical Society)

buses were purchased in 1916. They didn't do well in mud and snow, so they went back to the horses during those times. The wheels would come off, and runners went on. Electricity was added to the school in 1923. Enrollment peaked in 1917 with eighty-two students. In 1927 there was one graduate, and in 1929 the last graduation was held. The school was denied high school accreditation in the 1920s. At that time students were transported to schools in Worthington. The last year for ninth graders was 1938 as the state ordered the closure of the high school. The school was later razed.

A local history of Reading tells that in 1911 the bank was robbed. Sometime in the early morning hours, two men blew open the bank safe. The nitroglycerine blast shattered the bank building and shook all of Reading. The cashier, living across the street from the bank, grabbed his shotgun and opened fire on the front entrance of the bank. Escaping through the rear entrance, the robbers jumped into a horse and buggy they had stolen earlier and were on their way. The townspeople pursued and finally caught up with the bandits. A shootout occurred (at the Greene School). That robbery is considered the last horse-and-buggy robbery in America.

In 1960 a car accident near Reading claimed the lives of nine area residents. One of the cars was carrying shift workers from the nearby Campbell Soup Company in Worthington.

The post office was closed in 1985, and Reading became a community post office until 1997. It still retains its zip code. It is also still home to many, a busy burg and a community.

Be sure to check out the Nobles County Pioneer Village for a hands-on trip to area history.

ST. KILIAN

1892 - 1907

CLASS C

APPROXIMATE LOCATION:
County Road #18

Faith was important to the early settlers of St. Kilian. The first thing they did was build a church, and since they preferred to live near their church, a settlement grew up around it. Forty acres were purchased and in 1857m a thirty-two-foot-by-forty-eight-foot church building was constructed. Two years later a general store/post office, a blacksmith shop, and two saloons completed the village named for the church.

Sitting high atop the Buffalo Ridge, hopes were high that the Burlington Northern Railroad would build its line through the village. The hopes were dashed when the railroad bypassed the settlement. The new community of Wilmont was created along the new rail line, and soon St. Kilian businesses closed and others moved to Wilmont. The store and post office closed in 1917.

Today the church is still active and is listed on the National Register of Historic Places.

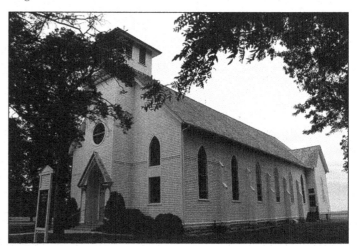

St. Kilian Catholic Church. (Courtesy of Tom McLaughlin)

PIONEER VILLAGE

Farm House. (Courtesy of the Nobles County Historical Society Pioneer Village)

General Store. (Courtesy of the Nobles County Historical Society Pioneer Village)

Grain Elevator. (Courtesy of the Nobles County Historical Society Pioneer Village)

Hospital and doctor's office. (Courtesy of the Nobles County Historical Society Pioneer Village)

Sod house. (Courtesy of the Nobles County Historical Society Pioneer Village)

Sod house. (Courtesy of the Nobles County Historical Society Pioneer Village)

The Red Garter Saloon. (Courtesy of the Nobles County Historical Society Pioneer Village)

Small prairie church. (Courtesy of the Nobles County Historical Society Pioneer Village)

Olmsted County

CHESTER (HAVERHILL)

1866 - 1957

CLASS A/G

APPROXIMATE LOCATION:
Immediately east of Rochester on County #14 near County #19 and #119

Deeming that law enforcement and other officials weren't doing enough to protect or recover their stolen horses, some residents of Haverhill formed the "Haverhill Anti Horse Thief Society." Sworn to assist each other in deterring and apprehending horse thieves in the area, the society had a slate of elected officers and riders. A Constitution complete with Articles and Bylaws was drawn up. One of the interesting facts of the society was that they allowed women to join the group. Olmsted County records do not note the capture of a single horse thief. As Olmsted County summarizes, the society seems to have developed into a social organization, which hosted many a picnic, oyster supper, and other social events.

Olmstead County history also adds that with the advent and popularity of automobile travel the society's purpose became obsolete. Still the members met, at least annually.

It is said that society members were victims of practical jokes. Such a joke occurred in Viola in the 1890s. As the Society members met, their horses were stolen. With the horses hidden away in a nearby school building, it was days before the members found their animals. No records exist of the society after 1905, so it is assumed they disbanded.

Haverhill's post office operated from 1866 to 1867. It then became the Chester Post Office, and that operated until 1957. The settlement was along the Winona and St. Peter line. Until 1885 the village was bustling and had a population of 130 residents. By the mid-1880s the town had declined to just a handful of homes, a store, the school, and the post office. As Rochester developed, Chester was eventually absorbed by the growing metropolis.

It is said that the land around Chester was black loam soil and was covered with hazel brush, a sure sign of excellent farmland. Some referred to the region as the "Garden Spot of Olmsted County."

CUMMINGSVILLE

1856 - (1960)

CLASS A

APPROXIMATE LOCATION:
Near Stewartville, State Highway #7 between Chatfield and Stewartville

After reading about the lives of teachers in long ago Minnesota towns, I'm glad I wasn't a teacher back then. According to a history written by Laura Tesca Smith, teachers had a rough go of it. As far as Cummingsville teachers, classes were first held in a log school building constructed in 1856. The teachers "boarded around," which, according to Smith, meant they stayed week by week in different homes in the district. The teachers shared a straw mattress bed with the children in the family. They were also expected to help the housewives with duties and chores both before and after school. Of course, women teachers were paid much less than their male counterparts, who also had no such duties assigned or shared sleeping arrangements.

Cummingsville was not ideally located being situated on the floodplain of the Root River just below the Stewartville dam. Persistent flooding occurred often and an especially hard one was in 1960. That flood left Cummingsville a virtual ghost town.

Cummingsville was established as a stage stop along the route from Decorah, Iowa, to Pleasant Grove via Chatfield. Several businesses operated in the settlement including a wheel wright, a blacksmith, a small store and post office, and a Presbyterian Church.

GENOA

1872 - 1902

CLASS A

APPROXIMATE LOCATION:
75th Street near Exchange Avenue

Several sawmills operated in Genoa as did three stores. The settlement was platted in 1865. The school was the feature of the settlement.

HIGH FOREST

1856 - 1902

CLASS A

APPROXIMATE LOCATION:
Near Stewartville

It is said that, as beautiful as the High Forest area is today, it was even more so in the earliest days of the settlement. Named for the region's high lands covered with lush forests, scenic waterways, and abundant wildlife of the area.

Officially established in April of 1856, early settler John Robinson platted the settlement around a village green. The next year an addition was planned. An early sawmill on the Root River supplied much of the lumber used in building the settlement. High Forest grew and grew rapidly. One early history refers to High Forest as "a wide awake" community. The history stated that, at one time, High Forest included five general stores (all doing a brisk business), two drug stores, three blacksmith shops, two hotels, a doctor's office, a lawyer firm, and a population of three hundred. High Forest had a large high school.

Early settlers were of a variety of nationalities and included Germans, English, Irish, Norwegian, and Danish. Many were immigrants themselves or children of immigrants who moved to the area from New England and New York. One early settler of note was Captain William Tattersall, an Englishman from New York. Throughout his lifetime, Tattersall served as post master, local official, and as state representative from his district. However it was his hotel, the Tattersall House, that garnered the most interest. Not only was it a local landmark but it even influenced the turn of local politics.

Captain Tattersall built the three-story hotel, said to be the best hotel in the county outside of Rochester. Some even said it was the best outside of the Twin Cities. It quickly became a center of travel as it was located along a busy stage line between Marion and Rochester. It also quickly became a social and civic center.

An early High Forest history tells that the building had an office, a bar, a post office, and a kitchen and dining room on the first floor. Five bedrooms were located on the second floor, and the top floor was a ballroom.

It is said that, in 1856, the Tattersall House played an important role in the location of the county seat in Mower County, in an incident referred to as the "Tin Box Courthouse." The county seat designation in Mower County was hotly contested. Austin failed to get the county seat by lawful and peaceful means, so they tried alternative methods. As the story goes, an official from Austin took the county records from Frankford and made his way to Austin. He stopped for the night at the Tattersall House. The "tin box" was given to Captain Tattersall for safekeeping. Meanwhile, the sheriff led a posse and followed the Austin official, finding him at the Tattersall House. The Austin official refused to give up the "tin box," and Captain Tattersall refused to tell where the box was hidden. The Austin official was arrested.

Another guest at the inn, took the "tin box" and buried it under the snow in the nearby woods, said to have marked its location in an definite but unconventional way. A detailed map was sent on to Austin. Men were sent out to retrieve the box. Austin was awarded the county seat designation.

The Tattersall House was sold and dismantled for the lumber in 1945.

High Forest had always hoped to become a railroad point and possibly the Olmsted County seat. Over the years the hopes of a railroad never materialized, and people began to leave the settlement. The charter was rescinded in 1919. By 1948, the village green could still be seen and a few buildings remained. Today the name is retained by the township.

JUDGE

1897 - 1902

CLASS A

APPROXIMATE LOCATION:
Just off Highway #63 near Rochester Airport

Judge was considered a convenient shipping station. It was located on the farm of Edward Judge, thus the name. Established in 1882, the settlement had a store, a post office, and an elevator. In recent years, Judge had an old wood building and a sign that read "Judge School 1906-1957."

PLEASANT GROVE

1854 - 1895

CLASS D

APPROXIMATE LOCATION:
County #1 and 105th Street SE

Memories and the end of an era were on the auction block that June day in 1990. After over fifty years of business in the small village, the remnants of

Flynn's Store were auction off. The store closed in 1982. A *Stewartville Star* article reported that the store was the last grocery in town.

According to area historian Belva duMez Bernard, the original store building had been a home. It was later used as a garage and repair shop before being sold, moved and used as a granary. In 1932, the Houghtons bought the building and remodeled it, using the top floor as living quarters and the first floor as a grocery store. A later addition was used as a storeroom and garage. A room built on the east side served as a tavern. In 1952 the Flynns purchased the building, added gas pumps and operated it until its closure in 1982.

In its earliest days (approximately 1854) Pleasant Grove was along a stage coach line. The settlement included a hotel, a post office, a doctor's office, and throughout its history many other businesses. Several homes were also part of the community.

An Olmsted County history tells of a tragic event in Pleasant Grove in 1860. The blacksmith and the grocer got into a heated argument over what has long been forgotten. The grocer threw the blacksmith out of the store, causing a fall that broke the blacksmith's skull. The store owner was indicted for murder, found guilty of manslaughter in the fourth degree and sentenced to one year in prison and fined $1,000. He was pardoned after six months.

Pleasant Grove was home to Olmsted County's first Masonic Lodge. Over the years it declined. With the closing of the store and the auction in 1990, Pleasant Grove's era was over.

POTSDAM

1860 - 1905

CLASS C

APPROXIMATE LOCATION:
County #247 near County #11

Lack of water power didn't stop the German settlers of Potsdam from building a flour mill. Instead they devised and constructed a wind-powered flour mill. A gigantic windmill was placed on the roof of the mill. Reports tell that for over fifteen years the mill ground flour for area farmers. Records also tell of two tragic deaths at the mill.

Potsdam, named for the Prussian city, was established in 1860. A harness shop and a blacksmith shop were the first businesses in the settlement. A store soon followed. Later a

post office and a hotel were added. The Immanuel Lutheran Church also became an important part of the village and is still active today.

Area residents may have been able to overcome the problem of no water power but were not able to withstand the lack of a railroad. Without a rail line, the town declined and eventually faded into the annals of lost towns.

PREDMORE

1892 - 1905

CLASS A

APPROXIMATE LOCATION:
Near Highway #52 and 75th Avenue Southeast

The small community of Predmore was a station on the Winona & St. Peter Railroad. At its peak it had just one store, a blacksmith shop, a creamery, and a few buildings.

ROCK DELL

1858 - 1895

CLASS D

APPROXIMATE LOCATION:
County Road #3 (6820) near Byron

The post office in Rock Dell has been gone for over 100 years. The creamery had a different history. Not many businesses can say they operated in three centuries, but the Rock Dell Creamery in Olmsted County can. Established in 1889 and still going strong today, the creamery operated in the nineteenth, the twentieth and now the twenty-first centuries. Certainly in the creamery's 126 year history changing technology and changing worlds have affected the creamery business and have required adjustments and reinventions. The Rock Dell Creamery has done all that.

The creamery celebrated its 100th anniversary in 1989. At that point, Rock Dell Creamery was the oldest cooperative creamery in Minnesota and that was twenty-six years ago! According to an article in the *Rochester Post Bulletin*, editor Harold Severson summarized the creamery's long history. First known as the Zumbro Cooperative Creamery, the original building burned, and the Rock Dell Creamery was rented and contin-

East St. Olaf Church. (Courtesy of the good people of St. Olaf's Church)

ued on. In 1954 the name was formally changed to the Rock Dell Creamery. In 1989 it was locally owned and very much in business. The original building burned in 1891 and the present brick building was built in 1919.

I visited with the long-time creamery manager and a newer employee. They told me that today the creamery sells ice cream treats, milk is sent right on to AMPI and a large portion of their business is feed.

Rock Dell Creamery. (Courtes of the Rock Dell Creamery)

Another business, the Rock Dell Garage is also going strong after all this time.

Rock Dell was settled by Norwegians. As with many communities, church was a priority. First services were held in private homes. In 1856, St. Olaf Church was organized and a cemetery was established. Today's church building is a local landmark and center of the surrounding area.

SIMPSON

1890 - 1964

CLASS D

APPROXIMATE LOCATION:
County #1 near County #16 and 68th Street SE

Once a busy burg, Simpson was originally established along the Winona and Southwest Railroad line in 1890. The original plat included ten blocks with a total of ninety-eight lots. The settlement became a full-service trade center and, over the years, included a full line of needed

Another view of East St. Olaf Church. (Courtesy of the good people of St. Olaf's Church)

businesses, including several stores, a doctor and dentist, a post office, dance halls, pool hall, shoe shop, a hardware store, a bank, carpenter shops, and, in later years, garages and filling stations. Interesting, in 1915 Minnesota was listed ninth in the number of automobiles. The early history also tells that a license could be earned by signing a form stating one was a good driver and paying a three dollar fee, which also earned two license plates for three years.

Simpson depot. (Courtesy of www.west2k.com)

Bird's-eye view of Simpson, postcard. (Author's Collection)

School postcard. (Simpson)

Viola creamery front view. (Courtesy of Viola Creamery, National Register of Historic Places, Viola Cooperative Creamery, Viola, Olmsted, Minnesota 99001310)

The community even had a park, known as Whitney Block. Picnics, ball games, concerts, farm markets, and more were held at the site. One of the largest events occurred in 1916 and was called the Young Settlers Day Celebration. Contests, games, music, ball games, and more were part of the day's activities. All proceeds went to the American Red Cross.

VIOLA

1862 – 1960s

CLASS D

APPROXIMATE LOCATION:
County Road #2 and 105th Avenue Northeast

Second only to the Kentucky Derby, Viola's Gopher Count Festival is America's second oldest, continuous festival. It's just one year younger than the Derby. 2015 was the 141st annual celebration in Viola. Each year on the third Thursday of June, teams would be chosen and off they would race to gather more gopher tails than the other teams. The losing team provided a picnic for the winning team. The events have changed over the years, but as the Gopher Count webpage tells "the common thread of a community coming together for fellowship and fun has continued for 141 years." Each year, events now include a family night, a talent show, the crowning of a king and queen, a five-kilometer race, soap box derby, pie eating contest, ladies nail driving contest, tug of war matches, Bingo, a street dance, and so much more. Learn more at www.gophercount.com.

The folks in Viola know a thing or two about longevity. Not only is the Gopher Count Festival among America's oldest, but the Viola Creamery is getting up there in years as well. A new creamery building was built in 1924, to replace the original building that was destroyed by fire in 1923. Well known for its butter, the brand "Viola's Creamery Special" was shipped for the last time. Advances in technology and the advent of refrigerated trucks made many small, rural creameries obsolete. A timeline provided by a one-time creamery owner tells of the creamery's history and milestones.

According to the time line, after the creamery closed in 1949, the building housed a cabinet maker and a boat builder among others. The creamery was sold in 1961 and was used for a hive-to-jar honey operation. It was closed down by the USDA in 1987. Again the creamery sat vacant, this time for nearly twelve years. Vandals wreaked havoc on the building. The cupola was stolen, and that allowed pigeons to infest the building, joining the mice who had taken over the other portions of the historic building.

Unable to stand the decline of the old building a brick-layer purchased the structure and, with lots of hard work, brought it back. The building was placed on the National Register of Historic Places in 1999.

Many more hours of work by the owners of the building changed it into the Viola Creamery Steak House. As told by the owner, financial setbacks, harsh weather, and a rural location off the beaten path, let to the steak house's closing. At last report, the creamery was being converted into a private home.

Viola, the village, was platted in 1878 as a station along the Eyota to Plainview rail line. The settlement included a grain elevator, store/post office, a hardware store, a drug store, two churches, a Modern Woodsman Hall, and the creamery. Several homes were also part of the community. The post office lasted until the 1960s and is now a rural route.

Though not officially a "town" Viola knows about community, and how to count gophers. Check it out next year and see how community lives on.

Viola Creamery, National Register of Historic Places, Viola Cooperative Creamery, Viola, Olmsted, Minnesota 99001310

Gopher County Days in Earlier Days. (www.gophercount.com)

Crowds at Viola Gopher County Days. (www.gophercount.com)

Pipestone County

The Arlie tornado, 1924. (Courtesy of the Pipestone County Historical Society)

AIRLIE (CLAUSEN)

1882/1934

CLASS A

APPROXIMATE LOCATION:
6½ miles west of Pipestone

Early Arlie. (Courtesy of the Pipestone County Historical Society)

Had Arlie been just one-half mile to the west, it would be a South Dakota lost town rather than a Minnesota lost town. One-half mile from the Minnesota/South Dakota border, Airlie was first known as Clausen. The settlement was founded by a Scottish land development corporation known as the Dundee Land and Improvement Company. Dundee had tried several times, all unsuccessfully, to establish exclusive Scottish colonies in southern Minnesota. Airlie, while prosperous for a short time, would also be an unsuccessful endeavor.

Arlie school. (Courtesy of the Pipestone County Historical Society)

The settlement's first sign of progress was the building of a grain warehouse in 1880. The next year a post office was established under the name Clausen. The next few years showed increasing growth and development. A general store was established. That same year Clausen became known as Airlie, named for the president of the Dundee Corporation, the Earl of Airlie Scotland.

During Airlie's existence the village included three elevators, a lumberyard, a depot, a blacksmith shop, a saloon, the general store, a school built in 1886, and a tavern. Airlie's greatest development took place in 1885.

Arlie elevator in more recent times. (Courtesy of Tom McLaughlint)

Arlie depot. (Courtesy of the Pipestone County Historical Society)

In May of 1899, Airlie was nearly consumed by a devastating fire. A 1984 Pipestone County history tells that the fire started in the Cargill elevator. Nearly 15,000 bushels of grain were lost as was the two elevators, the blacksmith shop, a house and barn, and several other sheds and structures. According to the history, Airlie did continue on albeit "limping along" until the 1930s. A 1924 tornado destroyed most of the rest of the town. For years a small renovated elevator marked the former townsite.

ALTOONA (CRESSON)

1894 – 1896 (1910s)

CLASS A

APPROXIMATE LOCATION:
Altona Township

Long after the small settlement of Altoona (Cresson) ceased to be, the elevator still stood sentinel over the surrounding prairie. The railroad tracks are long gone; the village streets have been reclaimed by nature and are indistinguishable from the prairie grass. It seems fitting that the elevator was still standing, being the last vestige of the farming settlement.

Grain production in the northwestern Pipestone County community necessitated access to transportation. In 1885 the Burlington Northern Railroad extended its rail line into Pipestone County. That same year, Altoona was platted and included fourteen blocks. Plans were made to build a depot, but there are no records indicating it was ever constructed. However, the grain warehouse was built in 1885. Nearly ten years later, a general store was built with a post office in 1895.

The store/post office burned to the ground in 1896. Temporary arrangements for the post office were in the works, but the post office was discontinued before anything could be done. Sometime around 1910, the village became known as Cresson. Around that time, the village itself had disappeared, becoming a flag stop along the Rock Island line. The village may have disappeared, but the elevator was a harvest time necessity. A succession of owners operated the elevator until 1969 when it was closed for good. In 1984, it still stood tall, being the last remnant of Altoona/Cresson.

CAZENOVIA

1885 - 1938

CLASS C

APPROXIMATE LOCATION:
Near intersection of #7 and #15

Once a busy trade center in Troy Township, Cazenovia is a rural hamlet today. It is still home to some, but as a town, itself, is lost.

Once located on the Rock Island Railroad, Cazenovia's heyday was in 1885. A post office did operate over fifty years, though, only being discontinued in 1938.

ETON (GRAY SIDING)

1890s

CLASS A

APPROXIMATE LOCATION:
6 Miles East of Pipestone

Confusion about similar sounding names necessitated a name change for the small station stop along the Omaha rail line. Originally called Gray Siding, that name was shortened to Gray. Gray was often confused with Cray near Mankato, both on the Omaha line. It was decided that one of the communities had to change their name, and according to Arthur Rose's early history, Gray was the loser in the lottery, so they had to change their name. In 1896 Gray became Eton, named for the English school.

Records tell that the main feature of the town was the elevator which operated until it burned in 1920.

JOHNSTON

1890s

CLASS A

APPROXIMATE LOCATION:
One mile North of Pipestone

Centered around a quarry, Johnston was established in 1890. At its peak, it had a frame hotel, and approximately forty families called it home. As quarries dwindled, so did Johnston. The hotel burned, and many homes were moved to Pipestone. According to a 1984 Pipestone

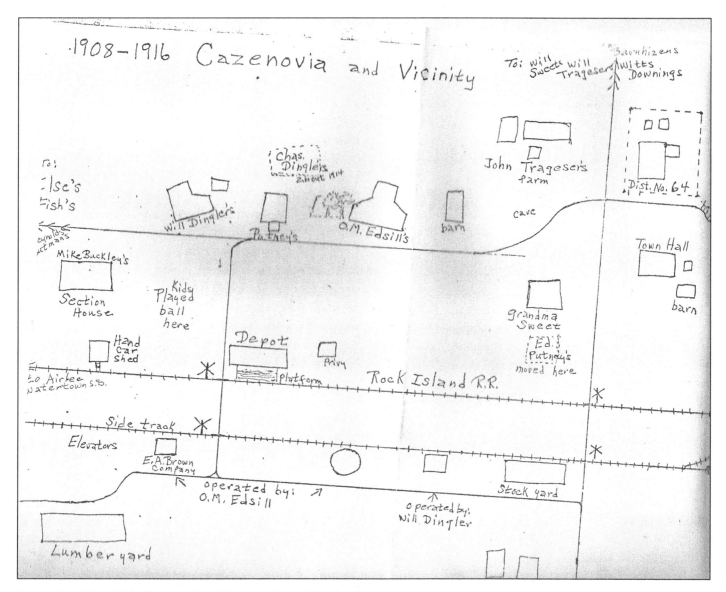

Cazenovia, 1908 to 1916. (Courtesy of the Pipestone County Historical Society)

County history, the last stones were quarried in the 1930s. In 1984 a few foundations remained as did the quarry.

LUCTOR (CHURCHVILLE)

1902 - 1905

CLASS B

APPROXIMATE LOCATION:
5 miles northwest of Holland

With a name like "Churchville," there can be little doubt as to what the early settlers deemed a priority. Church it was. In fact, the church was estab-lished at the same time as the community was settled in 1899. The early settlers, twenty-two immigrants, purchased ten acres of land and built the Dutch Reformed Church of Churchville and a parsonage.

As Churchville grew and developed, name changes oc-curred. According to early historian Arthur P. Rose, twelve years after the construction of the church, a store was estab-lished, and the community became known as New Chicago. The small community was at times referred to as Pumpkin Center. Lastly it was called Luctor.

The church was always at the heart of the community. The village was thriving around 1900 and prospered until the par-sonage was destroyed by fire in 1912. Through it was rebuilt, Luc-tor never had another resident pastor. Visiting clergy served the needs of residents until the church closed in 1928. The buildings were moved and repurposed, and soon Luctor was no more. The church cemetery still marks the settlement. Dormant for over seventy-five years, the last burial took place in 1940. A recent *Pipestone Star* article featured the cemetery and stated that twenty-seven tombstones and eight concrete enclosures still stand.

NORTH SIOUX FALLS

1891 - 1893

CLASS B

APPROXIMATE LOCATION:
3 miles northeast of Jasper

Lasting just over a decade, North Sioux Falls was a quarry town. The settlement was developed because of the quarry, thrived because of the quarry, and it died because of the quarry. Alternatively the settlement was also known as Pink Stone Quarry, so named because of the distinctive pink stone (Sioux Quartzite) quarried at the site in the settlement's four quarries.

Primarily a company town, everything in the village was geared to the quarry workers, which at one time numbered 221. Products produced included paving blocks, paving stones and crushed rock. A general store, built of stone, was constructed in 1890. A post office was established in 1891. That same year, a rail spur ran to the site. A 1984 Pipestone County history relates that the train was nicknamed "The Boozer," because an order could be sent to the liquor store, and it would be delivered by the train. A hotel/boarding house for the workers was also built in 1891. A blacksmith shop and a school also were part of the settlement. A few homes completed the community.

By 1905, the village was nearly faded. Records tell that the hotel was moved to a farm. A building constructed of the native pink stone was dismantled block by block and rebuilt in Jasper. For a time, it was an opera house, a grocery store for years, and was later a senior citizen center. In 1984 it was being restored as the "Bauman Hall."

For a short time in the 1930s, the quarry was reopened to provide stones for the dam construction at Ihlen. Broken stones still litter the prairie. The Split Rock Creek State Park is located nearby.

North Sioux Falls quarry. (Courtesy of the Pipestone County Historical Society)

Redwood County

Main house of the Springville gold mine. (Courtesy of Joshua Dixon *Redwood Falls Gazette*)

MORGAN

1878 - 1880

CLASS A

APPROXIMATE LOCATION:

Short-lived, Morgan was established in 1878, was first called Brookfield and was nearly gone by 1880. The post office operated those same years. At the post office's closing, just one store was still in business.

PAXTON

1879 - 1882

CLASS A

APPROXIMATE LOCATION:
Paxton Township

Begun in 1879, Paxton had all but disappeared by 1882. Originally platted with seven blocks, most of them were cut into fractions by rights-of-ways. A post office operated just three years, 1879 to 1882. A store, grain buying firm, and a blacksmith shop were the settlement's primary businesses.

RIVERSIDE

1875 - 1876

CLASS A

APPROXIMATE LOCATION:

The year 1875 was Riverside's big year. During one week in 1875, over five and one-half tons of butter was shipped out of Riverside. The wheat harvest was five hundred bushels a day. The hotel hosted a Grand New Year's Eve Gala. Tickets were two dollars and included a dinner, music, and dancing.

A March 1876 fire raged through the village. Only the post office and a small lean-to shed survived the inferno. The fire and dwindling riverboat traffic set Riverside's demise into motion. As nearby Redwood Falls developed, Riverside declined.

SPRINGVILLE

1894 - 1896

CLASS B

APPROXIMATE LOCATION:
1 mile east of Delhi, near the northeast end of Gold Mine Lake

Lively would be putting it mildly. The short-lived mining town lasted just two years, but, yes, Minnesota did have a gold mine. The cries of gold in the area ignited gold fever and Springville was the result. Area historian Duane Peterson wrote that Springville was a typical mining town with all the characteristics of a wild-west mining town, and included all the pertinent businesses associated with a mining boom town. They included a general store, a livery, a dance hall, hotels complete with "dance hall girls" or, as some called them, "ladies of the night." Peterson writes that the women would come from Minneapolis on weekends by train to Morton, then by stage coach to Springville. The roundabout travel route was necessary as Delhi didn't allow "sporting women" in their community.

In 2012 an amateur gold prospector visited the old town site. According to an article by Joshua Dixon of the *Redwood Falls Gazette*, a few specks of gold were found among the slag piles and old mine remnants. Today, the area is sometimes used as an unauthorized swimming hole and old mining remains can be found.

Miners, Springville, 1894. (Courtesy of the Joshua Dixon *Redwood Falls Gazette*)

Rice County

Christdala Church, Millersburg. (Courtesy of Christdala Church www. christdala.com)

Millersburg school. (Courtesy of Christdala Church www.christdala.com)

CANNON CITY

1855 - 1865

CLASS A

APPROXIMATE LOCATION:
5 miles northeast of Faribault near County #20 and Crystal Lake Trail

Grandiose would fit the hopes and plans of early Cannon City planners. One of Rice County's oldest communities, Cannon City was at one time in contention for the county seat designation.

During its heyday, Cannon City was home to three churches, two lawyer firms, a doctor's office, a two-room brick schoolhouse, two hotels, a harness shop, a cabinet shop, three blacksmith shops, a saw mill, a fanning mill, and more.

In 1855 school enrollment was twenty-five, then three years later it was up to nearly 100. But then, in 1865, the railroad routed through Faribault, which was the county seat. Cannon City decline rapidly.

EPSOM

LATE 1800s

CLASS A

APPROXIMATE LOCATION:
4 miles west of Kenyon on County #26

Primarily a shipping point for area farmers, Epsom had two elevators, a stockyard, a depot, and an area school. The Moland Creamery shipped their products out of Epsom.

As rail service declined, so did Epsom. The tracks were removed in the 1980s. The only visible sign of the community today is a wooded cemetery with approximately thirty graves.

LITTLE CHICAGO

1880s

CLASS A

APPROXIMATE LOCATION:
Between Lonsdale and Northfield on Highway #19 near I35

Just like its more famous namesake in Illinois, Little Chicago was said to be wild, windy and home to a wide-open liquor business. Established in the 1880s, Little

Chicago had a general store, a blacksmith shop, a skimming station, an implement dealership, a tool shop, and a lively tavern. As the railroad line created Lonsdale, Little Chicago declined.

In recent times, there were a few homes in the area and a nearby golf club.

MILLERSBURG

1858/1901

CLASS D

APPROXIMATE LOCATION:
Rice County #1 near Chester Avenue

Settled in 1855 and platted two years later, Millersburg was short-lived as a viable town. The community included two stores, three blacksmith shops, the Millersburg Hotel, a sawmill, and a post office. Then the railroad bypassed the community, and the settlement declined. In 1976 a few homes, the town hall, and the store were clustered near the old town site.

Nearby stands the original and historic Christdala Church. Listed on the National Register of Historic Places, the church has never been altered or moved. Though no longer an active congregation, the church is maintained by a preservation group and non-profit group. In 2007 the group purchased the old Millersburg School and maintains that as well. The school houses records and historical artifacts. Learn more at: http://www.christdala.com/

MOLAND

1882 - 1905

CLASS A

APPROXIMATE LOCATION:
Near Lamb and 270th Street

When the new Moland Creamery was built east of the store, it moved from Steele County to Rice County. Moland was established in the 1870s and included the store, a post office, the creamery, the Bethel Church, and the Shady Nook. The Nook was a gas station tavern and social center.

PRAIRIEVILLE (EAST)

1857 – EARLY 1900s

CLASS C

APPROXIMATE LOCATION:
3 miles east of Faribault

Early county officials predicted a lasting trade center and busy little burg. By 1930 all that remained was the school, the cemetery, and a few homes. Over the ensuing decades, the cemetery became abandoned and overgrown. With time nearly all remnants of the small community had faded into history. As area resident, Robert Delesha commented in a 2010 news article, other than a few exceptions, "Prairieville is long lost and forgotten." A small resurgence occurred in the later 1930s when a creamery and a few businesses were started, but they were short-lived.

In 1937, several ruins remained. Even then the cemetery was, as historian Lester Blais wrote, "hardly recognizable."

Enter Chelsea Bowege, an area high school student. Chelsea and her family lived near Prairieville. From her earliest days, she was fascinated with the long-gone village. A 2010 news article in the *Faribault Daily News* written by Derek Wehrwein recapped Chelsea's efforts to mark Prairieville with a highway sign. Encountering obstacle after obstacle, the young woman never gave up her efforts. She connected with the Rice County Historical Society, and together they pushed

forward. It seems she wasn't the only one working to preserve the history of the small community.

Tim Lloyd discovered that his great-great-great grandfather was buried in the Prairieville Cemetery. He went in search of the grave and found the cemetery in ruins. He helped to form the Prairieville Cemetery Association, and the group began to restore the historic grounds.

According to Wehrwein, the cemetery's last burial was in 1909 shortly before it was abandoned. Forty-five graves were found, including those of veterans from as far back as the War of 1812. A community effort ensued, and the cemetery was lovingly restored and is maintained.

Efforts to secure a highway marker continued. Wehrwein writes that one of the issues was the fact that there were two official Rice County maps, one showed Prairieville, the other did not. Once able to prove that Prairieville did indeed exist, the state erected the familiar green highway marker along Highway #60. A small brown sign also erected as part of the marker reads "Prairieville, established 1855 Rice County Historical Society."

Prairieville itself is long gone but far from forgotten. Thanks to the efforts of a few individuals working through a community.

RUSKIN

1903 – 1930s

CLASS B

APPROXIMATE LOCATION:
County #23, south of #60 between Kenyon and Faribault

Some lost towns do a pretty good job of staying hidden. Ruskin is one of those places. A 2002 news article by historical columnist John Cole, described today's Ruskin well. Once a busy railroad settlement, the tracks have long since been abandoned and removed. Today the old rail bed is a tree-lined driveway leading to Ruskin's one and only home.

Back in 1903 Ruskin lay along the Milwaukee Line Railroad route running from Faribault to Zumbrota. The depot was little more than a small three-sided shanty offering some but little shelter. In order to board the train, passengers had to flag down the train as there was no depot agent. Passenger service was dropped in 1926, and the depot was removed in the 1950s. Cole writes that the rail line continued until 1980 when it was abandoned and later taken up.

Prairieville Cemetery Marker. (Courtesy of Bob Lewandoski)

Two large elevators dominated Ruskin's landscape. Destroyed by fire, the foundations were still visible in 2002. Ruskin also had a store and a blacksmith shop.

Today even an observant traveler would have a hard time discerning Ruskin. Barely visible in 2002, time and nature will further erases any physical signs of the town.

SHIELDSVILLE

1854 - 1970s

CLASS D

APPROXIMATE LOCATION:
10 miles west of Faribault along the southwest shore of Lake Masaska

Still bustling today with Hirdler Park, the lakeside setting and several active community organizations, Shieldsville carries on the legacy of the 1850s village.

In its earliest days, Shieldsville the settlement included three or four blacksmith shops, two wagon shops, three grocery stores, a flour mill, a furniture factory, and seven saloons.

One early resident was said to be an aviation pioneer. Some say he was ahead of the Wright Brothers. A 1972 news article stated that he was diminutive with a full black beard. He was always building some kind of machine sometimes with a dog as a passenger. He later left Shieldsville and moved to Minneapolis.

With the idea to build a county park, the general store building was razed in 1973. Today Hirdler Park with its impressive Veteran's Memorial occupies the site. The park also includes an approach and access to Lake Masaska. Several organizations keep the community spirit alive. The lakeside hamlet is home to many residents and a few businesses. While the long ago village no longer exists, Shieldsville is still very much an active community.

TRONDHJEM

1860s - 1910

CLASS C

APPROXIMATE LOCATION:
1½ miles east of Lonsdale on Highway #19

Norwegian through and through, the large number of settlers chose to name their new home after their Norwegian homeland. Flourishing in the 1860s until

"Trondhjem Church." (By Elkman - Own work. Licensed under CC BY-SA 3.0 via Commons - https://commons.wikimedia.org/wiki/File:Trondhjem_Church.JPG#/media/File:Trondhjem_Church.JPG)

the early 1900s, Trondhjem was home to three stores, a post office, a creamery, a blacksmith shop, and the Trondhjem Lutheran Church.

Clearing the land was hard work. The land was hilly and covered with brush and timber that had to be cleared. Ditches were dug and drain tile laid in order to drain the swampy lowlands.

Mail was brought by horseback or by horse and buggy from Northfield twice a week, on Wednesdays and Saturdays. Some settlers walked over three miles to pick up their mail. By 1909, Trondhjem was a rural post office, but most the village was already gone. Two of the main factors in the demise of the community was the railroads bypassing the settlement and the subsequent growth of Lonsdale.

The Trondhjem Lutheran Church is still active and is the heart of the area. A new church was constructed in recent years, and the old building is preserved and maintained. In 2001 it was listed on the National Register of Historic Places.

WALCOTT

1856/1901

CLASS A

APPROXIMATE LOCATION:

Primarily a company town, everything in Walcott was dependent on the mill. The town grew up around the mill, and when the mill was destroyed by fire, the town, for all intents and purposes, was finished as well.

Walcott grew up around Walcott's Mill, and most of the people in the village were employed by the mill. All of the settlement's businesses were supported by the mill and its employees. In addition to the mill, two stores, a dance hall, a creamery, a hotel, a cooper shop, and about sixteen homes were in the village during its heyday. A post office operated from 1855 to 1862, and mail was brought by stage.

Mill maintenance was being completed in October of 1899 when a fire broke out. Because all of the equipment was shut down, there was no power to pump water, so the fire spread quickly. Faribault's Fire Department responded to the alarm, but their hand pump was unable to squelch the flames. Early historians tell that the heat was terrific and that everything north of the mill was burned. Haystacks over one-half mile away were also burned.

After the fire, mill owners reopened a closed mill in Faribault (King's Mill), but the Walcott Mill was never rebuilt. Walcott was unable to survive the loss of the mill.

Today a few houses, and old red barn, and Patti's Photography are at the former town site.

WHEATLAND

CLASS A

APPROXIMATE LOCATION:
3 miles from Lonsdale

Records can oftentimes be conflicting. One source on Wheatland says the community never amounted to more than a name and a building or two. One says a few businesses operated for short time. Another lists businesses in the community. One can only research, analyze and determine which information is most likely accurate. In the case of Wheatland, a report written by Lester Blais in 1937 is based on interviews with several residents of Wheatland, including town clerks, and the last village council. Seen if anyone should know the history of the community they should.

According to Blais's report, when the railroad was built, Wheatland had a population of 350. Numerous businesses operated and included a creamery, a general store (with an auditorium and dance hall), a hotel, a saw mill, two blacksmith shops, a livery stable, and a saloon.

In a rather odd combination, a village hall/jail building shared space with a kindergarten school. District #104 also had a school building in the community. It burned in approximately 1906.

Wheatland had a volunteer fire department, equipped with a hand pump mounted on a cart. A village water works with a 374-foot well and sidewalks made of wood but with a few concrete ones lined Main Street. A park and picnic grounds were also in the community. A boat launch was near the sawmill and was said to be a popular Sunday afternoon destination.

It was expected that the new rail line would route through Wheatland, but, at the last minute, the railroad had troubles obtaining rights-of-way. The railroad wanted to purchase the land at a nominal price. Unable to get the land at the low prices they wanted to pay, the railroad was rerouted. The new community of Lonsdale was established, and, as it grew, Wheatland declined.

The creamery was the first to pack up and move. Most of the other businesses soon followed. Some buildings were moved to Lonsdale, others torn down. In 1908 the village council met and voted to dissolve the incorporation. Wheatland was no more. Roger Langseth has traveled to most southern Minnesota lost towns over the years, and he writes that today Wheatland has six to eight homes. A historic wood shed, roped off, still stands.

Rock County

Kanaranzi building, (Courtesy of Tom McLaughlin)

Kanaranzi, Minnesota, (Courtesy of Tom McLaughlin)

ASH CREEK

1871 - 1894

CLASS A

APPROXIMATE LOCATION:
Clinton Township South of Luverne

Rock County's only post office in 1871 was in Luverne. Often the trip was quite an undertaking, so a second post office, that of Ash Creek, was established. Considered more a trade center and grain market than a full-fledged village, Ash Creek was named for the nearby creek.

In 1882, the farm upon which the station sat was sold to Colonel Grey, an English capitalist and large landowner. According to early historian Arthur P. Rose, Colonel Grey planned to build a flourishing town at the Ash Creek station site. Platted in 1883, the original plat included eight blocks. Several buildings to be used in farming and workers accommodations were built. A store was also constructed in 1884, and the post office was relocated to the store. In 1885, the railroad added a stockyard to the settlement. Folks believed that the railroad would establish a station at the site as well. A $15,000 bonus was offered to entice the railroad to lay its line so it passed through Ash Creek. Still the railroad station never materialized.

In 1889, the Congregational Church Society built a church. Progress was slow but steady. A school was built in 1903.

Little is known about the village's decline and demise.

BRUCE

1888 - 1936

CLASS A

APPROXIMATE LOCATION:
2 miles west of Hills

Built with high hopes and expectations, Bruce was platted in 1888. Sixteen blocks were laid out and included in the original plat.

According to early historian Arthur P. Rose, development began in earnest. A grain warehouse, a depot, a hotel, a store, and a second warehouse with a capacity of 30,000 bushels of grain were soon established. A second store also soon joined the village. Rose tells that efforts were made to establish a saloon.

The liquor license was denied. Not to be deterred, the owner set up business anyway. He was later arrested and convicted. A post office was established in 1888 and was discontinued in 1936.

With the establishment of the village of Hills, just two miles away, Bruce's fate was sealed. Hills was located at the junction of the Illinois Central and the new Sioux City and Northern Railroad lines. Bruce simply could not compete with Hills and soon would fade into history. The hotel, the store, and the blacksmith shop all moved to Hills. The few remaining buildings were soon abandoned.

Bruce experienced a bit of a resurgence in 1890. Two liquor firms, fleeing South Dakota's prohibition laws, were set up in Bruce, but were short-lived. By 1900 Bruce was at its end. Rose wrote that one lone resident, the postmaster and the only merchant still remaining in Bruce, tried to keep the village going. The local newspaper reported that it wouldn't be long before the post office and the only remaining Bruce business would relocate to Hills. They were right.

KANARANZI

1884 - 1992

CLASS D

APPROXIMATE LOCATION:
8 miles southeast of Luverne

Only in recent history, 1992, did the post office close. Kanaranzi has the feel of a roadside hamlet and community. People still call it home. Still Kanaranzi is considered one of Minnesota's Lost Towns.

With the expansion and extension of rail lines into Rock County, the creation and establishments of new settlements grew. Kanaranzi was one of the newly formed stations along the Burlington Northern Railroad in the 1880s. It took an entire year, until 1885, before townsite development began.

Primarily an agricultural area, the first building was a grain warehouse. A second warehouse was built that same month, September 1885. A depot was also constructed that fall. Soon a post office and several residents were a part of the settlement.

According to early historian, Arthur P. Rose, a heavy wind storm in August of 1887 destroyed one of the warehouses. It was quickly rebuilt.

Rose writes that for the first three years of the settlement there were no stores. By 1892 the village included a store/post office, a lumberyard, a blacksmith shop, the grain warehouses, and a school that was built in 1899.

MANLEY

1890 - 1914

CLASS C

APPROXIMATE LOCATION:
Near the intersection of #4 and #17

When the Sioux City and Northern Railroad (later part of the Great Northern Railroad system) was laying their line through Rock County in 1889, there were great hopes and expectations for Manley. According to a 1911 early history by Arthur P. Rose, residents of nearby Beaver Creek and Valley Springs offered substantial incentives to the railroad in return for a link to their communities. With visions of a new terminus at the junction of the Sioux City and Northern Railroad with the Chicago, St. Paul, Minneapolis, and Omaha Railroad, the offer was turned down.

A quarter section of land was purchased at a price of four thousand dollars. Platted as Hornick, the settlement later became known as Manley. The name was in honor of the cashier at the bank in Sioux City and who was also a leading stockholder of the Sioux City and Northern Railroad. The original plat included ten blocks. According to early historian Rose, invitations to nearby Beaver Creek and Valley Springs were extended, inviting them to join the new community before they would be forced to join.

Though development did occur, growth and a boom were not experienced. To encourage growth an aggressive advertizing campaign was launched. A land auction also spurred sales.

According to Rose, on sale day, a special, free, excursion train ran from Sioux City to Manley, transporting prospective investors to the auction. Rose wrote that nearly 600 people made the trip with seventy-five lots being sold. Little actual construction or development occurred.

A post office, a small bottling works, and the one and only store were established. Few additions to Manley were ever completed. The mill closed in 1892, and Manley's decline was rapid. Beaver Creek and Valley Springs prospered as Manley diminished.

The store and a few homes were eventually moved. In 1901 one of the elevators burned and the station closed. Rose concluded that by 1911 there were no residents in Manley proper.

Today there are a few buildings in the vicinity. Manley Tire is an active business.

Manley Tire. (Courtesy of Manley Tire)

Manley Tire office. (Courtesy of Manley Tire)

Steele County

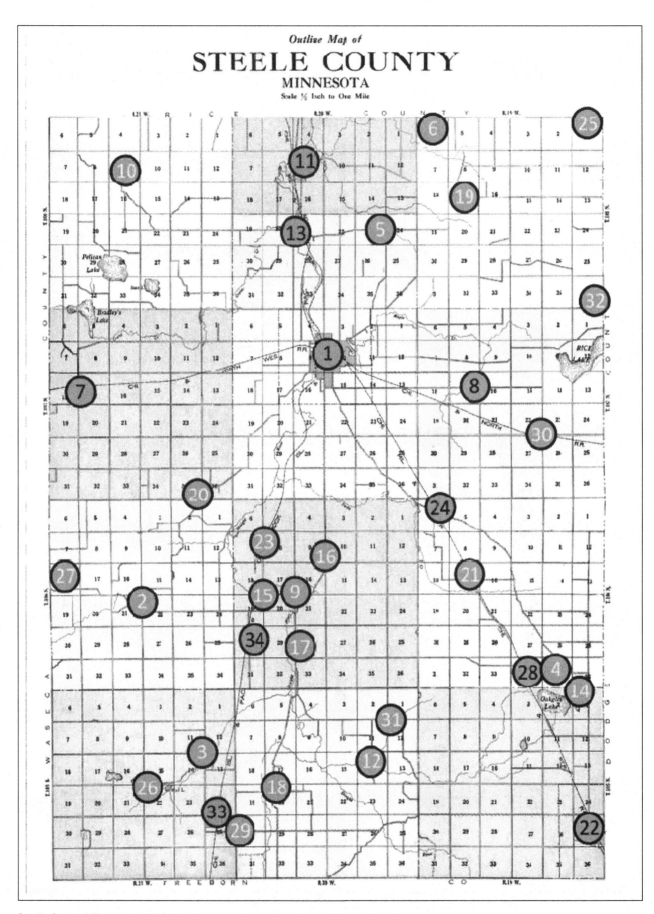

Steele County Village map. Numbers in description and location match numbers in map.

ADAMSVILLE (BERLIN)

1856 - 1904

CLASS A

APPROXIMATE LOCATION:
(3) Berlin (26)

On August 29, 1857, the Adamsville post office, which had only been in existence for fourteen months, closed. It reopened later that same day as the Berlin post office. In its short life as Adamsville, the community had a church, a barber shop, and a cheese factory. The Berlin post office operated at this location until 1884.

Confusing the matter, in 1884, the Berlin post office relocated to the Beaver Lake area. Beaver Lake became known as Berlin. In the late 1880s, Beaver Lake was a popular tourist resort area.

With the railroad's establishment of Ellendale in 1901, the Berlin/Beaver Lake post office closed in 1914. The village eventually faded away. According to Steele County historian Douglas Meyer, Beaver Lake remained a resort area until the 1920s.

ANDERSON (LYSNE)

1890s - 1910s

CLASS A

APPROXIMATE LOCATION:
(30)

Beginning its existence as Anderson (Station), the village was established in the 1890s and named for the landowner upon which the Winona & St. Peter Railroad station sat. A post office was established and later renamed Lynse. Later the post office became known as Anderson Station. The village faded after the post office closing in 1912.

AURORA CENTER (OAK GLEN)

1856 - 1871

CLASS A

APPROXIMATE LOCATION:
(4) (14) Steele County Map

Begun as Aurora Center in 1856, the post office would transfer to Oak Glen until it was discontinued in 1871. The stage coach stop is considered Steele County's ear-liest established stop. The coach stop would also be relocated to Oak Glen. Aurora Center vanished. Oak Glen would remain until the railroad created the village of Blooming Prairie. Oak Glen's post office closed in 1871 and as the stage coach ended, Oak Glen vanished.

AURORA STATION

1860s - 1890s

CLASS A

APPROXIMATE LOCATION:

(21)

Nearly wiped out by a devastating fire in the late 1880s, the village would exist until 1894 when the creamery and post office closed. Aurora Station was once a thriving village, a station along the Minnesota and Cedar Valley Railroad, established as the railroad line extended through Steele County in the mid 1860s.

COOLEYSVILLE

1858 - 1901

CLASS A

APPROXIMATE LOCATION:
(12) (18) (29)

Running from Owatonna to Albert Lea, the stage coach had three branches. The first routed through the Steele Center and River Point area. According to area historian, Douglas Meyer, just south of River Point the line veered east around a huge marsh in Summit Township. It was along this eastern route that a station stop was established. Cooleysville was that stop, and it was named after an early settler in the area, William Cooley. A post office from 1857 and was moved to Cooleyville's second location in 1862. The first village vanished.

In 1862, the stage line was re-routed to higher, more level land, a more direct route to Albert Lea. The post office operated until 1892 when Cooleysville was again relocated.

With the establishment of a creamery, the Berlin and Summit Creamery, Cooleysville was again moved. The creamery was built in 1891, and soon a small village grew around it. Since the previous Cooleyville's post offices were relocated, it again moved to this location. It also was known as Cooleyville. When the Cedar Rapids and Northern Railroad constructed a line into southern Steele County, a new station was established, Ellendale. Unable to compete with the new village, the Cooleyville Post Office closed permanently in 1901 and was moved to Ellendale. The creamery closed in 1912 and Cooleyville, in any location, was no longer.

An interesting footnote to the history of Cooleyville was found in a *New Richland Star* newspaper article in 2011. According to an article written by Carol Jolly, it seems there was gold mining in the community.

The article tells of the Patterson brothers. Folklore has it that the New Jersey brothers were told, in great detail of the gold in Cooleyville. The brothers were told to go the small Minnesota community where they would find a small girl swinging on a gate. Directly across from the gate would be the land upon which the gold would be found.

After arriving in Cooleyville, the brothers searched for two weeks until one day they discovered the girl swinging on the gate. They bought the land across from the gate and spent the next four years searching for the gold. They found none. They then contacted the medium who came to Cooleyville and immediately locating the mine. A shaft was dug. Some say small amounts of gold were found; others say nothing was ever found. The brothers spent the rest of their lives searching for gold.

DEERFIELD

1857/1906 - 1946

CLASS A

APPROXIMATE LOCATION:
55th Street/72nd Avenue (10)

Another location along the Owatonna to St. Peter stage coach line, Deerfield was settled in 1855. A post office was established in 1856 and was discontinued in 1886. Deerfield's most active period was after the Deerfield Creamery was established. Starting as a skimming station, it was later upgraded to a full creamery. The village faded away after the creamery's closing in 1946. Today there are a handful to homes, a church, and cemetery in near the old village site.

DODGE CITY

1856 - 1894

CLASS A

APPROXIMATE LOCATION:
(6)

Not the Kansas frontier town of fame, Dodge City, Minnesota, was first settled in 1855. An early store operated in the community as did a post office from

1856 to 1894. In the 1890s a cream skimming facility was in business in 1893. By 1895, the skimming business moved to Rice County and Dodge City faded into history.

EAST MERIDEN

1867 - 1898

CLASS A

APPROXIMATE LOCATION:
(20)

Other than the dates listed in post office history (1867 to 1898), we know little about East Meriden. The village was located along the stage coach route from Owatonna to Mankato. There was a District 16 school established there.

ELLWOOD

1856 - 1871

CLASS A

APPROXIMATE LOCATION:
(5) Steele County Map

Home to one of Steele County's earliest rural schools, Ellwood was platted in 1854. A post office operated from 1856 to 1871.

ELMIRA

1857 - 1858

CLASS A

APPROXIMATE LOCATION:
(15)

Rumors were rampant. The railroad was going to extend its line through the area. In anticipation of the booming economy that was sure to follow the arrival of the railroad, a dam was constructed, a sawmill was built, as well as several other buildings. In 1886 the Winona & St. Peter Railroad did route through the area, but went through Owatonna and not through the small community of Elmira. With the bypass, development stopped, and Elmira soon became a lost town. A ghost town maybe, but perhaps the only ghost town with its own Facebook page, "Ghost Town of Elmira."

HAVANA

1856 - 1911

CLASS A

APPROXIMATE LOCATION:
(8)

Name changes were common for new, small communities. Established in 1856 in Dodge County Havana became part of Steele County in 1856 and was known as Lafayette. The township changed names, settling on Dover. When the Winona & St. Peter Railroad reached Owatonna the village was known as Havana, or Havana Station.

According to Steele County historian, Douglas Meyer, the community was an important destination. A post office operated under the various names from approximately 1856 until 1911/1917.

The Havana Creamery was established in 1893 and closed in 1944 when the station stop was also closed. Today the area has several homes.

HOBSON

1894 - 1943

CLASS A

APPROXIMATE LOCATION:

Life in Hobson revolved around the creamery. First established as a skimming station in 1894, the next year it became a full-fledged creamery. A post office was in operation from 1898 to 1905. Operating as the Maple Creek Creamery Association, it served the area hamlet until 1943. Once the creamery closed, Hobson declined. The creamery building was converted to a residence, and for a while operated as the Rice Lake Store.

LEMOND

1856 - 1906

CLASS A

APPROXIMATE LOCATION:
County #4 (2) (27) on Steele County Map

Existing as both an early pioneer village and a turn-of-the-century settlement, Lemond was situated in two Steele County locations.

Early Lemond Township settler's cabin. (Courtesy of the Steele County Historical Society, Village of Yesteryear)

The original location for Lemond (2) was along the 1856 stage route from Owatonna to Mankato. A post office operated sporadically from 1856 to 1886. Lemond's economy was based almost entirely on the stage coach traffic. The Buckhorn Inn, a local landmark, was built in the late 1850s and operated until the stage coach became obsolete in the early 1880s.

Lemond's second life began at its new location in 1886 with the transfer and relocation of the post office. The center of this Lemond location was the creamery begun in 1891. In 1916 the creamery left Lemond and relocated. That move signaled the end of Lemond. The post office was discontinued in 1916.

There were a few vintage homes/buildings, an old store front and service station at the village site in recent years.

MERIDEN

1856 - 1992

CLASS C

APPROXIMATE LOCATION:
(7)

Today's small hamlet of a few houses and an elevator was settled nearly 150 years ago. In December of 1856, the Winona & St. Peter Railroad routed their line from Owatonna through Meriden. The post office was established in 1856 and operated nearly 140 years.

Meriden's Blacksmith Shop was unique in that the top floor served as the town hall. That building still stands and is on display at FarmAmerica near Waseca Minnesota. The blacksmith's forge is, on occasion, fired up and run.

FarmAmerica is a non-profit group and site dedicated to education and preservation. Educating today's youth, and

Meriden Blacksmith and Town Hall. (Courtesy of FarmAmerica www.farmamerica.org)

Meriden Depot. (www.west2k.com)

Christmas on the Farm, Meriden. (Courtesy of FarmAmerica)

Meriden Depot side view. (www.west2k.com)

those of all ages, is their primary mission. Not only are farming and farming practices preserved, but the group illustrates the importance of agriculture to our everyday world. It was created in 1978 by the Minnesota Legislature as the Minnesota Agriculture Interpretive Center.

FarmAmerica has several displays including a Prairie Interpretive Center, an 1850s settlement, a one-room school house, a country church, a 1930s farmstead, the blacksmith/town hall, and a feed mill and grain elevator.

Several annual events are hosted by the group and include "Taste of the Farm," "Tractor Rides," Farm Camp, which allows students to spend two days living and working the farm, a Fall Fair, a Haunted Corn Maze, and Mill, Hayrides, All Hallows Eve (horrible spooks come out after 10:00 p.m.), and Christmas at the Farm.

Take the family out to FarmAmerica, any season, any time, it is not only educational but fun as well.

MERTON

1862 - 1903

CLASS A

APPROXIMATE LOCATION:
(19)

Name changes were the norm for Merton, going through at least four before a post office was established in 1862 under the name Merton. The town started as Union Prairie, then became Orion, then Lyon, and finally Merton. The post office operated until 1903. A creamery operated from 1900 until 1943, after which time the community faded.

MOLAND

1862 - 1905

CLASS A

APPROXIMATE LOCATION:
County Road #13 and 89th Avenue NW (25)

Taking the term "crossroads community" to a new level, Moland was located one-half mile east of the juncture of Steele, Rice, Dodge and Goodhue counties. A pioneer village existed in the 1860s, a post office was established in 1862 and operated until 1905. Thirty years after the establishment of the village (1896), a creamery was built. The early community also included a blacksmith shop, a barber shop, and other essential businesses. The creamery was the livelihood of the community for over seventy years, closing in 1967.

The Moland Lutheran Church was and still is the area's social center. Each year the church hosts a Strawberry Festival.

RIVER POINT

1859 - 1895

CLASS A

APPROXIMATE LOCATION:
County Road #3 (17)

Aptly named, River Point was located near the point where all four tributaries of the Straight River converged to form the river's main channel. The community had a post office and a creamery from 1899 to 1938. The village vanished after the creamery's closing. An old "River Point" sign, a white house with pillars, and two chimneys marked the old town site in recent years.

SACO

1860s - 1962

CLASS A

APPROXIMATE LOCATION:
7 Miles south of Owatonna, Near Intersection of County #31 and 32nd Avenue SW (23)

Religion and faith were important to most early settlers but especially so to the Catholic Bohemian settlers of Saco. Saco was in fact a direct result of the 1860s set-

Saco Church. (Courtesy of the Steele County Museum- Village of Yesteryear)

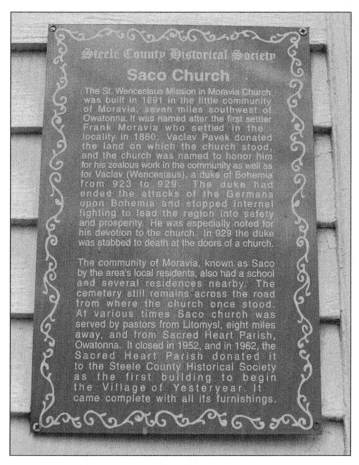

Saco Church Marker. (Author's Collection)

tler's formation of the Moravian Mission and at one time the settlement was known as Moravia. The congregation first worshipped in the district schoolhouse that had been established in 1871. A church was built in 1891.

Businesses in Saco expanded when the Burlington (Rock Island) Railroad established a station in 1902.

The St. Wenceslaus congregation lasted for many decades until 1952. In 1962, the Sacred Heart Parish donated the church and all of its original contents to the Steele County Historical Society/Museum to be the first building in the county's Village of Yesteryear.

The Village of Yesteryear is located at the Steele County Fairgrounds and houses approximately fifteen buildings. They include the Saco Church, the Chicago & Northwester Rail Depot, a Duluth and Iron Range caboose, two log cabins, and an 1850s town hall, a blacksmith shop, a general store, and more. Several annual events are held at the Village of Yesteryear, including Christmas in the Village, which features sleigh rides, wassail and cake, a visit from Santa Claus, and more. Other events are also hosted, and the church is available for rental for such events as weddings. Learn more at http://www.steelehistorymuseum.org/index.php/village-yesteryear/.

Four to five homes are at the village town site. The cemetery that once was across from the church is still at the village site as well.

SOMERSET

1857 - 1859

CLASS A

APPROXIMATE LOCATION:
(9)

Primarily a post office and stage coach stop, also known as South Lemond, Somerset was short-lived. First settled by folks from New England and New York, a post office was established in 1857 and closed in 1859.

STEELE CENTER

1893 – 1902 (1960s)

CLASS A

APPROXIMATE LOCATION:
(16)

Not so long ago, Steele Center was still going. Lasting until the 1960s, that is in most of our lifetimes. While all lost towns are intriguing, towns that vanished in our lifetimes are especially so.

Steele Center was the first stop along the original stage coach line form Owatonna to Albert Lea. A post office operated from 1858 to 1902. In 1892 the village had a creamery, a gas station, a garage repair shop, and a general store. The creamery closed in 1957 with the other businesses following. According to area historian Douglas Meyer, Steele Center vanished in the 1960s.

In recent years there were a few homes near the village intersection and a "River Point" sign attached to a garage.

SUMMIT

1898 - 1958

CLASS A

APPROXIMATE LOCATION:
County #27 and #27

Beginning with and ending with the creamery, Summit was established in 1893 when the creamery was built. A post office, under the name Omro, operated from

1898 to 1902. The creamery closed with Summit following suit in 1958.

A handful of homes, including a home that was converted from the creamery mark the village site.

Wabasha County

Jarrett millstone. (Courtesy of Wabasha County Historical Society)

Millstone

This millstone was in service for almost half a century in a grist mill along the Zumbro River, Hyde Park Township, in the village of Jarrett. The village was founded in 1878, the same year that partners Kimball and Kitzman started their milling operation. The mill, along with a general store and the Minnesota Midland Railroad Depot, became the milling and trading center for the settlers for miles around. The mill contained several sets of millstones including the one on display and were used to grind grains for flour and animal feed.

A water wheel was the source of power for the mill. The lower bedstone was stationary while the runner or top millstone was turned by the mill's water power. The grain was fed into the center of the top millstone and the ground grain would exit from between the outer edges of the two millstones. The miller could adjust the top millstone for the desired grind.

In 1884, F. G. Colburn, the new owner, installed a modern steel roller reduction process to produce flour. Because the millstones were superior to the steel rollers for producing animal feed, the mill continued to use the millstones throughout its history with several different owners until 1926 when the mill was destroyed by fire and was never rebuilt.

Over time, the Zumbro River overflowed and covered the remains of the mill. In the 1950s, Arthur Olin excavated this only remaining intact millstone.

Jacksonville school. (Courtesy of Wabasha County Historical Society)

Jarrett marker. (Courtesy of Wabasha County Historical Society)

St. Julius at Jacksonville. (Courtesy of Wabasha County Historical Society)

WABASHA COUNTY

Research as I could, I was unable to find any significant information on Wabasha County's lost towns. Try as I might, the only items I could find told minimal to nothing on the county's communities. Other than a post office establishment and discontinued date, there was little information available. If readers have any information on Wabasha County lost towns, please send the information to me and perhaps we can update this county at a later date.

Some early settlements in Wabasha County included:

Bear Valley – North of Zumbro Falls on Highway 3, PO – 1847 to 1902

Bremen – County Road #23, 1 Mile north of Olmsted County Line PO 1872 to 1888

Conception – Countys #14 & #18 PO 1894 to 1902

Cooks Valley – 1858 to 1873

Dumfries – Valley between Zumbro River and Highway #60 1899 to 1912

Glasgow – 1863 to 1879

Gopher Prairie – 1860 to 1872

Jarrett – Along Zumbro River near Silver Spring Creek – PO 1879 to 1919

Keegan – 1879 to 1917

There are several other post office locations listed for Wabasha County but how large the adjoining settlements were is unknown.

Waseca County

Last residents of Okaman. (Courtesy of Joyce Kaplan, Okaman Elk Farm)

Sorgum Mill. (Courtesy of Joyce Kaplan, Okaman Elk Farm)

Gift Store interior, Okaman. (Courtesy of Joyce Kaplan, Okaman Elk Farm)

Okaman school, Haley-Kaplan. (Courtesy of Joyce Kaplan, Okaman Elk Farm)

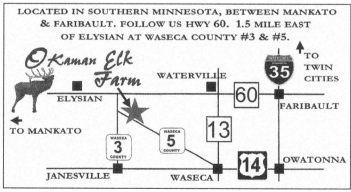

Okaman map. (Courtesy of Joyce Kaplan, Okaman Elk Farm)

ALMA CITY

1870 - 1963

CLASS C

APPROXIMATE LOCATION:
On County #9 one mile west of County #3

After the removal of the Winnebago tribe from the region, Alma City was platted (1866). The village was named for the founder's first school teacher. A post office operated for nearly one hundred years.

Another long-time village fixture is the St. John's Lutheran Church. The church celebrated its 100th anniversary in 2010. The building has stood in the village since its construction in 1869. Serving several denominations and congregations, St. John's first service was in January 1910. At one time a Christian day school was part of the congregation; however, that closed in 1970.

St. John's Lutheran Church, Alma City. (Credit)

CREAM

1895 - 1903

CLASS A

APPROXIMATE LOCATION:
2 Miles Southwest of Pemberton

Originally wholly located in Blue Earth County, expansion of the settlement spread into Waseca County. A post office was established (in Blue Earth County) in 1905 as was a creamery, a cheese factory, a general store, a barbershop, and a box-car depot.

Even with a temporary depot, the railroad decided to build the permanent depot at Pemberton. With completion of the depot, most of Cream moved out. Within a few years Cream was gone.

MATAWAN

1907 - 1972

CLASS D

APPROXIMATE LOCATION:
County #11 & #28

The early twentieth century saw the establishment of Matawan. In 1907 a railroad depot was built on the Brubaker Farm. Matawan was the name chosen by the railroad. An eighty-acre plot was platted and also laid out by the railroad.

Matawan in the 1920s had a creamery, a lumberyard, a post office (which had a long life), a school, a church, and other businesses.

Matawan is home to the Byron Town Hall. In 2012 the township hall was applying for entry into the National Register of Historic Places.

Matawan Depot. (www.west2k.com)

OKAMAN

1858 - 1882

CLASS C

APPROXIMATE LOCATION:
County #5 near Elysian

Native American for "good place to tarry" or "heron" the ninety-acre village was split between Waseca and Le Sueur counties.

OKaman-Cervidae Elk Farms

ELK HERD ● FREE PETTING ZOO

GIFT STORE ● VINEYARD

HANDMADE ART, WOODCRAFTS & HOME FURNISHINGS

UNIQUE JEWELRY & KNIVES ⬩ ANTLER MOUNTS & PIECES

DELICIOUS, NUTRICIOUS ELK MEAT ⬩ TROPHY BULLS

SO MANY ANIMALS: DONKEYS, ALPACAS, GOATS, HORSES, PIGS, RABBITS, CATS

FUN & ENJOYMENT FOR THE ENTIRE FAMILY

YOUR HOSTS ● THE KAPLANS ● Elysian, Minnesota

Top: Elk farm card; bottom: Elf Farm scene. (Courtesy of Joyce Kaplan, Okaman Elk Farm)

Barn close up. (Courtesy of Joyce Kaplan, Okaman Elk Farm)

Kiddie train. (Courtesy of Joyce Kaplan, Okaman Elk Farm)

Okaman was established in 1857. John Buckhout built a sawmill, a flour mill, storehouses, and farm buildings. The flour mill operated twenty-four hours a day. Farmers came from miles away, some as far as the Iowa border. While in Okaman, they stayed in Buckhout's hotel and and brought their supplies at his store.

The Financial Panic of 1857 hit Okaman hard. The following year, bad weather destroyed the crops. That double-whammy nearly did the little settlement in. However, the final blow was when the railroad bypassed Okaman. Without rail service, settlers moved across the lake to Janesville. Many settlers used teams of horses to pull their buildings across the frozen lake. Okaman soon declined and rapidly.

A 1993 *Mankato Free Press* article stated that historian James Childs dates Okamans demise to 1864. However, local historian Patti Hoversten has found evidence that Okaman survived into the 1870s. Ironically, the Chicago, Northwestern Railroad did come along to Okaman in the 1880s long after the community's demise.

Today, Don and Joyce Kaplan live at the old town site. They also operated the Okaman Elk Farm. They have an original sorghum mill on their site. They also have a petting zoo and elk farm with meat for sale. They have a gift shop, and offer special events throughout the year.

In 1993 a later owner of Okaman donated part of the old village site to the county, and it is now a county park.

CLARENCE H. JOHNSTON

While researching and learning about lost towns is rewarding in and of itself, it is the people, past and present that bring the history to life.

One day, I received an email from the Hoverstens in regards to Waseca County, specifically Okaman. In following up with the email, I learned of Clarence H. Johnston, a Minnesota architect of note. Patti Hoversten told me that Clarence had been born in Okaman, the grandson of founder John Buckhout. That was the tip of the iceberg. I had to know more. I learned he was the architect behind one of my favorite Minnesota destinations, Glensheen Mansion in Duluth. As Patti told me more, I found Mr. Johnston fascinating, much as she did when she first learned of him. We aren't the only ones impressed. Twin Cities Public Televsions (TPT) produced an hour-long documentary on Mr. Johnston's illustrious career titled "Gracious Spaces."

Recapping Patti's extensive research I summarize Mr. Johnston's life and career:

Patti first learned of Mr. Johnston while on a 1976 tour of the Skinner House on Summit Avenue in St. Paul. The tour was sponsored by the Friends of the Minneapolis Institute of Art. The brochure mentioned the Waseca-born architect. Having just moved to Waseca from St. Paul, her curiousity was peaked. Wanting to learn more, she began looking for a book on his life and work. None existed. She began her research, in pre-Internet days. Somewhere she learned Mr. Johnson had been born on the northeast shore of Lake Elysian, in a Waseca County ghost town—Okaman. Thus began five years of research. Here is what she learned.

Clarence H. Johnston was the Minnesota State Architect from 1901 to 1930. He designed numerous homes, many on St. Paul's Summit Avenue; Glensheen (Congdon Mansion), colleges, businesses, medical buildings, and more. Johnston was an early friend and contemporary of Cass Gilbert, architect of Minnesota's State Capitol. The two often competed for same the same projects, including the State Capitol project.

Delving deeper Patti visited the Northwestern Architectural Archives (University of Minnesota). There she had the honor of seeing Johnston's original blueprints, read letters between

Gilbert and Johnston and held Johnston's Grand Tour of Europe sketches.

Patti wrote an extensive biography. Copies are on file at the Waseca County Historical Society, the Minnesota Historical Society, and the Ramsey County Historical Society.

The Johnston family was so appreciative, they asked Patti to write a longer biography. Thinking it was beyond the scope of her expertise, she declined. Paul Clifford Larson, a professional author and historian took on the project. His book is *Minnesota Architect: The Life and Works of Clarence H. Johnston.*

Palmer Creamery. (Courtesy of Robert Hagen)

OLD JANESVILLE

1860 - 1870

CLASS A

APPROXIMATE LOCATION:
Just outside today's Janesville

First named St.Ceaser, then New Albany and lastly Janesville, the little burg was bustling, home to several stores, a hotel, a mill, and a saloon.

When the railroad expansion was being surveyed in the late 1860s, a nearby landowner offered free land if the railroad route ran just south of the community. Accepting the offer, East Janesville was platted. All of Janesville's buildings were eventually moved to the new location. In 1870, the new Janesville was incorporated, and the old location lost.

Palmer Depot. (Courtesy of Robert Hagen)

PALMER

1885 – 1901 (1947)

CLASS A

APPROXIMATE LOCATION:
County #22 near 110th Street

Palmer Methodist Chcurch. (Courtesy of Robert Hagen)

Every lost town needs, and deserves a champion. For long-ago Palmer, Robert Hagen is that champion.

Hagen, a life-long resident of Waseca County, tells that he was always aware that Palmer existed, he just never thought much about it. That was about to change. As a child, he and his father would take care of and maintain the Palmer cemetery. His father maintained the cemetery for over forty years. As he got older Robert began to give more thought to local history and that of Palmer. Thus began Robert's three

years and counting journey to learn more about the long-ago community. His end goal, his only goal, was to bring awareness to Palmer and to erect a sign marking its location.

Other than knowing of Palmer's existence and recalling conversations about the town Robert overheard as a youngster, he had little to go on. His first stop was the Waseca County Historical Society. They had a few photos and a bit of information they could share with him. They had several other resources, but none were indexed or cataloged so Robert had to

Palmer Methodist Church as it looked in 2015. (Courtesy of Robert Hagen)

Palmer schoolhouse. (Courtesy of Robert Hagen)

Palmer road sign. (Courtesy of Robert Hagen)

Robert Hagen and Palmer sign. (Courtesy of Robert Hagen)

Even with all of the information Robert has compiled, he is still garnering more. There are still questions to answer, including why the village was named Palmer. There is still more Robert would like to know.

Hagen's goal of getting a location sign erected was another long journey. Permission from landowners had to be obtained. Local governments, the Iosca Township Board had to approve the placement of the signs. They approved and gave the go-ahead. Next Waseca County had to approve. They granted approval but with the stipulation that Hagen had to pay for the signs.

As Sam Weidt wrote in a recent *Waseca County News* article, deciding on the signs' color was another decision. Highway markers are typically green and historical markers are brown. Palmer fit both. Deciding on green signs, Hagen purchased three, two for County Road #22 (one from each direction) and one for his office.

Hagen learned that purchasing the signs was only one step. The site had to be surveyed and deemed safe for sign placement. Since County Road #22 had recently been sealed, and all the signs removed, they all had to be resurveyed for placement. The Palmer sign could go with the others.

On August of 2015, the 100th anniversary of Palmer's establishment, Robert Hagen's signs were posted. Hagen's years-long journey had "saved" Palmer from oblivion. Not only did Robert Hagen leave a well-document history of Palmer, he ensured that Palmer's location would not be lost or forgotten. Hagen has given Palmer its place in history. Palmer may be long gone, but as long as someone or something is remembered, it lives on.

go through nearly everything piece by piece, making notes of all he found. Pulling together all of the information, he learned more than he could have imagined. Robert has created a fully documented history of the village including photos, then and now, postcards, papers, stories, dates, and more. He also conducted extensive interviews, gleaning information not found anywhere else and preserving it for future historians.

Summarizing Robert's extensive findings, I credit this information to Robert Hagen:

Beginning its existence as Palmer Station, the village was along the Minneapolis and St. Louis Railroad. Originally a "whistle stop," the town was not platted until 1915. Over the years, Palmer would consist of four general stores, a post office (1895 to 1901), a creamery, a stockyard, a school house, two train depots, a blacksmith shop, a church, and a grain elevator. The store operated until 1945.

Palmer is so much more than its business register and its dates and buildings. It is about its people. Robert has done that justice and has included in his history the story of the people and the place.

With time and a changing world, Palmer declined and eventually faded into history. Robert believes the automobile hastened the village's demise. The ability to travel further distances made small towns unnecessary.

PEDDLER'S GROVE

1800s

CLASS A

APPROXIMATE LOCATION:

Names sometimes tell the story. Such is the case with Peddler's Grove. Supposedly, in the settlement's early days, itinerant merchants sold goods to early settlers. Not allowed in the village, the merchants camped for the night at an isolated grove of trees.

Peddler's Grove consisted of four stores, a saloon, a hotel, and a school house. When Wilton was named the county seat, the Mankato, Wilton, and Owatonna stage made stops in Peddler's Grove. Unable to compete with Alma City, Peddler's Grove declined. One the cemetery remained in later years.

ST. MARY'S

1856/1873

CLASS A

APPROXIMATE LOCATION:

I never knew county seat designation was such a big deal. I learned that the loss of it could and did signal the end of a village while it virtually assured the county seat village would prosper. St. Mary's was one village on a long list of Waseca County communities that vied for the designation and one of the many that failed.

Settled in 1855 and platted in 1857. St. Mary's included a shingle factory, a saw mill, a flour mill, a hotel, a drug store, a blacksmith shop, and a saloon.

Once Wilton was chosen as the county seat, growth halted abruptly in St. Mary's. The Civil War further accelerated the village's decline. The final blow was the railroad's decision to bypass St. Mary's. St. Mary's never recovered. In 1873, parts of the village reverted back to farmland, and in 1926 the remaining portions were legally vacated.

The Church of the Nativity of St. Mary's was the village's heart. Established in 1856, the first church building was constructed in 1858. A larger church was built in 1880. It burned in 1885 and was rebuilt in 1887. That 1887 building served until the church was disbanded in 1973. The Waseca County's Historical Society purchased the building hoping to preserve it as a historical site. However, the cost of the upkeep was too much. It was also determined that the church could not be saved. An auction was held to sell the building and its contents, all except for the bell.

In 1978 the building was razed. A memorial to St. Mary's was erected in October of 1979.

Today the area houses the historical stone enclave marker and the bell.

WILTON

1856 - 1888

CLASS A

APPROXIMATE LOCATION:

Once the Waseca County seat. Once the village that all other area lost towns competed against and lost out to. Once a thriving village platted the same year as Minneapolis, 1856. Within a year of platting, home to several stores, hotels, homes, two newspapers, a doctor's office, and two lawyer firms.

Once the Winona, St. Peter Railroad was surveyed and laid out, all of Wilton's "onces" no longer mattered. In 1869, upon Waseca's incorporation, a vote was held to determine where the county seat would be located. Waseca won by 215 votes and Wilton's end was in sight.

Watonwan County

Godahl school. (unknown)

Godahl store in the early days. (Courtesy of the Godahl Store)

Godahl store. (Courtesy of the Godahl Store)

ECHOLS

1901 - 1925

CLASS C

APPROXIMATE LOCATION:
Highway #4 – 4 miles south of St. James

Lasting just twenty years, the railroad village of Echols was the area's social center. Platted in 1899 along the Minneapolis and St. Louis Railroad, seven blocks were laid out. One block was designated a park but that never materialized. Soon after the railroad began its operations, Echols was home to several businesses, including a depot, an elevator, a creamery, and a store/post office.

The depot lasted only a short time. It never had an agent on duty, and passengers had to flag down the train if they wanted to board. As farmers acquired their own separators, the creamery became unnecessary.

A Farmers Club was established in 1913, and a hall was built next to the store. The club and Echols's social events kept the community going. Dances and meetings were held in the hall and in vacant buildings as needed. Many credit the Farmers Club with keeping Echols viable into the 1920s. The club members met weekly, every Friday, and a program, lunch, and social hours were part of the meeting. In later years, the club declined and only met monthly. Every year between Christmas

and New Year's they had a community dinner. Rook parties were also popular. Talent shows and carnivals were held on occasion. February meant the oyster stew dinners. The young would play basketball and roller skate. Immunizations and extension lessons were also offered in the community. Red Cross Sewing Circles were held during World War I.

All that came to an end in 1925 when the hall and adjacent store burned. A new hall was built a short distance away but it was never the same. Lucille Howe wrote that, by that time, everyone had their own car, and distance was no longer an issue. One by one the businesses closed. The railroad stopped operations, and the rails were removed. A few buildings and homes remained, but Echols the village was no more.

GODAHL

1894 - 1907

CLASS C

APPROXIMATE LOCATION:
On the Brown/Watonwan County line, On #4 between Sleepy Eye and St. James

Once home to several businesses, today there is only one in Godahl. But what a business it is. Established in 1894 as a co-operative endeavor, it is considered Minnesota's oldest co-op stores. The first members bought

Godahl Building. (Courtesy of Tom McLaughlin)

Godahl store interior. (Courtesy of the Godahl Store)

Godahl store today. (Courtesy of the Godahl Store)

Godahl store interior today. (Courtesy of the Godahl Store)

shares at a cost of $20.00 each. With a total pool of $5,000, stock was purchased, and the store opened in 1894.

At the time Godahl also included a creamery, a blacksmith shop, a post office (1894 to 1907) and in later years also included two gas stations and a pool hall/restaurant. In the 1980s the population was just under twenty residents.

One resident, Vera Rossbach, wrote that, as long as the creamery operated, the store thrived. Wives would accompany their husbands, or send a shopping list with them, to town on cream-hauling days.

Over the years, the community and other businesses dwindled. The store continued on despite a declining customer bases and rough economic times. Things looked especially bleak in 2005. A committee to save the store was formed. A bake sale and other fund raisers were hosted. An annual Godahl Labor Day Celebration brought hundreds of people to the village.

Not only is the Godahl Store a business, it is also the area's social center. Just as it was in the early days, the community

works to keep the store going. Many events are hosted throughout the year. You can learn more at the stores Facebook page: https://www.facebook.com/FriendsOfTheGodahlStore/.

Better yet, visit the store in person. It's a treat for the senses.

GROGAN

1891 - 1932

CLASS C

APPROXIMATE LOCATION:
#13 & #16

Under orders from the United States Post Office, Watonwan County's community of Lincoln, had to change its name. Another Lincoln existed in Morrison County, and they wanted to keep the name. So a name change was necessary.

Rosendale Grogan Church. (Courtesy of Tom McLaughlin)

According to a 1974 *Waseca County Plaindealer* article, the Lincoln creamery had twelve stockholders. Each wrote their last name on a slip of paper and put the paper in a hat. The name drawn out would be the community's new name. The odds might have been stacked for "Grogan" as five of the twelve shareholders had that last name. Chances were good "Grogan" would be drawn. It was!

At its peak Grogan had two elevators, two stores, a lumberyard, a stockyard, a school, a depot, and several homes. In 1942 the depot was sold, split in half and moved. One half became a home and was used until it burned in 1997.

Primarily a residential community by 1974, the elevator and depot were gone. The school, though not in use, was still standing.

SVEADAHL

1860s - 1907

CLASS C

)APPROXIMATE LOCATION:
On #18, south of #1 and #18 intersection

Sveadahl, including both east and west, may have faded over the years, but its churches and its community know a thing or two about longevity. Swedish for "Swedish valley or dale" the first settlers came to the area in the late 1860s. Building a church was of the utmost importance, so the settlers pooled their resources and established the West Sveadahl church and congregation. Land was purchased and a building purchased in Comfrey was moved onto the property. The next summer a tornado destroyed the building, causing one fatality. A new building was completed in 1890. The present church was then built, and the old building moved just north. It later became a private home.

West Sveadahl church. (Courtesy of Tom McLaughlin)

East Sveadahl church. (Courtesy of Tom McLaughlin)

Records indicate a conflict between church members. Two churches seems to be the outcome. I'm unsure as to when the two churches began, before or after the tornado. At some point, the congregation split and the East and the West Sveadahl churches were established. In the 1980s, both churches shared one pastor.

Sveadahl also included a blacksmith shop (1893), which later became the Sveadahl Service Station (1938).

Long lived the Sveadahl Store was built in 1894. It carried a full line of goods and included a locker plant. A creamery operated for over fifty years from 1906 until 1951.

Area historian Shirley Knudson wrote that in the 1980s Sveadahl was quiet, the vacant creamery and store still stood.

Winona County

Beaver flood. (Courtesy of the Winona County Historical Society)

Beaver school. (Courtesy of the Winona County Historical Society)

BEAVER

1857 - 1906

CLASS A

APPROXIMATE LOCATION:
Now part of the Whitewater Wildlife Management Area,
adjacent to the Whitewater State Park

Recent news reports, photos, and video footage of the mud slides showing cars, semis, and trucks under six feet of mud is hard to fathom. Seeing Mother Nature's destruction brought to mind Beaver in Winona County. The small community faced similar circumstances and eventually succumbed to nature's wrath. As one writer wrote, the scenic rugged valley went from wilderness and back in the space of one hundred years. It is ironic that what first attracted the settlers to the region would tragically spell the demise of the settlement.

Early settlers chose the location because of its proximity to the intersection of the Beaver Creek and the Whitewater River. Water power was readily available for milling, and the farmland was fertile. Abundant natural resources were also very appealing. There was a nice variety of trees, fruit, and wild game. Indeed, it seemed to be the perfect spot to settle down, build a life and a community. For a while, it was, at least in the early years from 1854 to the early 1900s.

The first house and first store, a fourteen-by-twenty-foot log structure, was built in 1856. A blacksmith was also established that year as well as a post office. The excellent water availability was used to power the first sawmill. In 1857, the sawmill switched to grinding grain, fifty bushels a day. The name of the village, Beaver, the oldest in the Whitewater River Valley, was selected because in the early days, a dam built by Beavers was there.

The settlement was platted in 1856. The forty-acre plat had twenty blocks, ten lots to a block. Soon the settlement included a grocery store, a blacksmith shop, a Methodist Church, a Woodman's Hall, a school, and a town hall. The Beaver Hotel was built in 1865, and it quickly became a popular stop over for settlers traveling from Rochester, and settlers hauling grain to shipping points.

Things began to change in the early 1900s. With the clearing of the higher lands and hills and poor farming practices, the area became even more prone to flooding. It was no longer possible to count on crops or for farmers to make ends meet.

Bird's-eye view of Beaver. (Courtesy of the Winona County Historical Society)

Beaver Cemetery. (Courtesy of J. Boice)

CLYDE

1873 - 1902

CLASS B

APPROXIMATE LOCATION:
Southeast of St. Charles, at junction of Winona County #5 and #35

Many began to relocate. The persistent floods forced others out.

In the 1930s the State of Minnesota began to buy up abandoned farmsites in the valley. Plans were to create a game preserve and state park. A 1935 *Winona Daily News* article summed up the flooding issue with its headline "Soil Washed Down Hill and Village Disappeared." The article reported that some fields were filled in with sand and mud ten to twelve feet deep. Roads that had been built six feet above flood stage now were suddenly six feet lower than the surrounding land. Bridges that had been ten feet above the water line became entirely buried in the silt and sand. Crops flooded three times a season, and it became so bad that it was hard to tell where the hillsides and valleys began and ended. One report that a barn, recently torn down, was found covered in eight to ten feet of muck. The cattle were standing on ground that had originally been the hay mow loft.

In 1938 the creek overflowed twenty-eight times. A mass exodus began from Beaver in 1943. At that time, the Pitman and Robinson Act allowed the government to purchase land in the settlement. By 1955 Beaver was abandoned. In 1960 a former resident and author of a book on Beaver wrote that he visited the old town site. It had changed so much he could not find the spot where he was born and lived for sixteen years.

Today the area is part of the Whitewater Wildlife Management Area and the adjoining Whitewater State Park.

Decrepit but still standing in 1991, organizers hoped to host the first annual Clyde School reunion. The building's roof was torn up and nearly gone, letting the elements inside. The only thing inside the building at that time was an old dismantled Chevy.

The school was built in 1927 to replace an earlier brick building. Enrollment once reached forty students strong and was as low as ten in the mid-1940s. Other than the school building, little remained of the small Scottish settlement that at one time peaked with 125 residents. The community was named after the River Clyde in Scotland.

In 1991, Cassidy Edstrom, a reporter for the *Winona Post and Shopper* told that, when she visited the site, the dilapidated school, the Masonic Lodge, and one house with a dog that could only be appeased with potato chips tossed at it, was all that was left of the village.

Organizers of the reunion hoped for a good turnout and requested that all attendees bring a pot luck dish to share.

Speaking of the Masonic Lodge, it was long-lived, the longest of anything in Clyde. Chartered in 1864, the lodge celebrated its 100th anniversary with a dinner in 1964. The lodge originally shared space with a lower-level store. The lodge occupied the top floor. The store closed in 1908, and the building was given to the lodge.

Debating was a popular form of entertainment in Clyde's early days. People came from all around to attend the debates. A creamery, noted to be Minnesota's third co-operative was called the Saratoga Creamery and was also part of the community. In 1945 all that remained of the creamery was the well.

FREMONT

1876 - 1910

CLASS C

APPROXIMATE LOCATION:
Near Junction of #6 and 5 miles southwest of I-90

Fremont Store 1914. (Courtesy of the Fremont Store)

Local folklore tells that the small settlement of Fremont was first known as Neoca. The Neoca post office began in the 1850s and was named after an Native American legend. The community later changed its name to Fremont after John C. Fremont, one-time presidential candidate had traveled the Territorial Road and spent the night at the hotel. Since it was so unusual to have a general of such magnitude visit the community, the townsfolks decided to rename the settlement in his honor.

Once a busy burg of fifty, Fremont was located along the Chicago, Northwestern Railroad line and also along the Territorial Road. A post office operated from 1876 to 1910. At one time housing two stores, the Fremont Store still stands today and is still operating. What a store it is.

Many will attest to the fact that it is not just a country store. It is in the words of many "cool." It's worth going out of the way to visit the historical business. Take the kids, the grandkids; they too will think it's cool. The store is planning its 160th anniversary in 2016. Check out the stores Facebook page at: https://www.facebook.com/The-Fremont-Store-232862293403930/

Freemont Store. ("FremontStoreMN" by Jonathunder - Own work. Licensed under GFDL 1.2 via Commons - https://commons.wikimedia.org/wiki/File:FremontStoreMN.jpg#/media/File:FremontStoreMN.jpg)

BIBLIOGRAPHY
SOUTHERN EDITION

"4,000 at old Cedarville History outing." *Fairmont Daily Sentinel.* August 28, 1933.

Adams, Cynthia. E. "East Prairieville – In a Personal Setting." May 1939.

Adams, W.B. "East Prairiville." May 1939.

Allsen, Ken. "Old Frontenac Minnesota: Its History and Architecture." Charleston. 2011.

"Amiret." Web. April 18, 2015.

Amo, Drew. "Alma City Church celebrates 100 years." *Waseca County News."* June 22, 2010.

Anderson, Torgny. "Centennial History of Lyon County, Minnesota." Marshall. 1970.

Andries, Jennifer. Email. April 28, 2015.

Beis, Jessica. "Bernadotte 'cow lady' opens 'mooseum' for holiday open house. *St. Peter Herald.* November 22, 2013.

Beitler, Stu. "Neighbors Save Town of Prosper." *La Crosse Tribune.* www3.gendisasters.com, July 25, 1913.

Bernard, Melva duMez. "Research Study of Pleasant Grove Township, Olmsted County, Minnesota 1852 – 1960." N.d.

Best. Barba K. Email. June 19, 2015.

Best, Barba K. Email. July 5, 2015.

Beyers, Pat. "Historic Schumann home originally Cazenovia Store for many years." *Pipestone County Star.* April 16, 1981.

Beyers, Pat. "Nothing Left but memories of Pumpkin Center Store." *Pipestone County Star.* August 5, 1982.

Beyers, Pat. "Towns gone but not forgotten." *Pipestone County Star.* April 12, 1981.

"Bicentennial Review of the Village of Pleasant Grove." Old Settlers Association. July 1954.

Blais, Lester. "Village of Walcott." Unpublished paper. N.d ca 1937.

Blais, Lester. "Wheatland Village (abandoned)." Unknown. October 20, 1937.

Blais, Lester. "Prairieville, Abandoned Village." Unpublished. October 13, 1937.

Blanchard, Barbara. "East Chain calls old age 'Best Part of Life.'" Unknown. N.d.

Blanchard, Barbara. "East Chain Ranks as Never-Never Land. Unknown. N.d.

Brookens, Jenn. "Friends recall Erdman's wisdom, love of life." *Fairmont Sentinel.* August 7, 2012.

Brookens, Jenn. "Kimball Korner store prepares to close down." *Fairmont Sentinel.* December 26, 2012.

Brown, John A., editor. *History of Cottonwood and Watonwan Counties, Minnesota.* LaCrosse. 1916.

Busch, Fritz. "Godahl Store lives on." September 7, 2010.

Busman, Caryl, Clercx, Diane, editors. *Murray County Minnesota: 1857 – 2007: A Scrapbook of Memories.* 2007.

Busp, Lillian. "The High Forest Story." *Stewartville Star.* June 10, 1971.

Campbell, Marian and Dahle, Kermit. "The History of Clyde." June 17, 1945.

Carlson, Lorne. "The Norwegians in Olmsted County." Unknown. N.d.

Carpenter, Fred. *The Good Life: A Sort of Auto Biography.* 1977.

"Carson Church to hold reunion 1875-2005." Unknown. N.d.

"Center Chain." Martin County Historical Society files. N.d.

Christensen, Gail. Letter. "Dotson" December 17, 1980.

Cole, John L. "Epsom, Minnesota Elevator, School started near tracks my Chicago, Milwaukee Railroad in 1903." *The Kenyon Leader.* January 29, 2003.

Cole, John. "Ruskin, Minnesota." One-time community was located between Kenyon and Faribault." *Kenyon Leader.* August 7, 2002.

Cottonwood County Historical Society. *Centennial History of Cottonwood County.* 1970.

Cottonwood County Historical Society. *Cottonwood County History.* 1970.

"Creamery proved to be major Delft industry." Unknown. N.d. Files of Cottonwood County Historical Society.

Crippen, Ray. "Busy Days at Org." Nicollet County Historical Society newlstter. April 1995.

Croes, Shelley. "Boom town goes bust: Although Okaman bustled briefly, a railroad route sealed its doom." *Mankato Free Press.* March 1, 1993.

Crouch, Charles. "Wasioja: Rooted Yet Ever Growing." Tempe. 1977.

Curtis-Wedge, Franklin. *History of Freeborn County.* Chicago. 1911.

Dahlin, Curtis A. *Dakota Uprising Victims: Gravestones and Stories.* Edina. 2007.

Daniels, Evelyn. "Nashville." Unknown. N.d.

Davis, L.G. "Ghost Towns of Brown County." *Sleepy Eye Herald.* February 19, 1942. Mt. *Lake Observer.* 1970.

"Delft established by the railroad was named after two Dutch cities."

"Delft Immanuel final worship services in 'old church' Sunday. Unknown. July 15, 1979.

DeRuyter, Ann. "Abandoned Cemetery gets Facelift." *The Journal."* September 23, 1980.

DeRuyter, Ann Marie. "Local Residents Discuss History of Golden Gate." *Sleepy Eye Herald Dispatch.* March 30, 1978.

"DeSota." Martin County Historical Society files. N.d.

Dineen, Mike. "Iberia" Files at Brown County Historical Society n.d.

District 183 Students, "Iberia School District." Brown County Historical Society files, unpublished. 1971.

Dixon, Joshua. "Backward Glances." *Redwood Falls Gazette."* June 28, 2012.

Dixon, Joshua. "Gold Found in Redwood County 2012 edition." *Redwood Falls Gazette.* October 1, 2012.

Dodge County Historical Society. "Towns and Ghost Towns of Dodge County." Unpublished Manuscript. Mantorville. 2015.

Drache, Barb. Map. "Moland." N.d.

Duncanson, C.A. "Highlights of Early Days in High Forest Township." N.d.

Dungay, Neil S. "Cannon City." August 22, 1946.

"East Chain shows village can thrive without a railway." Unknown. N.d.

"East Chain to get "Lit Up" for first time. " Unknown. N.d.

Eastmans, Gladys. "Creamery general store thrived at Center Chain." Unknown. N.d.

Edstrom, Cassidy. "Clyde School to hold reunion." *Winona Post and Shopper.* July 17, 1991.

Else, Loren. "68 Men Left, only 1 Returned." November 5, 2011.

Engebretsen, Gyda Jackson. "Notes on history of Palmer." 1980.

"Farewell to Org, New Sweden and Willow Creek." *Minneapolis Tribune Picture Magazine.* March 6, 1977.

Fillmore County Historical Society. *Fillmore County, Minnesota.* Dallas. 1984.

"Fire at Airlie: The little village nearly wiped out of existence." Unknown. May 1, 1899.

Flo, Harold Olaf. *Childhood Memories Growing Up in Rapidan, MN.* 2003

Franklin, Jim. *Pioneering Goodhue County.* McGregor. 2003.

Freeborn County Historical Society. "Freeborn County Towns and Villages." N.d.

Freeborn County History and Genealogy Society. *Freeborn County Heritage.* 1989.

Ganske, Donna. "Golden Gate." Unknown. N.d.

Gehl, Robert C. "Yucatan is Sunday night town: People gather from afield." *LaCrosse Tribune.* N.d.

German, Roger. "For butter or wurst." Unknown. N.d.

Goertz, Tonial "Do you Remember . . . Reminisces of Verdi." *The Pipestone Star.* January 31, 2008.

Goertz, Tonia. "Verdi, Highlights in the history of Verdi." *The Pipestone Star.*" January 31, 2008.

Goff, Al. editor, *Nobles County History.* St. Paul. 1958.

"Golden Gate Village Site." *Sleepy Eye Herald Dispatch.* March 23, 1978.

Goodell, David. Email. July 8, 2015.

Goodell, David. Telephone. July 7, 2015.

Goodhue County Historical Society. "The Goodyear County Historical Society is commemorating ghost towns." Web. May 14, 2015.

Graf, Crystal. "Historic-minded to mark "lost towns." *Fairmont Sentinel.* September 7, 2001.

Griswold, Burr F. "Remains of a Village: An anvil and a vice." Houston County Historical Society files. N.d.

Griswold, Burr F. "Yucatan dwindles but it won't die." *Mabel Record.* May 14, 1967.

"Grogan's name was selected by drawing chance from a hat." *Watonwan County Plaindealer.* 1974.

Grundmeier, Shirley. "Once Again a Boom Town." *The Blue Earth County Historical Society Newlsetter.* Summer 1997

Guthrey, Nora H. "Notes on Early Years of High Forest Township." April 1948.

Hagen, Robert. "Palmer" unpublished paper. August 2015.

Hanson, Jess. "The Rediscovery of Kerns: Belgrade Township, Nicollet County, Minnesota." North Mankato. 1995.

Harren, Heather. "Rapidan" email. May 5, 2015.

"Haverhill Anti Horse Thief Society." Olmsted County Historical Society files. N.d.

Hiebeat, Gareth. "No one smokes, drinks, dances in Delft." *St. Paul Sunday Pioneer Press.* November 27, 1960.

Herbst, Gordon H. *Minneinneopa State Park: 150 Year History.* Janesville. 2007.

"History of Minneopa." Transcript as performed for "Ghosts from the Past." *Blue Earth County Historical Society Newsletter.* November 1992.

"History of Nashville." Martin County Historical Society files. N.d.

"History of the North Star Peace Church." Martin County Historical Society files. N.d.

Hodgson, R.E. "Peddler's Grove, one of memory cities in Waseca County History." *The Waseca Herald.* March 15, 1963.

Hoefs, Dennis. *Chain of Lakes Country.* Virginia Beach. 2007.

Houston County Historical Society. "Anything quiet as a Bee?" Unknown. N.d.

Houston County Historical Society. "History of Houston County." Dallas 1982.

Houston County Historical Society. "Newhouse just withered away: The speculators sold out fast." Unknown. N.d.

Houston County Historical Society. "Remains and history of a once booming village." Unknown. N.d.

Houston County Historical Society. "River caused citizens to change town's site." N.d.

Houston County Historical Society. "Stone lady on the hill watches over tiny Black Hammer Village." Unknown. N.d.

Houston County Historical Society. "Trails, Villages can still be found." Unknown. N.d.

Hoversten, Patti. Okaman. Email. September 28, 2015.

Howe, Lucille. "Vanished Town lives in minds of those that loved it." Unknown. N.d.

Huegel, Donna. "Log home a stop on Territorial Road." LaCrescent Area Historical Society. November 10, 2005.

Hughes, Thomas. "History of Minneopa State Park." 1932.

"Iberia" Map. Brown County Historical Society Files. Unpublished. November 1973.

"Iberia" Unpublished Manuscript. Brown County Historical Society files. N.d.

"Imogene." Jackson County Historical Society. "History of Jackson County, Vol. II.) Lakefield. 1979.

Jensen, Kathy. "Clark's Grove: A Place We Call Home." Clark's Grove. 1990.

Johnson, Fred. "Ghost Towns of Goodhue County: Great Expectations." *Goodhue County Historical News.* March 1987.

Jolly, Carol. "A Gold Mine of History." *New Richland Star.* March 30, 2011.

Jorgenson, Karen. "Historical Society marks sites of Dodge County "Ghost Towns." August 9, 2015.

Keller, Walter George and Mary O'Brien Tyrell. "The Box Man: The Autobiography of Walter George Keller." St. Paul. 1996.

Kirchmeier, Michael. Email. March 28, 2015.

Kirk, Jenny. "Praise, Prayers and . . . Angry Birds?" *Marshall Independent* February 13, 2015. www.marshallindependent.com

Klossner, Ruth. Email. July 8, 2015.

Klossner, Ruth. Email. July 9, 2015.

Klossner, Ruth. "Hebron History Remembered." *Lafayette Nicollet Leader.* N.d.

Klossner, Ruth. "Kern's History is topic of NCHS program." N.d.

Klossner, Ruth. "Like so many others, St. George Store fades into history." *Lafayette Nicollet Leader.* November 4, 2010.

Kochendorfer, Ann. "Recalling Pixley . . . Center Chain." *Fairmont Sentinel.* November 4, 1989.

Krueger, Coralee. "75 years of service, final postmark stamped at Delft Post Office Friday." November 1, 1990.

Lake Benton Chamber of Commerce and Convention and Visitor's Bureau, "Relics of a mad elephant." Email. April 20, 2015.

Lamp, Daisy. "Legend of High Forest." 1921.

Larson, Eldred Klose. "The Story of Echols." March 1970.

Leavenworth Wilder, Lucy. Ed. *Old Rail Fence Corners: Frontier Tales Told by Minnesota Pioneers.* St. Paul 1976 (1914).

Leonard, Honorable Joseph A. *History of Olmsted County, Minnesota.* Chicago. 1910.

"Lime Creek." Murray County Historical Society files. N.d.

Lincoln County Historical Society. "Lincoln County, Minnesota 1873-1975." Lake Benton. N.d.

Lindemann, Don. "Dotson (Bedford) MN." Unpublished November 3, 2001.

"Local residents convert Delft Fellowship Hall into coffeehouse." October 13, 2010.

"Lodge at Clyde Marks 100th Anniversary." *Winona Sunday News.* October 18, 1964.

"Lone Cedar." Martin County Historical Society files. N.d.

Lundin, Vernard. "Growing Up in Judson." *The Blue Earth County Historical Society Newsletter.* January 1987.

"Manyaska and Lone Cedar." Martin County Historical Society files. N.d.

"Martin County Ghost Towns." Martin County Historical Society files. N.d. January 1, 1928.

McMillan, John. "Friends for Golden Gage Cemetery Restoration Voted." *The Journal."* September 23, 1980.

Messinger, Mrs. Lewis. "History of Eden." Unpublished Manuscript. Files of Dodge County Historical Society.

Meyer, Douglas. "Steele County Villages." Steele County Historical Society. 2015.

Meyer, Jerome. "Remembering Ghost Towns of Faribault County." Unknown. *Albert Lea Tribune.* May 22, 2013.

Meyer, Roy W. "The ghost towns and discontinued post offices of Goodhue County." Red Wing. 2003.

Meyer, Roy W. "The Story of Forest Mills: A Midwest milling community." *Minnesota History.* March 1956.

Mileham, Robin. *A Century of Memories: Imogene, Minnesota.* Dallas. 2001.

"Minnesota 50 Years Ago – Potsdam." *Minneapolis Journal.*

Monoreif, Mattie Maxwell. "A Family Record of Dotson Family." Unpublished. N.d.

"More lost towns of Martin County are remembered." Unknown. N.d.

Morris, Anne. "The country store: A lingering memory." Unknown. N.d.

Mower County Historical Society. "Mill on the Willow: A History of Mower County, Minnesota, 1984." Lake Mills. 1984.

Muchlinski, Jim M. "Lyon County Ghost Towns." N.d.

Neill, Reverend Edward D. *History of Fillmore County, Minnesota.* Salem. 1882.

Nelson, Arthur M. "Know your county." *Fairmont Sentinel* articles. July 27, 1960. September 14, 1961.

Nelson, Howard M. "Early History of Nicollet County." St. Peter. 1972.

Nelson, Major Arthur M., "Know Your Own County: A History of Martin County, Minnesota. 1876-1947." Fairmont. 1947.

Nelson, Mrs. Thomas. Letter. "The Swedish Settlement at Millersburg." October 24, 1938.

Nicklay, Deb. "Residents say goodbye to Flynn's." *Stewartville Star.* June 12, 1990.

"No Trace Remains of Martin County's Lost Village, Lake Is Gone." Unknown. August 20, 1944.

"Norse Ceremony Recalls Olmsted Early Settlers." *Rochester Post Bulletin.* May 27, 1925.

Norseland Community Anniversary Committee. *Norseland: Where the Big Woods Meets the Prairie.* Decorah. 2008.

"North Star" Martin County Historical Society files. N.d.

Palmer, Gail. "Beauford Corners." *The Blue Earth County Historical Society Newsletter.* July 1988.

Palmer, Gail. "The Ghost Town: Mankato Mineral Springs." *The Blue Earth County Historical Society Newsletter.* June 1986.

Palmquist, Anity Lee. "Say you're a Yankee, or else." Unknown. N.d.

Paris, Donna Petrowinc. *History of East Chain, Minnesota.* 1992.

Peterson, Duane. "Springville." n.d. Web. May 15, 2013.

"Pioneer Village." Nobles County. www.thudscave.com.

Pipestone County Historical Society. *Pipestone County History.* Dallas. 1984.

"Pixley." Martin County Historical Society files. N.d.

"Pleasant Grove Township History." Olmsted County Historical Society files. Unknown. 1945.

"Remembering 14 Communities that were founded, flourished and are no longer." 2015.

Rietsema, Rachel. "Refurbished Byron Township Hall something to behold. " *NRHEG Star Eagle.* March 28, 2012.

"Rock Dell Resident Seek Tax Law Change." *Rochester Post Bulletin.* April 15, 1959.

Roberts, Mrs. "Early History of Eden Township Told: Mrs. Roberts reveals that Lone Tree is a ghost town, once active." *Independent Review.* April 23, 1953.

"Rock Dell Township." Olmsted County Historical Society. Unknown. 1883.

Rogers, Ruth. "Who got all the Money?" Houston County Historical Society files. N.d.

Ronan, Thomas. B. "Free Enterprise." Rochester. 1969.

Rose, Arthur P. *An Illustrated History of the Counties of Rock and Pipestone, Minnesota.* 1911.

Russell, William. "The Early History of High Forest." June 24, 1979.

Sandeen, Bob. "Economic Conditions Created Nicollet County's ghost towns." *The Free Press.* October 5, 2013.

"Sauntering Around in Olmsted County – Potsdam." Unknown. N.d.

Schmidt, Janet R. "West Newton, then and now." N.d.

Schrader, Julie Hiller, ed. *The Heritage of Blue Earth County.* Dallas. 1990.

Schreiber, Pauline. "Millersburg was mecca for Swedish settlers." N.d.

Schroeder, Sharon. Eighth Grade Class "Preview and Added Information of Lone Tree." 1980.

Scottston, Barb. Email. May 6, 2015.

Scottston, Barb and Atherton, Terry. "Winnebago Valley, the town a creek runs through." Unknown. N.d.

Scobie, Elizabeth. "What About Golden Gate?" *Sleepy Eye Herald Dispatch.* June 29, 1976.

Severson, Harold. "Rock Dell Creamery Celebrates 100th Year." *Rochester Post Bulletin.* August 14, 1889.

Shannon, Ed. "Bancroft: More than just a prairie ghost town." *Albert Lea Tribune.* March 6, 2005.

Shannon, Ed. "Ghost Towns of Freeborn County." *Albert Lea Tribune.* April 16, 2012.

Sioux Valley Lutheran High School. "The Experience."

Smith, Jason. "Flensburg Files." September 2015.

Smith, Jason. "Jackson County" Email. September 27, 2015.

Smith, Laura Tesca. "The History of Cummingsville from 'Hope' town to 'Ghost' town." N.d.

Sobotik, Jerry. "Godahl Store Bids for Survival." *The Journal.* July 27, 1986.

"Soil Washed down hill and Village disappeared." *Winona Daily News.* November 19, 1955.

Solinger, Sue. "Preserving History is aim of Cemetery Restoration." *Sleepy Eye Herald Dispatch.* February 7, 1980.

"Son of Iberia Pioneers Returns Brown County Visitor after 40 Years finds many changes." *Sleepy Eye Journal.* July 14, 1949.

Steil, Mark. "Minnesota's Oldest Coop Store may close." Minnesota Public Radio. August 10, 2005.

Stelplugh, Alice. "Money Creek Township and Village." Houston County Historical Society. Unknown. 1982.

Stewartville Area Historical Society. *The Stewartville Area.* Charleston. 2009.

Stitt, James. "The History of Le Sueur County's Ottawa Stone Church honored." *Le Center Leader* August 23, 2013.

"Stories Tell of Six Generations." *Byron Review.* September 28, 1988.

Swanberg, L.E. *Then and Now: A history of Rice County, Faribault and Communities.* Faribault. 1976.

Swanson, Claude N. ed. "East Chain pioneer challenges." N.d.

"Tenhassen." Martin County Historical Society files. N.d.

"The Meighans and Forestville: Part II: The Boom Is Over." Web. May 12, 2015

"The Meighans and Forestville: Part Four: The end of Forestville and a new beginning." Web. May 12, 2015

Theobald, Paul. "Sleepy Eye area can boast of its own ghost towns." *Fairfax Standard.* April 16, 1981.

Timm, Jaimie. "Looking Back: Settling Johnsburg." *Austin Living.* May/June 2015.

"Town of Amiret." History and Description of Lyon County, Minneosta. 1884.

Trace remains of Martin County lost village, lake is gone." Martin County Historical Society files. N.d.

Ulmen, Steven. "Shadows of the Past: Lost Villages of Blue Earth County." *The Blue Earth County Historian.* Vol XVI No. IV Fall 2008.

Unknown. "The Heritage of Faribault County." Dallas. 1987

Upham, Warren. "A Geographical Encyclopedia." Minnesota Historical Society. 2009. Web. November 2012

Vance, Daniel. "The Dam Store." May 1994.

Vander Linden, Tom. "A long day to reach South Ridge: Stage coach travel remembered." Unknown. N.d.

Velishek, Jon. "What a place was Prairieville." Unknown. N.d.

Vogel, Russ. "The Death of North Sioux Falls: And the three lives of its cornerstone." *Worthington Daily Globe.* August 11, 1980.

Watonwan County History. Dallas. 1995.

Webb, Wayne F. "Redwood, the Story of a County." St. Paul. 1964.

Wehrwein, Derek. "Prarieville, signs of life." *Faribault Daily News.* June 13, 2010.

Weidt, Sam. "Finding Palmer: Waseca man's research helps memory town live on." *Waseca County News.* August 21, 2015.

Weidt, Sam. "The town that was no more: Waseca man works to find the story of tiny Palmer, Minnesota." *Waseca County News.* August 14, 2015.

Winnebago Valley Hideaway. 2015.

"Who Recalls Golden Gate?" *Sleepy Eye Herald Dispatch.* March 4, 1978.

Winona County Historical Society. "The Beaver Story: 100 Years in the Whitewater Valley." Winona. 1962.

"Wirock." Murray County Historical Society files. N.d.

Zschetzsche, John. "This town . . . No, he says, Village . . . Well, Actually calls it a thriving ghost town, has a population of 9 (count 'em) and is still on the map. *New Ulm Journal.* September 22, 1963.

"Zumbro Dairy at Rock Dell shows gains: Creamery near here one of the first formed in the State of Minnesota." *Rochester Post Bulletin.* June 3, 1949.

INDEX
SOUTHERN EDITION